AYA GODA returned to Japan from her travels in 1998, and lives today in Hokkaido, in northern Japan, where she spends much of her time painting. *Tao* is her first book, for which she won the prestigious Japanese Noma Prize for Literature.

ALISON WATTS was educated in Adelaide, Australia, before taking an MA in Advanced Japanese Studies at the University of Sheffield. She now works as a freelance translator from the Japanese, currently living in Ibaraki, Japan.

From the reviews of *Tao*:

'As well as poetic descriptions of the land, Goda gives an insight into recent history from both an outsider's and an insider's view. More than just a travel book, *Tao* works on many levels; think *The White Masai* meets *On The Road*.' **Real Travel**

'Good travel books, like travel itself, open the door to new worlds. In the strongest works the author's vision becomes our own, especially if his or her subject is a distant destination. For most of us, northern Russia will forever be defined by Colin Thubron's *In Siberia*. Antarctica is Sara Wheeler's *Terra Incognita*. No matter how many times I visit India, Delhi will always be for me William Dalrymple's *City of Jinns*. Now, an arresting book is about to take hold of our collective vision of rural China. The book brings the reader new insights into Han racism, sky burials and the wholesale eradication of Tibetan rights and culture since the Cultural Revolution. Most movingly, *Tao* is a spare, heartfelt work of love that captures the thrill of a young woman discovering the world in all its beauty and troubles, from everyday pleasures (tripe soup, Wanzi tea, love-making beside a mountain lake) to haunting terrors. A dozen film producers would die to adapt this book into an irresistible road movie, if only Beijing would permit filming in Tibet and China.' **Rory MacLean,** *Guardian*

'A riveting narrative of political repression and intellectual rebellion in China at the time of the Tiananmen massacre in 1989... Goda's style is captivating in its matter-of-fact tone... The narrative is strikingly self-effacing, foregrounding the charismatic personality of Yong.' *Mslexia Magazine*

TAO
AYA GODA

TRANSLATED BY ALISON WATTS

Portobello
BOOKS

First published by Portobello Books Ltd 2007
This paperback edition published 2008

Portobello Books Ltd
Twelve Addison Avenue
Holland Park
London
W11 4QR, UK

The translation of this book into English is supported
by the Arts Council.

Designed by Nicky Barneby @ Barneby Ltd
Typeset in 11.25pt Monotype Sabon by
Avon DataSet Ltd, Bidford on Avon, Warwickshire

Printed in Great Britain by CPI Bookmarque, Croydon

I.

THE ARTIST WHO FLEW IN ON A FIGHTER PLANE

1. THE WANDERING ARTIST

26 August 1988. Poplar trees silhouetted against the purple afterglow of sunset. I'm cycling towards the centre of Kashgar from the tree-lined outskirts. Uighurs heading home by donkey- and horse-cart wave and call out greetings as they pass, curious about a stranger travelling on her own. Whenever I dismount to ask the way, I'm surrounded; it's hard to make progress, and I'm late returning to my hotel.

Kashgar is the Silk Road capital in north-western China. But it's more Uighur than Chinese; the Uighurs' Muslim culture lives on here in Xinjiang Province, with its desert ruins and desolate wildernesses. The gorgeously coloured shawls that envelop the women stand out vividly against the desert; old men loiter around the town centre holding the reins of the donkey- and horse-carts that function as taxis; and stalls in the bazaar sell handmade ice cream out of copper containers, all kinds of lamb dishes, freshly cooked nan bread, mountains of watermelons, *manaizi* grapes and yellow *hami* melons. I've come overland from Hong Kong, arriving after three days on a bone-shaking bus from Turfan.

It's just before midnight when I return to the Oasis Hotel. Although in this vast country where there's no time difference between east and west, things don't always move according to a timetable set to accommodate Beijing. Here in the far west of China the sun never sets, or rises, until very late, and in Kashgar right now it's really still only seven in the evening.

Back in the hotel I pay 6 yuan at the service counter, return the bicycle, then go upstairs to the dormitory. Thirteen beds line the large room, which is unappealing in the way of a school classroom, but one night here costs only 6 yuan – cheap accommodation that attracts backpackers who've made the long journey to Kashgar.

When I sit down on my bed beside the window to look through my pack for a face towel, I notice an enormous dark-green rucksack on the bed next to mine. A newcomer has arrived. I do hope there isn't some weird person sleeping next to me in the unsegregated room of this cheap hotel. The rucksack is good-quality mountain climber's gear emblazoned with an American brand name. It's scuffed and covered with mud, and some of the straps are broken – I can't imagine what travels it's been on. And what could it contain that makes it bulge so? Lying next to it is a long cylindrical object wrapped in a dirty cloth.

I sense that the owner of this pack isn't Japanese. It's too dirty to belong to a Westerner, and too modern to belong to a Pakistani. I want to find out about the owner, but nobody else has returned to the dormitory yet – everyone is outside, relaxing at the food stalls in the cool summer night.

Every evening shish-kebab stalls appear on the street in

front of the Oasis Hotel. Directly across the way is the Seman Hotel, a slightly more luxurious lodging that is full now because it's the peak summer-travel season. For travellers who stay at less expensive establishments, these stalls provide places to hang out and relax. I go back downstairs, my mind filled with the thought of shish kebab.

Smoke from the grills rises to meet me, and the smell of chillies and cumin tickles my nose. As I expected, a crowd of familiar fellow-travellers has gathered: some lively Hong Kongers, another Japanese who was on the bus with me from Turfan, two young women from Osaka, a group of three from the Waseda University Expedition Club and a middle-aged man from Kyushu.

'What happened? You've been gone for quite a while.'

I sit down on a bench and accept a beer from the middle-aged man, who's been travelling for a long time.

'I went to the Abakh Khoja Tomb today and met some Uighurs. *Liang ge*.' I order two shish kebabs from a tiny ancient Uighur man. Just as I'm being served the freshly grilled meat dripping with fat, I hear someone call out, 'Hey, it's the Tibetan! You're back!'

A young Asian man has appeared on the scene. Balancing a large watermelon in one hand, he's wrapped in crimson clothes, with a woven Tibetan sash tied around his head. His face is bright and smiling, and his body is brimming with vitality.

'He arrived this afternoon. Says he lives in Lhasa, in Tibet,' one of the young women from Osaka informs me. Lhasa? Could he be Tibetan?

The young man plonks the melon down on the edge of

the bench and begins dividing it up efficiently with an old dagger he wears at his waist.

'Please, please.' Perhaps this is meant in place of a greeting, for he smiles at the seated travellers as he hands them melon slices before biting into one himself. I hold a piece of melon in one hand and a shish kebab in the other, taking bites from each in turn, but all the while my eyes are riveted on this guy.

He's of medium height and lean, though his arms and legs bulge with muscles, and he's obviously been on a long journey. His dishevelled, shoulder-length hair is matted like mud-hardened yak fur, his shirt and trousers the colour of lamas' robes are torn in places, and worn-out shoes flap open. He has a large nose with flared nostrils, thick lips and pointed eye teeth peeking out from his laughing mouth. His eyes remind me of a wild wolf. The sash around his forehead bears the Buddhist symbol that resembles a swastika. Our eyes meet. He laughs and hands me another piece of watermelon.

I feel certain that this is the owner of that peculiar rucksack.

When I return to the dormitory later, the Tibetan comes in soon afterwards. As expected, he approaches the bed next to mine. He looks at me, then laughs when he sees me unwinding the strip of cloth I've wrapped roughly around my toes to prevent blisters from my ill-fitting Chinese leather sandals, indifferent to how it makes me look. I smile wryly – he's in no position to laugh at other people's appearance! – and say hello. He writes something in Chinese characters on a piece of paper. If he can write characters, then he must be Chinese.

'My name is Cao Yong. I am an artist. I live in Lhasa, Tibet,' he writes. 'My mother is Nepalese and my father is Chinese, but he lives in Bangkok. I am an art teacher – in name at least – at Tibet University in Lhasa.'

'I am an art student at a university in Tokyo. My name is Aya Goda.'

I had left my home town on the northern Japanese island of Hokkaido to enter an art university in Tokyo but had soon grown tired of life there. To be sure, there were many opportunities to see new exhibitions, avant-garde theatre, concerts and films, but once I'd taken in what there was to see, I came to feel that I was merely killing time in tiny spaces around the city. Nothing about contemporary art impressed me. Before I knew it, I found myself travelling to China whenever there was a long holiday break.

'Do you paint too?' Cao Yong asks.

I show him my student ID in reply because it's quicker that way. We can both read and understand the Chinese characters that are common to the Chinese and Japanese languages, even if we don't pronounce them the same way. Yong pulls out his work ID The card says that he's a teacher in the Art Department at Tibet University. Born in 1962. Only five years older than me and already a university teacher at the age of twenty-six!

Cao Yong smiles and opens his bundled-up cylinder. Inside there are canvases. He carefully spreads one out, and I see a picture of a beautiful Asian woman dancing and a captivating bodhisattva, drawn in fine lines like an Indian miniature. It's the first time I've seen this kind of erotic Tibetan religious painting.

'This is something I copied in Ali. It's not my own work.'

Yong proceeds to unroll other pictures to show me. I sense considerable ability in the flow of the precisely drawn lines. The guy's appearance is bizarre, but it does seem possible that he is an extraordinarily talented person.

'These wall paintings in the Guge Kingdom are absolutely exquisite. I really love it there.'

My Chinese is limited to greetings such as *ni hao* for 'hello' and *zaijian* for 'goodbye', or survival phrases for asking prices and numbers, so to communicate with me Yong uses a little English mixed with body language, gestures, written characters and pictures.

'I've been travelling for nearly a year. I went to Mt Everest, Mt Kailas, the Shiquan River and Ali, and then came to Xinjiang. My life during that time is recorded on the film in there. Shame I can't show you,' he says, pointing to the tremendously heavy rucksack.

The rucksack is crammed with photographic equipment, masses of film, camping gear, canvases for painting and a disassembled rifle complete with bullets. Inside the cylinder are dozens of reproductions of Buddhist pictures and as many as a hundred rubbings of ancient stone Buddhas. Yong had journeyed through the Tibetan wilderness on horseback and on foot, arriving in Kashgar via Yecheng. Before that, he'd been living in the ruins of the ancient Guge Kingdom – a Buddhist kingdom invaded by solders from Ladakh three hundred years ago.

'Ali is uninhabited. Not a single tree or blade of grass grows there. I lived for ages in that wasteland and survived by hunting.' Yong has an air of wild strength about him;

his body exudes the smell of the wilderness and he brims over with energy. He appears to be a person who pursues his dreams and hopes, realizing them exactly as he wishes to. I envy him.

'I climbed Everest up to 7000 metres. But it was excruciating. My lips were swollen. It was so tough I thought I'd die! In the camp there I found some Japanese climbing rations – rice processed in May 1962 and dried fish. I ate them because there was nothing else, but they had no flavour at all. Probably because they were even older than me! The air was too thin at that altitude for them to rot.' He goes on to tell me about climbing Everest without oxygen or any other equipment, just a down jacket and sleeping bag. I listen attentively, fascinated by Yong's lively chatter and richness of expression, and lose track of the time. It's as if the wanderer I've yearned to meet ever since I was a little girl has suddenly appeared before me.

It begins to grow light outside, and, not surprisingly, we begin to feel tired, so we end our conversation. Everyone else has been asleep for hours, but the lights were left on for us. Even with them off, Yong can't seem to fall asleep and pulls a book from his pack. 'I'm a nocturnal animal. Will you lend me a torch so I can read? Where are you planning to go after Kashgar?'

'I thought I'd go to Urumqi. I'll go back to Japan before university starts in mid-September.'

'I'm going back to Lhasa after this. Let's go to Urumqi together.'

'All right,' I reply and close my eyes. I recall how, before travelling to Kashgar, I'd blown 10 yuan in Foreign

Exchange Currency as an offering when I prayed to a
Buddha image in the caves at Dunhuang: *Let me meet the
Little Prince in the desert.*

Next day, in Yong's company, a completely new city
appears before my eyes.

'*Chi shenme?*' In the bright morning, he asks if I want to
eat something.

'*Zhua fan,*' I reply, thinking of the delicious Uighur dish
made from chunks of lamb on the bone and carrots cooked
with rice. Yong grabs a passer-by and asks where to find a
zhua fan restaurant. We find one, go inside and sit on a red
woollen carpet on the floor.

'*Zhua fan, duoshao qian?*' Yong asks for prices.

'*Xiao wan, liang yuan, da wan, san yuan.*' Two yuan for
a small bowl, three yuan for a large one.

'*Liang ge da wan, cha.*' Yong orders tea and two large
bowls of food. After a while they're brought out, but there
are only two pieces of meat and bone topping the carrot-
coloured rice.

'*Rou tai shao!*' Yong, who has rapidly calculated the
price for each piece of meat and deduced that there
isn't enough, jumps up and goes into the kitchen to
complain. I'm open-mouthed when he returns beaming
triumphantly and holding chunks of lamb which he places
in our bowls.

'Aya, I'll buy you a bus ticket to Urumqi at the Chinese
price.' Fares are three or four times higher for foreign
travellers than they are for Chinese citizens.

In high spirits, Yong insists that we go to the bus
terminal. Once there he hands me a pack containing his

valuables and plunges into the dense throng of people, squeezing skilfully into the queue. He's soon at the front, but when he reaches the window, a fearsome-looking ticket-seller screeches at him, 'You're a Japanese student, aren't you? You have to pay in Foreign Exchange Currency! Don't think you can fool me!'

She won't believe that Yong is bona-fide Chinese despite the identification card and work ID that prove it. 'You probably got this forged in Hong Kong,' she says accusingly and refuses to sell him the tickets.

'It's no good. Let's try again tomorrow.' With a scowl on his face Yong gives up and we leave. What does this mean? Why can't he buy a ticket in China even though he's Chinese?

'I can't stand those ticket-sellers. Their only entertainment is to find fault with other people. I've been called Japanese many times. Hong Kongers often say I'm a Japanese *ronin*. What in heaven's name is a *ronin*?' Yong asks me bitterly.

'A *ronin* is a wandering samurai.' I burst out laughing at the thought. He probably gets called that because his hair is long. I certainly haven't seen any other Chinese who look the way Yong does – everyone dresses alike in Mao suits with cropped hair. I suppose people who are a bit different, like Yong, are constantly challenged by other Chinese who thrive on finding fault and petty meddling. But on this occasion I'm not surprised that the ticket-seller was suspicious; after all, Yong was trying to get her to sell a ticket for me – a foreigner – too.

On our way back to the bazaar, some Uighur girls yell out 'Savage!' and jump out of our way. Yong smiles wryly.

He's been in the wilderness for too long and looks like a wild man come to the big city.

Along the way we stop in one of the People's Parks – so common in China – that always have a statue of Mao Zedong standing in them. We sit down on a bench under a tree and begin another conversation-in-writing.

'I'm sorry to cause you trouble over the ticket,' I write.

'I'm so happy to be with you. I love you very much,' Yong replies abruptly. 'I will definitely come to Japan to look for you in future.'

What?! His reply astonishes me. After all, we only met last night. Is he just some Don Juan?

'I haven't seen so many flowers and trees for ages,' Yong continues. The next moment, he's hugging me tight and kissing me.

'Savage!' I yell and slap him hard before I know what I'm doing. I get up to leave, but Yong writes furiously to explain himself.

'Why aren't you sure if I'm a good person or not?'

'You're a savage. I've only just met you.'

'It's okay to get mad. But I want you to understand how I feel. I have to be honest with you. There's no need for deception. I hate lies,' he writes, stringing the Chinese characters together as only a native can.

'I always think I'd like to be reborn as a man.'

'But you're a woman, and a good one at that. Don't think such strange thoughts.'

'I've always travelled alone.'

'I've always travelled alone too, but since meeting you I want us to be together. If you'd like to, would you become my wife?' Now, out of the blue, he's proposing to me!

'Not possible.'

'Don't you want to get married?'

'I'll never marry. I'm too selfish.'

'But I don't want to part from you. You have a good character. I feel at peace when I'm with you.'

'We've only just met. How can you know my character?'

'You have a strong will.'

'I do believe that you're a good person. We can be friends. All right?'

'If we can be together, anything is fine by me.'

We set off together again.

In the bazaar, hunting for souvenirs, I linger at a stall lined with rows of knives. While I'm absorbed in looking at them, all different shapes and decorated with elaborate Uighur designs, Yong suddenly grabs the knife-seller and picks a fight with him.

'Hey pal, are these lousy knives 30 yuan? Don't make me laugh.' Is this a kind of entertainment for Yong? I don't know why, but for some reason he seems to be well informed about the quality of the knives and where they come from, and is relentless in his criticism.

'Damn it!' Although the Uighurs are cool, practised salesmen, the man finally explodes, his face turning red as he stamps his feet.

'It's hopeless. These knives are duds. Don't buy them. Let's go,' Yong says and walks away quickly. After all he said before about Chinese people finding fault with others, he's one to talk!

We proceed through the vibrant bazaar thronged with shoppers, weaving through the crowd and gazing at the rich display of goods: colourful hats adorned with embroidery and ornaments, flamboyant shawls and fabrics, copies of the Koran and all sorts of other things.

Suddenly Yong darts ahead. Wondering what has happened this time, I see him grab an Uighur man by the scruff of the neck and start to punch him. A commotion breaks out, and in no time a wall of people surrounds us. What's going on? Is it that this guy just loves to fight? Yong berates the man and jerks his arm up, at which point a small radio slips out of the jacket hanging over his arm.

'Prick! Fucking bastard!' Standing firmly in the middle of the road with the radio in his hand, Yong draws himself up to his full height as he loudly hurls abuse. The man had stolen Yong's radio from the pocket of his backpack.

'This radio is my precious travelling companion,' Yong says, lovingly stroking the Sony shortwave radio. 'When I was alone in the wilderness, it provided my only contact with the world.'

I'm astonished by the intuition that alerted him to the pickpocket.

It's strange how there's never a quiet moment around Yong. On our way back to the hotel, his attention is caught by a big sheep's skull in the midst of the miscellany of goods spread out for sale at the side of the road.

'This is called a *ye pan yang*,' he explains delightedly.

'*Ye pan yang*?'

Yong's eyes sparkle. 'How much is it?'

'It's not for sale.'

Despite this blunt reply, Yong enthusiastically begins bargaining in Chinese mixed with Uighur. Yet again we find ourselves surrounded by people watching the spectacle. Isn't it supposed to be possible to tell the age of animals like this from the number of rings on their horns? I bend over to count the rings and discover that there are more than sixty. Wide as outstretched arms, the curve of this magnificent example looks heroic.

'No. I won't sell.'

'Fifty yuan.' Behind the stall-holder stubbornly shaking his head, an elderly man sitting down to smoke a pipe intervenes in the bargaining.

'Too expensive. Sell it to me for 20.' Yong tries obstinately to beat down the price.

'Thirty yuan, then. Take it!' With these few words from the old man, it's decided. Yong is jubilant as he grasps the skull and lifts it high over his head.

'I love these things.'

'So do I. Such beautiful horns! But can you carry it all the way back to Lhasa?' What is he thinking of buying this heavy skull, considering that he already has that heavy rucksack to carry?

'Sure I can! I'll get a sutra carved into the brow and hang it up for decoration!'

We return to the Oasis Hotel, where Yong rushes to the washroom. Bits of rotting brain still cling to the skull, and the back of it teems with tiny, squirming insects. He flushes water through the eye sockets in order to clean it, causing a cascade of rotting brain and black insects to come pouring out.

'Oh no! You're crazy!'

Some Westerners come in and yell in disgust before fleeing again, but Yong continues what he's doing amidst the commotion. Even if this is a cheap hotel, washing a rotten skull in the communal bathroom is a breach of good manners, I think, and the thought prompts me to fetch some insect repellent and spray it into the skull.

'It might be better if we kill the insects with this.'

Yong turns a beaming face on me, overjoyed that someone approves of what he's doing.

Yong doesn't hesitate in acting if there's something he wants to do; satisfying his desires and impulses appears to be his main aim in life, and thus it's quite impossible for him to be sensitive to other people's feelings. But I'm comfortable with such outrageous behaviour. Watching him reveal himself to me naturally and without affectation, little by little I'm coming to understand the kind of person he is.

We leave Kashgar together, Yong carrying the hugely heavy rucksack and enormous sheep's skull. Yong's pack looks as if it weighs a hundred kilos and I can't even lift it, but he picks it up easily. The sight of him walking along carrying the huge skull with both hands is sufficiently awesome to send people scuttling out of his way.

29 August. Morning. Yong and I set out for the bus terminal by donkey-cart and then board a long-distance bus bound for Urumqi. The journey takes three nights and four days, but now I have a travelling companion it doesn't feel the least bit long.

On the bus we continue our conversation-in-writing without let-up, and my diary becomes completely covered with characters and sketches in no time. When we get onto the subject of art, Yong's attitude takes a surprisingly serious turn. I still have difficulty believing that he could be an artist, but whenever I ask him something relevant, he instantly responds with a sensitive reply.

'Are you free to pursue your art in China?'

'The Communist government controls every aspect of life in China. Art over the last few decades has become a victim of politics. But I've always painted pictures to express my feelings.'

'Do Chinese people understand art?'

'The answer to that question fills me with rage and indignation. The government only wants flunkeys who do what they're told, just like dogs. It has no sense of humanity or respect for human rights. People are little more than bricks to be stacked into place. There is absolutely no tolerance of art that expresses individuality or sincerity.'

'Japan is very free, but there are still problems. These days Japanese society is too soft, so it's only rarely that anything good is produced. Adversity is the best possible condition for producing art, I believe. Therefore China may be able to produce good art in the future. I've seen some films made recently by Chen Kaige and Zhang Yimou, and they were fabulous,' I answer, thinking of *Red Sorghum* and *Yellow Earth* at the Tokyo Asian film festival.

'I've seen Japanese art magazines like *Geijutsu Shincho*. I have a reasonable understanding of Japanese art. I really love *ukiyoe* prints. But it's strange that even though Japan today is an international economic power with highly developed science and technology, in the arts it is, if anything, boring. Art has been reduced to decoration.'

I'm amazed he knows *Geijutsu Shincho*.

'The true value of art is surely in the ultimate spirituality with which all of humankind can identify,' Yong continues. 'It's difficult for you and me to exchange words, but our feelings are the same. By looking at my paintings, maybe you can begin to understand my emotions. Words can't take the place of pictures. Only through painting can I express the pain and other emotions in my heart. When I paint, only then can I enter my own transcendent world. Art is living spirit, one eternal soul.'

There's a compelling power in Yong's gaze. Although I still haven't seen his own work, his way of expressing himself conveys a burning passion to paint from the heart. Yet I really can't understand the anguish and suffering that lie behind his words. What is it exactly that has caused him so much bitterness and sorrow? His words could be taken from a novel or a film, but they aren't a fabrication or a performance; they're uttered straight from his heart ... and render me speechless.

'Japanese people can probably hardly imagine the hardships of the Chinese. What they understand most clearly are the atomic bombs dropped on Nagasaki and Hiroshima. In China, the government itself is a nuclear bomb that could explode at any time. Moreover, it always explodes over the heads of the Chinese people. On the surface, China appears to be free, but in the near future this bomb is likely to explode again.'

'There are some very serious problems, aren't there,' I respond, but I personally have no real feeling for the suffering people experienced in Nagasaki and Hiroshima.

'The Chinese people's vicious cycle of hurting and

deceiving one another deeply distresses me,' Yong
concludes passionately.

'Where were you born?'

'I was born in Henan Province, in Xinxian, which is
below the Yellow River and above the Yangtze, at the base
of the Dabie mountains. All my life I've been tossed about
by circumstances. My family were classified as landowners,
and life ever since I can remember has been a brutal
struggle.'

But hadn't Yong told me that his mother was Nepalese
and his father was a Chinese living in Bangkok? Why
would he lie like that?

'You aren't mixed race, then?'

'No, I'm pure Chinese. There are plenty of arseholes in
China. If they knew I was a Chinese travelling about freely
like this, they'd soon interfere.'

'Can't Chinese people travel freely?'

'No, of course not.' He pulls out the dagger he carries at
his waist to show me. 'This is the dagger my maternal
grandfather used. He was already an army officer by the
time he was my age. It's a great pity he was assassinated
before he turned thirty. I always carried this dagger while I
was travelling through Tibet. It looks menacing and has
tasted the blood of many people. It gives me courage. If I
put it under my pillow at night, not even evil spirits will
come near.'

Yong quickly blacks out the words he's written and
signals with his eyes that it's risky to let anyone see what
we're writing. Then he starts asking the questions.

'Where are you from?'

'A place called Noboribetsu, in Hokkaido.'

'Hokkaido. I've see it in a film. Takakura Ken was in it. Hokkaido is a place of white birches; it snows and it's very cold, isn't it? Is it beautiful there?'

'Yes, it's very beautiful. Noboribetsu is close to the Pacific Ocean and has lots of farms, so I grew up drinking milk.'

'Milk?!' Yong is astonished. 'You drank milk when you were growing up?'

'Yes, every day. Is that strange?'

'I never had anything like milk to drink when I was growing up. We were lucky to get soya milk occasionally. It's incredible that you could drink as much milk as you wanted.'

'I've never experienced having nothing to eat.' Yong's description of his early life sounds worlds away from mine.

'Haven't you?' He's momentarily speechless. 'When will the road under the sea be finished?'

'You know about the Seikan Tunnel? It was finished in March of this year.'

'Japan is so small. Just the distance we've travelled today on the bus would probably be enough to cross the country.'

'Maybe. It takes eighteen hours by boat from Tokyo to Hokkaido.'

'Car journeys in Tibet are calculated in days. It takes more than ten days to drive from Lhasa to Chengdu.'

'If you were born in Henan Province, when did you start living in Tibet?'

'I first went to Qinghai and Xizang – that's Tibet – when I was at university, and I became crazy about the highlands the moment I arrived. I felt that my spirit could be at peace there. I took up my teaching post when I graduated from university.'

'Do you really teach art at a university?'

'Yes. But I soon got tired of being around a bunch of fools and wasting my life. I love the nomads' way of life – being close to nature and living in freedom. That's why I'm always travelling. For years I've been interested in the religions of the Himalayas. On this trip I photographed rock paintings and temple paintings in Ali. Many Westerners visit Lhasa, and they snap up my paintings. A lot of people like them. I have a good American friend who is a collector. He promised to come to Lhasa in October to buy my paintings. My plan is to return in time to meet him.'

Yong did seem to know some Westerners who had arrived in Kashgar with him. I remember a young American buying one of his Guge Kingdom Buddha rubbings for several hundred yuan. Ordinary Chinese workers barely receive a hundred yuan for their monthly salaries, but Yong makes several hundred in one shot; that's a huge sum in China. This financial base is obviously what supports his freedom.

'Next spring,' Yong continues, looking intense, 'I intend to hold an exhibition of my work in Beijing. I've been planning it for many years. There's a chance the government will intervene and cause trouble. Work that expresses humanity or feeling is never permitted, but whatever happens, I'll show you that I can do it.'

'This is your appeal to the people of China, isn't it?'

'Absolutely! I'm destined to fight on their behalf!'

'That must be a wonderful feeling!'

'I hope with all my heart that when the exhibition opens, you'll come and see it.'

'Sure. That'll be right in the middle of the spring break. But be careful. Don't get yourself killed in the process.'

'I intend to leave China after the exhibition.'

'Leave China? Do you mean defect?'

'This is the situation: I've known some Germans for a long time. One of them works for Greenpeace. He buys many of my paintings, and he's someone with influence. He wants to show my work in Germany, but I want to do that after I've had my first exhibition in China. When it's over, I'll contact him. But if the worst happens, I'll go straight back to Tibet and then on to Nepal. There'll be no problem – I know all the escape routes along the Tibetan border.'

Why does Yong need such preparation and determination just to put up an exhibition? Instead of asking him, I pull out my Walkman and get him to listen to some avant-garde music.

'This music is great. Who wrote it?'

'A German group. If you like it, I'll give it to you.'

'It's fantastic!' His eyes shine as he listens intently to *Songs of Byzantine Flowers* by SPK. I feel happy at being able to have even the tiniest bit of influence on him.

'This should be listened to full blast.' Yong persuades the bus driver to turn off the popular Chinese songs he's playing and put on SPK instead. When the avant-garde music resounds throughout the bus, however, the Hong Kong passengers boo loudly.

'What's this weird stuff? Put the other music back on!'

Yong throws them a ferocious look. 'You pieces of dog shit.'

He listens to the Walkman again for a while, then picks up his pen. 'This music is really wonderful. When I hear it, I shiver with sadness, and my heart feels like melting. It's like being led away to an eternal, distant world of dreams. I do not have the words to express this melancholy state. I wish I could stay like this, nestled in a boat of music. Drift ... drift ... and return to my mother's womb. Drift ... and reach the firmament of the eternal spirit.'

The rapturous, intoxicated characters are strung together like a poem.

'I love you. You are the only one to whom I can open the door of my heart and express sincere passion – at last that seems possible. I've been to hell and back. Ever since I was a child I've experienced hardship and had many bitter experiences. I've looked death in the face over and over again. But from the moment I met you, I felt like I'd found the companion I was seeking.'

Yong's words rock me to the core.

When we arrive in Urumqi, we make our way to Heaven Lake. This stunning lake, surrounded by steep, pine-covered slopes and overlooked by Mt Bogda in the Heavenly Mountain range, brims with limpid azure water. We walk past some Kazakh yurts and follow a small, clean river that feeds into the lake high up on the slopes, breathing in the cool, soothing air. Deep in the uninhabited mountains, the atmosphere around Yong finally becomes calm.

This artist carries with him all he needs for camping and also turns out to be a crack shot. After pitching his tent, he picks up his rifle, asking me to confirm that he has only seven bullets, then goes into the woods, returning a short time later holding seven wild birds he's brought down. He skilfully plucks and guts them by the river, and without further ado prepares wild-bird soup in a large enamel mug.

'Mmm, this is delicious.'

We eat the soup with some nan bread, savouring every mouthful. I've never eaten such fresh, delicious food before.

'This is my outdoor menu.' Yong draws pictures to show me what he ate while living in Ali: yaks, sheep, donkeys, pigeons, rabbits, squirrels, crows, mice and wolves. 'Out in the wild, the only way of getting food was to catch it myself.'

Sitting by the campfire and looking up at the starry sky, we let our imaginations wander, talking of our dreams: to roam far and wide and build a house in the place we like best; to travel around in a horse and cart, painting as we go; to go round the world by bicycle, starting in the Himalayas. Such dreams ...

'We'll go to Africa too. To the vast deserts. And when we're ready to stop travelling, we'll settle down in a pristine forest somewhere and paint for a living. I've dreamed of doing this all my life. I swear I'm going to make it happen! I'm not a gregarious person. I live in tune with nature. If you're with me, you won't have to worry about food.' Yong smiles as he speaks, his face full of confidence.

Suddenly he grabs the rifle and, pointing it to the sky, pulls the trigger. 'There are wolves nearby. I'm just giving them a scare. They won't come any closer if I do this.' Now his face is serious.

'There will come a time when you and I will be together, I'm sure of it.' His voice is charged with conviction.

I answer him with a story. 'Do you know that in Greek myth men and women were joined together along their backs? People had four arms and legs, and two faces, and were very wise and strong. They used their arms and legs to move swiftly, just like a wheel. But they were too clever for their own good and plotted to rebel against the gods. The gods became angry and cut them in two. So now men and women, who've lost pieces of themselves, endure lonely, tormented lives as they search for their lost halves. Since I met you, I hope I may have found my missing half.'

'Yes, I knew I'd found my missing half when I met you. Together we are a perfect whole.'

The days at Heaven Lake fly by like a dream, and the time comes when Yong must return to Lhasa to prepare for his exhibition and I must return to Tokyo for university. We go from Urumqi to Dunhuang, and catch a bus to Golmud.

'Don't write to me at Tibet University; send your letters care of my friend Xiaoming. In Beijing you can write care of my painting teacher Yu Ren. And here's my home address.'

13 September. I board a train for Xining.

'Be sure and come to my exhibition in Beijing. I'll write. I'll be waiting.'

'I'll come, you can depend on it. And I'll study Chinese too.'

We exchange promises again at the entrance to the carriage, then Yong leaps onto the platform from the already moving train.

'*Mingnian, jian*! See you next year!' he yells.

I watch him standing on the platform until he disappears

from sight as the train gathers speed. In the plane from Hong Kong to Tokyo, all I can think about is how to learn Chinese as quickly as possible. The moment we land at New Tokyo airport, I buy a Chinese dictionary.

2. REUNION

5 February 1989. The chilly morning air of Guangzhou rouses me the moment I stumble drowsily off the night ferry from Hong Kong. I pass through customs and jump into a taxi. '*Guangzhou huochezhan*,' I say to the driver, who takes me through the still-empty streets to the train station. When he stops the car I clamber out and thrust some *renminbi*, left over from my travels last summer, into his hand.

'What's this? Hey, you're a foreigner! Pay in *waihui*!' the driver yells, objecting to my use of the currency reserved for Chinese citizens. This moment fills me with a real sense of being back on Chinese soil.

Guangzhou Station is quieter than usual because most people have already returned home to celebrate Spring Festival. It looks like it might even be possible to get a hard-sleeper ticket by waiting in the queue at the ticket window, but just to be on the safe side I buy a relatively expensive ticket from the Uighur touts hanging around in front of the station.

Clutching my ticket printed with the words 'Guangzhou

to Beijing, No. 48, departing 21.05', I dash to the telegraph office in front of the station and punch out a telegram to Yong care of his teacher Yu Ren. At last I can relax. Time flies by while I make the usual preparations for travelling in China: at the Dong Fang Hotel I exchange traveller's cheques for Foreign Exchange Currency, which I then change into *renminbi* with an Uighur black-market money-changer. Finally I'm on the train pulling out of the station for the three-day journey north to Beijing, with the sound of Spring Festival firecrackers ringing a send-off in my ears. It's been five months since I said goodbye to Yong, and now here I am again being jolted about on a Chinese train as the opening day of his exhibition finally draws near.

After I returned to Japan, Yong kept me up to date with constant letters and telegrams. And I kept my promise to begin studying Chinese. From Yong's letters I learned that, after returning to Lhasa, he was occupied with trying to raise the money to finance his exhibition. Luckily, he met many Western collectors who bought his paintings and managed to put together a sufficient war chest. In November he gave up his room in Lhasa, disposed of his possessions and set out for Beijing, stopping at his parents' place in Xinyang to get his paintings ready for the show. After arriving in Beijing, he seemed to struggle hard to find a venue, before eventually succeeding. The exhibition was set to open on 14 February.

'Come quickly!' Yong wrote. 'Let's have the exhibition and a wedding at the same time. Get permission to defer your studies and come to Beijing right away!'

My classmates watched in wonder as I studied Chinese during our French classes.

'I met an amazing guy in Kashgar. I really think it was meant to be.'

'It can't be as romantic as all that,' my friends said. 'Look, isn't this guy just about to escape overseas if there's trouble when he has his exhibition? That's why he wants to get married. Don't you keep hearing about Chinese people desperate to leave their country?'

I tried to be rational. First of all, we couldn't possibly build a marriage when I was so offbeat. More important, though, was whether a person like Yong could ever settle into family life? After all, artists do spend their lives drowning in a sea of self-love. It's in their nature to be self-centred – they're just like drug addicts. And how could I make a decision anyway, after spending only eighteen days with him? Who knew what would happen? My friends had to be right – he was asking me to marry him with the intention of leaving China. The sensible thing to do would be to keep the beautiful memory at the back of my mind and have done with it.

But some time later, a thick, heavy envelope landed in my letterbox. Inside, I found several photographs of Yong's work – paintings beyond the scope of my imagination – and my soul was rocked by their impact, so much so that it scared me. It's difficult to appeal directly to someone's heart in words if they speak a different language. But paintings are different. Paintings don't need interpretation. Paintings are direct reflections of a person's heart. I began to get a sense that their intense messages written on thin Chinese letter paper were a cry from Yong's soul, that he was calling to me with an inescapable sense of urgency.

Then, shortly after that, I received one more photograph: Yong, stark naked with the world's highest peak, Mt Everest, in the background. In the picture he was shouting as if he was challenging the mountain – or no, maybe that wasn't it: he seemed to be crying out his desire for union with it.

I lined up the photographs of Yong's paintings and thought long and hard. In the end, I concluded that I had at least to go to Beijing. As if to hold me to my resolve, Yong kept up his campaign of daily telegrams and phone calls.

'I love you! I'm waiting! Hurry up and come!'

I left Japan as soon as spring break started.

It's impossible to sleep under one thin blanket in the freezing-cold hard-sleeper carriage of this northbound train. Before the second night is over I get up and sit by the window, gazing out at dawn breaking over the grey landscape. I haven't slept a wink.

Exactly one year earlier, I'd made the same journey, to see the magnificent Forbidden City of the film *The Last Emperor*. But I'd come to hate Beijing; I'd found it an unfeeling, grey city where people were cold and hard-hearted. If it were not for Yong's exhibition, I wouldn't be going there a second time.

The train arrives at Beijing Station. The air is dry and the weather fine, so I don't feel the cold all that much. Once again, the station is quiet because of Spring Festival. Despite the telegram I sent from Guangzhou, there's no sign of Yong. My feelings, running high at this much-anticipated reunion, turn to disappointment, and I grimace in anger as my temper rises. That my arrival in Beijing should be like this – after having made such a long journey across sea and land to see Yong again!

With me is Nakamura, a young Japanese guy I met on the train who's visiting China for the first time. Together we board a bus to go in search of accommodation. We get off at the Beijing-nan stop and walk along the canal to the Qiaoyuan, a hotel with cheap dormitory rooms for foreign travellers where I stayed on my previous visit. In fact I'd been worried that Yong would be so frantically busy preparing for his exhibition that we might somehow miss each other, so I'd told him that I'd be at the Qiaoyuan.

Feeling like a tour guide, I stand at the reception desk. 'Excuse me,' I begin, flaunting my newly learned Chinese, 'do you have any rooms?'

'*Mei you*. We're closed for Spring Festival.' *Mei you* – those words again! The invariable response of Chinese 'service workers' to any request. The girl behind the desk shakes her head and glares at me, so I withdraw timidly, intimidated as always by these fierce young women workers.

'Listen,' I tell Nakamura, 'she said that they're closed because it's Spring Festival – you know, the old Chinese New Year.' Disappointed, we catch the bus back to the city centre. I figure that once we find a hotel and get rid of our heavy packs, I'll be able to think about what to do next. If I go to the contact address Yong gave me for his teacher Yu Ren, then I can probably find out where the exhibition is being held. But every hotel we try is closed for Spring Festival. Eventually, Nakamura and I reach the Jianguomen district in the centre of Beijing; we've been tramping around for hours and are now in a real pickle.

'It's okay. Let's keep looking,' Nakamura is kind enough to say, but he knows little about China and looks anxious.

The sun is already low in the sky. Staring at the cars rushing to and fro along the roads of Jianguomen, I begin to get seriously worried about what we will do for accommodation tonight.

'Aya!'

Someone behind me calls my name, and I turn around in amazement to see Yong on a bicycle! I'm too stunned for words. Yong, tight-lipped, glares first at Nakamura, then at me. He's misread my relationship with Nakamura!

With bowed head, Yong mutely walks away, pushing the bicycle. I too say nothing, still angry with him for not coming to meet me at the station. To think that this is the moment of our great reunion!

Eventually my patience runs out, and I break the silence. 'Yong, why didn't you meet me? Didn't you receive my telegram from Guangzhou? We've been looking for somewhere to stay. This Japanese guy is in China for the first time, so I offered to help him find a hotel. That's all.'

'Telegram? I didn't get any telegram,' Yong says, looking up at last. 'Perhaps the Telegraph Office has closed for Spring Festival.'

Is it possible that a telegram could still not be delivered after three days? I'm speechless.

We walk until we reach the Dongdan district, where we enter the narrow lane of the Hongxing Hutong. It's lined with *siheyuan* – the characteristic old-style residences built around courtyard gardens – but now, with an extension or shed added on to every single one, not a trace of the original designs remains. In the corner of one compound live Yong's friend Shi Benming and his wife. Apparently they're letting Yong stay there during Spring Festival while they return to their home town.

Standing in front of the brick house, Yong calls out, 'Liao Hong! Liao Hong!' The door opens and a tall, fair-skinned youth appears.

'Aya, this is my friend from university, Liao Hong. He came from Henan to help me with the exhibition.'

'*Ni hao*, Liao Hong.'

'*Ni ... ni ... ni hao, A ... Aya, qi ... qingjin, qingjin.*' Liao Hong has a slight stammer, but with his red lips and fair skin he's a very handsome young man indeed.

Yong invites Nakamura in too, telling him that he'll help him find a hotel later. Nakamura looks flustered at being invited into a Chinese person's house.

'Aren't you lucky to be having this kind of experience so soon after arriving in China? You don't often get such an opportunity, you know.' I try to reassure him.

It isn't easy for foreign travellers to visit Chinese people's homes. Apparently this has become slightly easier in recent times, but the government strictly regulates its citizens' contact with foreigners. Those who do have personal contact with foreigners are watched closely, informed on and sometimes even accused of being spies and severely punished.

Inside, the house is divided into a spacious reception and living area and a bedroom. The living room contains a sofa, a stereo and a table with the implements for ink painting laid out on its top. Several modern abstract ink paintings executed in strong lines decorate the walls.

'This is Shi Benming's work. He's an artist,' Yong informs me.

'*He cha, he cha.*' Liao Hong offers us tea in the Chinese style, pouring hot water over leaves in glass cups.

'This place is close to the gallery. It's perfect for storing my pictures,' says Yong.

'So the venue's fixed?'

'Yes, it's the Artists' Gallery in the Beijing Music Hall, close to Tiananmen Square.'

Having drunk their tea, Liao Hong leaves with Nakamura to help him find a hotel. Now that I'm feeling more relaxed and comfortable, I'm able to make out the Yong I met five months ago, but after the misunderstanding around our reunion, our words are few and awkward. He's wearing the heavy German climbing boots he wore on his Tibetan travels along with army-style camouflage clothes. He's much thinner than he was and looks tired and pale, but his eyes sparkle more than ever. Under his camouflage gear he wears a T-shirt finely embroidered with a sun and a moon, and printed with the words 'Don Carroll Productions'. It's a very elaborate design.

'What's that T-shirt?'

'This was a present from my American friend Don Carroll. He's a photographer. When he saw my paintings, he told me that if I took them to New York, I'd be sure to get a huge response. He gave me this shirt … and the dream of going to America.'

'Ah, the Don Carroll you told me about in your letters, right? The person who bought your paintings in Lhasa?'

'That's right. We can really relate to each other. Someday I'm going to America!' Yong stands up and prods me to go outside. 'Come and look at my paintings.'

The paintings are in a storehouse next to the main building. One by one he brings them out and lines them up in the twilight against the brick wall for me to examine. I had no idea from the photographs that they were this big – taller than a person. It's incredible to think that he lugged several dozen of them all the way to Beijing on his own. There are, of course, no door-to-door parcel-delivery services in China. Yong carried the paintings several thousand kilometres, travelling by bus and train. With no rail connection to Lhasa, first he would have had a day-long bus journey to Golmud, then another day by train from Golmud to Xining, and finally a further three days being jolted on a train to Beijing.

'Oh, look, they're peeling!' Yong frowns and points to scratches on the paintings. 'The bus rolled over.'

'The bus?' I don't understand what he means, but I let it go, for I am transfixed. The canvases, made of sheets and rags patched together, are stretched over frames of wooden scrap. It's too bad that the pictures should have become creased, with big patches of oil staining the backs of several of them.

The paintings vibrate with outpourings of feeling, depicting the cries of a soul unmasked. They've been painted using classic Western techniques, yet the skill and expression aren't borrowed – these express Yong's own vitality. It's as if the pictures are breathing. I find it difficult to look at them square on; if I don't keep myself steady, I feel I might lose my balance and fall over. I believe that paintings are the tracks of people's spirits, but what form and dimension of spirit passed over these canvases? Although Yong is only twenty-six, I don't know any other living artist who can paint pictures of this calibre.

As the last rays of the sun fade away, I finally finish my viewing. At that instant, Yong embraces me.

'Aya! I thought you wouldn't come. I love you. I need you. Let's get married!' His insistence is frightening.

'I'm still a student; I can't even think about marriage. I only came to see your exhibition,' I answer eventually, feeling confused.

Lowering his head, Yong returns to the house without another word.

Once we're both inside, I ask about everything that's happened since we parted.

'I couldn't write everything in my letters because I was afraid they would be censored,' he tells me. 'After I returned to Lhasa, I was trying desperately to raise the money to hold my exhibition. I didn't know how much I'd need for this kind of one-man show in Beijing.' Yong tells me how he amassed several thousand American dollars – a huge sum – but has already used up most of it on preparations. I'm amazed he managed to get hold of that much money. He has a wad of American dollar bills sewn into his jeans.

'I left Lhasa in November taking only the essentials with me. I removed my paintings from their frames and carried them rolled up. Once the exhibition is over, I'm ready to escape abroad if I have to.'

'Your German friend will help you leave, won't he?'

'No, we're not in touch any more.'

'Then what will you do?'

'I've been to Nepal without a passport before. It'll be okay. I'll go to Burma from Yunnan.'

'You'll cross the border?'

'I'm just thinking ahead. I'm not sure there'll be trouble over my show.'

'What was that you said earlier, about the bus rolling over?'

'There was an accident during the night after we left Lhasa.'

'You mean to say that the bus you were on rolled over?!'

'That's right. The day I decided to leave, I rushed to the station to catch a bus to Golmud, but it was already full. So I asked the driver to let me sit on the seat over the engine, next to him.' Yong goes on to tell me that the driver fell asleep at the wheel and the bus swerved off the Qinghai–Tibet Highway, plunging into pitch-black wilderness. It rolled over several times, but at the first roll, Yong, who'd been asleep, flew through the windscreen like a bullet. As soon as he collected his wits, he realized that he was unharmed. However, when he saw the bus only a metre away with its wheels buried in the ground, he broke out in a cold sweat.

The bus lay on its side in the moonlit wilderness, bent and crushed out of shape, while injured passengers moaned and screamed – truly a scene of pandemonium. Yong could just make out that the luggage, which had been loaded on the roof, now lay scattered all over the ground.

'My pictures! What's happened to them?' Yong scrambled up and went to check his things. There were engine-oil stains on the canvases that had been fastened to a pole next to the driver's seat, but otherwise they were undamaged.

'Kill the driver!' the Tibetans began to yell in unison. Looking over, Yong saw a man stand up, holding a large dagger. The Tibetans whose relatives had been killed in the accident wanted revenge, so the driver, terrified by the sight of the man brandishing his dagger, hid behind Yong.

The dagger-brandishing Tibetan violently shoved Yong aside, but Yong did his best to plead on the driver's behalf, saying that it had been an accident. Yong persuaded the angry man that they needed to help the injured passengers first, and at last all of the Tibetans drew back.

The driver was grateful to Yong for helping him to escape death. 'It doesn't look like we'll be leaving here tonight,' he said.

Yong was used to these kinds of accidents in Tibet, so he got out his sleeping bag and prepared to go to sleep. Later that night, another bus driver noticed the accident scene from the highway and stopped. The second bus was owned by the same company, and the drivers knew each other.

'Oy! Can you take the injured passengers to hospital in Golmud for me? And take this fellow too, would you?' The driver arranged for Yong to get a ride on the other bus in gratitude for saving his life.

'It was 1.03 a.m. when the accident happened. I know because that's when my clock stopped.' Yong shows me a broken digital clock he carries with him as a souvenir. 'I was wearing this jacket then too. It's a bit torn, but I wasn't hurt. Only a few scratches. I can't help feeling that this jacket protected me. Anyway, after I arrived in Beijing, I went to all the galleries and museums looking for a venue, but at every place I tried they called my work "obscene" and refused to exhibit me.'

'Obscene? That's why you were rejected?' I don't understand. I thought any gallery would naturally want to show work of this quality.

'This is China, you know.' Yong seems to think that these words explain everything.

In Japan, anyone can rent a gallery and hold an exhibition for a small fee. In China, though, it's almost impossible for anyone apart from those authorized by the government to display work they've created outside the system. Since the Cultural Revolution, art has existed only to serve as propaganda and praise the socialist state. Writers who espoused freedom of expression were massacred, while most people kept their mouths firmly shut and repeated the sayings of Mao Zedong. After going through such times, free expression was locked up in the depths of people's hearts.

Nevertheless, things appear to be becoming a bit freer, with the work of younger artists like Luo Zhongli, Chen Danqing and He Duoling being recognized. But their paintings are realistic representations of farming life and cultural minorities that can be said to fall within the framework of Socialist Realism. In contrast, Yong's work strikes me as revenge, at long last, for the government's denial and suppression of human expression ever since the Cultural Revolution. In his paintings, Yong explodes all kinds of oppression: sexual, religious, human. Of course this is a country where people are given the death sentence for possessing pornographic videos, so powerful depictions of women's bodies, emphasizing their genitals, and of

Tibetan lamas could cause problems here.

'Three months ago, when I showed other artists my work and told them my plan for a one-man show, they laughed at me. Everyone said I couldn't do it with these paintings, that it was absolutely impossible. I began riding around Beijing on a bicycle looking for a venue.'

I heard later that the word amongst Beijing artists at the time was that a 'madman had arrived from Tibet'.

'All the official museums and galleries refused to take my work. I was worn out, but I never even thought of giving up. Then a friend introduced me to the Artists' Gallery. I met the owner, Mr Fu. He's passionate about presenting public exhibitions and is also involved in introducing young Chinese artists overseas. When Mr Fu saw my work, he said, "Let's have an exhibition." I couldn't believe my ears! My artist friends were all astonished too – they said it was a miracle. And so at last it was settled.'

Several creases carved into his face provide graphic evidence of Yong's difficult struggle so far. But having only just arrived from Tokyo, I can't quite grasp the situation. It all seems quite different from the understanding I have of what's involved in holding an exhibition. There's tension here, as if a battle is about to begin. Indeed, in his camouflage jacket, Yong appears ready to throw himself into whatever confrontation might occur. I have a definite sense that events of tremendous import are about to happen and feel that I very much want to be there to see it all unfold, to be of some help.

3. THE OPENING

8 February 1989. The next day, Yong takes me with him wherever he goes. Early in the morning, a group of five or six Canadians, Frenchmen and Mexicans visit Shi Benming's house to see Yong's paintings. They reserve two pictures to buy after the exhibition closes.

Next, we go to the coffee shop of the Jianguo Hotel, where Yong has promised to meet a young painter from Chengdu called Xue Mingde. Yong tells me that Xue Mingde belongs to the Stars Group, formed in 1979 by artists who sought freedom and democracy. We find a table and Xue looks at photos of Yong's paintings for a while, making admiring sounds. Then he speaks, a serious expression on his face.

'Cao Yong, listen carefully. I was inside for ten years. Things have got a lot better now, but even so, you'd better be ready to do at least half of that.' Xue Mingde has recently been released from prison for his participation in Wei Jinsheng's democracy movement. Yong merely knits his brows and lights a cigarette.

In the evening, we visit a friend of Yong's called John

Morrison, the vice-consul at the Canadian Embassy, at his flat in the embassy district. We receive a warm welcome and are shown into a beautifully decorated living room where Yong's work hangs on the walls. Mr Morrison speaks fluent Chinese. He'd been intrigued by rumours about Cao Yong when he'd gone to Lhasa and, on seeing Yong's work there, had promised to help when he had an exhibition in Beijing. Mr Morrison's assistance took various forms, including paying high prices for Yong's paintings to help fund the show.

'At last you've managed to have your exhibition. I'm delighted. I'll let other foreigners in Beijing know about it,' he assures Yong, beaming as he holds up a bundle of leaflets announcing the show.

9 February. Yong has received an invitation to make a presentation at the Youyi Friendship Hotel, where a dozen or more visitors from France, America and Spain have gathered to view a slide show of his work. Americans and Germans take most easily to his paintings, he tells me.

'Only once did some Japanese buy one of my pictures. It was so unusual that I asked this couple where they were from, and it turned out they'd been living in Canada for a long time.'

'That'd be right. Japanese people look at paintings with their ears, not their eyes.' I smile wryly.

10 February. In a back street of Dongdan, close to Shi Benming's home, we find a small Xinjiang restaurant selling *yangrou baozi*, steamed buns filled with lamb. A delicious smell fills the shop. We order ten buns from the

young Hui waiter for 7 jiao each. We marvel at how delicious the buns are – the thin wrappings stuffed to bursting – and order extra servings. The lamb-based cuisine of the Muslim Hui minority is the perfect source of energy in the cold Beijing winter. In China I get intense cravings for fatty food I could never imagine eating in Japan; the different environment requires it. If I ate Japanese food like buckwheat noodles or sashimi, I'd probably never have the strength to run for a seat on a train or squeeze into a queue to buy tickets, or the energy to give someone the brush-off or bargain while I'm shopping. Chinese people eat fatty food all the time because their daily lives depend on it.

Silently we stuff the fist-sized buns dripping with fat into our mouths. Yong scoffs them down at a great rate. The Hui youth gasps when he comes over to our table; I see that all the buns we ordered have disappeared. Yong is equipped with a unique stomach that enables him to cram in great quantities of food at one sitting.

'The modern-art exhibition opened at the National Art Museum on the 5th. Do you want to see it? There're two pictures of mine in it.'

Entitled *China/Avant-Garde*, this is the first exhibition of contemporary art ever mounted in China. Organized by a passionate young critic called Li Xianting and others, it displays work by young artists from all parts of the country. The exhibition slogan is 'No U-Turn'.

We walk through the chilly streets to the museum, where it becomes apparent that there's some kind of disturbance; security police surround the building, and a large crowd of young people is sitting in the grounds. We leap over the barriers, and Yong looks around for someone he knows.

'Hey, what's going on here?' he asks.

'On opening day Tang Song and Xiao Lu fired two guns at their work, calling it performance art. The police moved in straight away and closed down the exhibition. But it must stay open until the last day! That's why we're all protesting.'

A prominent 'No U-Turn' banner hangs over the front entrance, which has been closed off by the security police. As many as a hundred people sit in protest with their arms linked.

On 11 February the exhibition does re-open, and we pay a visit. Apparently since Tang's father is a high-ranking official, he and Xiao Lu have been released.

There's an extraordinary atmosphere in the museum, more akin to a revolution than to an exhibition. As we step through the entrance, I immediately notice that the walls are completely filled with groups of works, reaching all the way up to the third floor. There's such a variety, including strange objets d'art and several large pieces of paper printed with Mao Zedong's face in modern styles. They may be rough around the edges, but each and every one of the works on display conveys passion. Their unrefined yet tremendous vitality and insistence are overwhelming – I've never felt anything like it at exhibitions in Japan.

'This is pretty interesting, isn't it?' Yong points to a piece of paper hung from the ceiling that traces a curve through the air on which countless hieroglyphics have been printed. 'These are seals carved by Xu Bing. They look like genuine characters, but they're all invented.'

I have to take my hat off to the artist who hand-carved tens of thousands of these made-up characters, one by one.

Yong's paintings are on the second floor. He's only showing two small pictures because of the overlap with his private show, yet even amongst the many unconventional works on display, his paintings of rocky mountains shaped like praying hands that tower over a moonlit wilderness stand out from the rest.

In the evening we go to the Central Academy of Art to attend a debate on the modern-art exhibition. The auditorium is filled to capacity with hundreds of young people from all over China, and the atmosphere buzzes with excitement. A balding, pot-bellied, middle-aged man – one of the show's organizers – steps onto the podium and begins pontificating to the audience. Many of the hot-blooded young people sitting towards the front begin to boo. There's a rumbling of jeers from every corner of the hall that doesn't quite crystallize into words.

Yong sits there listening to the speech for a while, then leaps to his feet and begins arguing loudly with the speaker. The auditorium immediately falls silent at the sound of his booming voice, but a moment later it's thrown into a furore, with clapping and all manner of abuse being shouted. It's as if Yong has struck the spark that everyone was waiting for. A number of people gather around in a show of support. With Yong at their centre, they light up cigarettes and puff away, although smoking is forbidden in the auditorium, and vigorously carry on their dispute. It isn't clear to me whether this is a serious discussion or just a quarrel, but it goes on for some time.

The expression on Yong's face suggests that nothing is being achieved. 'We can't waste our time on this boring stuff,' he tells his supporters and leaves the hall. He's like the ringleader of a kids' gang recruiting followers. It's interesting to glimpse this bad-boy side of Yong, but I can't follow the tirade of Chinese.

'What were you talking about just now?'

'That idiot giving the speech was posturing about how "it is absolutely necessary that artists be part of a movement. Art is activism"! But I think that's rubbish. Artists create because they're moved by individual passions. It's got nothing to do with group movements. Didn't we come to Beijing because we wanted to show our work?! I said this kind of debate was meaningless and boring.'

I'd thought they were picking a quarrel, but it was in fact a debate on serious issues. There's a sense of tremendous pent-up energy in the young people who've gathered here this evening which feels like it could explode at any time. They're like volcanic magma seeking an outlet and waiting for the person who will inspire them.

The air in Beijing is dry in February; the sky is clear every day. I look over at the portrait of Mao Zedong in Tiananmen Square – on the red wall it stands out vividly against the deep blue sky – as we cycle down Changan Avenue. The still-new Beijing Music Hall, where the latest contemporary music in China is presented, comes into view on our left.

'The exhibition space is on the second floor.' Yong leaves his bicycle in the Music Hall car park, and I follow him up the stairs at the side of the building to the Artists' Gallery.

The long, narrow exhibition space is empty, waiting for Yong's show. On one side is a large window designed, I suppose, to enable works to be viewed in natural light. Several sofas are placed beneath the window.

'There's Mr Fu, Aya.'

A small, slightly overweight middle-aged man appears from the back of the gallery. '*Ni hao, ni hao*, your show's starting at last, then. Would you like to have a look at the permanent exhibition?' Mr Fu leads us to a room at the back. 'This work has been exhibited in Japan too.' He points to a small picture.

Mr Fu is bright and cheerful. While Yong discusses details with him, I look around at the permanent display of works depicting village life, realistic landscapes and young girls from China's ethnic minorities.

Next morning, Yong sets to work getting ready for his exhibition. Together with Liao Hong, he stacks his paintings onto the carrier rack of a borrowed bicycle. The stack of paintings wound round with rope looks alarming. Will Yong really be able to move such a large load? In fact when he pushes down hard on the pedals with his big mountain-climbing boots, the bicycle moves off smoothly towards Changan Avenue with its cargo intact. Somewhat disbelieving, I follow along behind.

Yong's threads his way through the throng of bicycles along Changan Avenue and Tiananmen Square. Friends who've come to help with setting up wait in front of the Music Hall, including a student from the Central Academy of Art, an artist visiting from Tianjin and others.

'Aya, would you draw me a sign for the exhibition?'

I'm happy to be entrusted with this important task. With

prayers for the exhibition's success, I draw the Tibetan deity Samvara.

That night, with everything in readiness, we all gather to eat lamb hotpot and toast the exhibition's success. Shi Benming and his wife, Sun Min, back in Beijing now the Spring Festival break is over, also join us. Shi Benming has a carefully tended moustache and exudes a refined air. Like her husband, Sun Min is also an ink artist. These friends of Yong have taken good care of him during his time in the capital.

'I've had one surprise after another ever since this one came to Beijing,' a slightly drunk Shi Benming declares. 'He's not an artist – he's a warrior. He was so fired up it was frightening. Desperately trying to economize even though he's got some money, saying he didn't know how much the exhibition would cost. He was eating stale pork every day, you know! Everyone's talking about him – "Cao Yong, the savage from Tibet, is in town, up to who knows what." But he actually pulled it off. I'll be damned. I really can't believe it!'

'Did you know everyone's saying Cao Yong is a soldier who stormed Beijing on a fighter plane from Tibet?' one of the young artists asked, laughing.

Aha, so it's not just me. I've been thinking that the reason an artist like Cao Yong seems so out of the ordinary is because I'm Japanese, but Chinese people think the same thing. When I hear everyone's impressions like this, it becomes clear to me that Yong's efforts to get this far with his exhibition have indeed been heroic.

'When Cao Yong arrived in Beijing, he slept in his sleeping bag on a bench in a public bathhouse for 8 jiao a night,' Liao Hong informs us. Beijing bathhouses rent out their changing rooms at night as cheap lodgings. Such places are crowded with labourers and peasants who've come to find work in the city.

On this night, though, we move from Shi Benming's house to stay at the Central Academy of Art, in the studio of Lao Fan, a student there. Couples without a marriage certificate can't stay together in hotels in China, and this rule is particularly strictly enforced in Beijing. The space that Lao Fan has cheerfully offered us is a sprawling one. Artists' implements lie scattered around, and the air smells of oil paint.

'Is this all right?' Yong asks me with a slightly worried expression. But I'm well aware that we're in no position to be fussy about accommodation. Still buoyed up by exhilaration, it doesn't bother me at all.

We make a simple bed with whatever rags we can find in a corner of the studio and retire early. Lights go out at ten at night at the academy to save on electricity, but in the candlelight I can see that Yong is having trouble falling asleep.

We leave for the gallery by taxi early the next morning. The series of forty or so works on show is entitled *The Split Layer of Earth – Mt Kailas*. Mt Kailas, Kang Rinpoche in Tibetan, is a holy mountain in the westernmost part of Tibet. In Buddhism, it is the centre of the world, and means 'navel of the earth'. 'The Split Layer of Earth' refers to the strata that created a fissure within the Himalayas when they were formed by a rise in the level of the ocean floor.

Opening time arrives as the staff are finishing

preparations for the party. Streams of people enter, and, in no time at all, the gallery is crowded with Westerners, Chinese, newspaper reporters and the media from many countries. Mr Morrison taps Yong on the shoulder and shakes his hand to congratulate him. More than anyone else, he knows how long and hard Yong has struggled to make this exhibition happen. He introduces Yong to his friends with great fanfare.

Amazingly, the show has attracted all the prominent foreigners in Beijing. The bureau chief from the *New York Times* is here, as are a CNN reporter, a manager from the West German company Siemens, staff from the American and French embassies' cultural sections, Spanish and Bolivian diplomats, representatives from the bureaus of overseas newspapers and staff from many other embassies. But I feel disappointed that amongst the embassy personnel, I don't see a single Japanese.

Mr Fu makes an introductory speech: 'The gallery is extremely honoured to hold this exhibition by Mr Cao Yong. We are tremendously proud that China is producing great young artists in these times. Cao Yong is a highly individual artist who has lived for a long time in Tibet and travelled through the uninhabited wilderness there while living off the land by hunting. To those of us living so far away, Tibet seems like a frightening, uncivilized place, but the culture, nature and way of life there have had an enormous impact on this artist's creativity. I hereby open this exhibition of paintings by Cao Yong, who was inspired to produce them by the land of Tibet. The exhibition runs from today until the 18th. Please enjoy yourselves.'

Journalists start interviewing Yong, and there's flickering

light from camera flashes. Yong looks larger than life, responding with shining eyes to the well-wishers who come up to shake his hand and embrace him. Reactions to the pictures vary: some people smile, some groan and weep, some frown and some exclaim in surprise. One woman is crying and throws her arms around Yong. People's masks fall away; their souls are revealed for all to see.

Yong stands at the heart of all this, in the centre of the gallery, pumping out a continuous supply of blood to his paintings.

A flurry of people comes and goes; right up until closing time we barely have a moment to breathe. And Yong has promised to meet someone called Chen Jun and his English wife, Jenny, at the coffee shop of the Jianguo Hotel afterwards. Born in Shanghai, Chen Jun has American citizenship. He's a young democracy activist, involved with editing the party organ of the Chinese Alliance for Democracy – also known as China Spring – which is mainly active in America, but he also manages the JJ Art Bar in Beijing.

On 6 January, the dissident physicist Fang Lizhi sent a letter to Deng Xiaoping calling for a release of political prisoners. In the letter he pointed out that China had to resolve its human-rights problems; he also called for a nationwide amnesty and the release of Wei Jingsheng and other political prisoners, this year being the fortieth anniversary of the founding of the People's Republic of China, as well as the seventieth anniversary of the May Fourth political and intellectual movement. Wei Jingsheng was an activist who'd written and placed a poster advocating individual rights on the so-called Democracy Wall in Changan Avenue in 1978. Chen Jun has links with Fang Lizhi and others, and is using the JJ Art Bar as a base from which to contact young artists who've come to Beijing for the modern-art exhibition, and to further his plan to start a democracy movement calling for the release of political prisoners.

We meet Chen Jun in the Jianguo Hotel. He's a slight young man with fair skin and intelligent features. Jenny is tall, blonde and beautiful. Yong has been in contact with Chen Jun since meeting him in Beijing. This evening Chen Jun appears to be trying to convince Yong of something, engaging him in deep discussion for a long time. On the way back to the studio, Yong explains: 'Chen Jun was asking me to join the movement to release political prisoners. He wants me to meet Fang Lizhi and the others and join with them to try and free Wei Jingsheng. But I've been turned off the business of politics and that kind of stuff for a long time. Besides, I didn't come to Beijing to get involved in politics. I came to show my paintings.'

Chen Jun was probably counting on Yong's ability to stir up young people. The debate about the modern-art exhibition that took place at the Central Academy of Art comes to mind.

'My grandma often used to say, "*Lingxiu* soon gets soiled",' says Yong.

'*Lingxiu*?' The word is new to me, and I don't understand.

'*Lingxiu* means the leaders at the top in China, but *ling* is a homonym for *collar*. *Xiu* is *sleeve*. On clothing, the collar and sleeve are the first parts to get dirty, aren't they?'

'Uh-huh, I get it.'

Many Chinese people wish ardently for the democratization of China. For interested overseas Chinese and those like Chen Jun who have American citizenship, there's little to lose if they become involved in political movements. It isn't so easy for Chinese living in the country, for they never know when the situation will change and disaster befall themselves or their families.

There are fewer visitors on the second day of the exhibition; nevertheless, a constant stream of people continues to flow through it. Yong appears to be terribly on edge and observes every visitor carefully. His nervousness puzzles me.

'It's the plain-clothes police,' he whispers with a serious expression. 'A man just happens to appear at my side whenever I speak to someone.'

I think of the closure of the modern-art exhibition, but then that was because of the shooting incident in the galleries, wasn't it? If someone fires a gun indoors, there are bound to be problems, no matter what country it happens in. Why would the police come to Yong's exhibition?

That evening we go to the Spanish Embassy, where Yong has been invited to give a lecture. A crowd of Westerners waits in the large hall. He's going to show slides of his own work as well as of wall paintings in the ruins of the Guge Kingdom. This event has been planned in conjunction with his exhibition as an introduction to Tibetan culture and to deepen understanding of Yong's own work. Midway through the twentieth century, the Italian Tibetologist

Giuseppe Tucci visited the Guge Kingdom to study the ruins there, but Tibet has been largely cut off from the outside world since the Chinese invasion.

Projected onto a large screen, the Guge Kingdom wall paintings' impact is breathtaking. Aside from the power of these pictures being unveiled for the first time, it's obvious even to an amateur like me that they are magnificent, technically superb works. The audience gazes intently at the screen. Vividly coloured murals depict Hell, sky burials, bodhisattvas and the birth of the Buddha Sakyamuni. These aren't just religious paintings: they have a mysterious attraction that springs from something even deeper. Yong stands before the large crowd and begins to speak about the Guge Kingdom. The room falls silent.

4. DAYS AS A KING

'After graduating from university,' Yong began, 'I took up a post as an art teacher at Tibet University. There's an old Chinese saying: "The mountains are high, the Emperor is far away." That's what I thought Tibet would be like; being far from Beijing, it would be freer – a better place to pursue my art. But as it turned out, I wasn't suited to the profession of teaching. Before long, I became captivated by the wilderness and vanishing religious culture, and began walking from one end of Tibet to the other.

'As an artist, I felt respect and some kind of responsibility for the temple paintings that were disintegrating gradually due to neglect and the weather, and so I began to make reproductions of them. I'd like to tell you about the months I spent as king of the uninhabited castle in the Guge Kingdom.

'Less than two hundred years have passed since Tibet became known to the outside world. Tibet was a mysterious land – completely isolated in a rugged geographical environment, and with a primitive way of life in which Buddhism occupied an absolute position. In 1904, the British Indian army sent an armed mission to open the gates of this forbidding snowy region and discovered a world beyond their imagination – of Tibetans whose lives remained as they had been in ancient times. The average altitude in Tibet is 4000 metres, and it was the surveyor-general of British India, Sir George Everest, who also discovered that Chomolungma, as the mountain is called in Tibetan, is the world's highest peak.

'Western Tibet is the bleakest and most desolate area of the country. This is the region of Ali, situated between the Himalayas and the Gangdise mountains, a thousand kilometres or so from Lhasa. When I dug up fossilized marine plants and shells from the strata there – the "split layer" – I realized the truth in the words of the bespectacled geographer who surmised that this uninhabited area had once been covered by a sea. Now Ali has finally been uncovered too, just like those fossils.

'The Guge Kingdom ruins are at the westernmost edge of the Changtang Plateau in Zanda County, bounded by India to the west and south, and bordering Kashmir on the north-west. The population is just over four thousand.

'The Guge Kingdom and one of its two capitals, Tsaparang, fell into ruin in the 1630s. It had attracted the interest of historians, archaeologists and Tibetologists for some time, but the remote location and forbidding environment kept visitors away. Even before the famous Tucci visited, however, an Englishman called Captain Young journeyed there along the Xiangquan River from India. He carried out detailed research, which he published in 1919 in an article entitled "A Journey to Tholing and Tsaparang in Western Tibet".

'The founder of the Guge Kingdom had been a descendant of the Tubo Kingdom, centred in Lhasa. Therefore, to relate the history of the Guge Kingdom, we must look back to the final period of the Tubo Dynasty.

'The Tubo Kingdom posed a threat to the Tang Dynasty to the east and Nepal to the west, and exerted power over central Asia, but by the middle of the ninth century it was in decline. There was a violent split in the royal family as a result of King Lang Darma's oppression of Buddhism. The kingdom fell into chaos, and at the end of the century, Bekotsang, son of O'sum, was assassinated. Bekotsang's son, Gyide Nyimagun, crossed the snowy mountains and fled to the vast, boundless wilds in the west. Thus the descendants of the Tubo set the stage for the seven-hundred-year history of the Guge Dynasty.

'The king of the land to which Gyide Nyimagun had fled welcomed him as a son-in-law and successor. Three sons were born, and the land was divided amongst them. The eldest, Ribagun, ruled Moyu; the second son, Zhaxi Deguan, ruled Purang; and the third son, Dezogun, ruled Xiangxiong, which is Ali. Moyu, in southern Kashmir, became the Kingdom of Ladakh; Purang, which bordered Nepal, became the Kingdom of Purang; and the Guge Kingdom was established in Xiangxiong. Ali entered an unprecedented period of prosperity. However, the division of territory into three planted the seeds of later conflicts.

'At the beginning of the fifteenth century, the Kingdom of Ladakh began a war with the Guge Kingdom. Then in the early sixteenth century, the Guge king married off his daughter to the twenty-first king of Ladakh, and relations improved temporarily as a result. By the end of the century, however, the conflict had intensified, and the people and monks of Guge joined with the Ladakh army to attack the royal palace. After the battle, Ladakhi troops took the Guge king and royal family away as prisoners of war, thus bringing down the curtain on the history of the Guge Kingdom.

'Peace came to Ali once again. All that remained of the illustrious Guge Dynasty was their castle. Today, the ruins of the kingdom look weathered and worn, as if they have been excavated from the bottom of the sea. Only the thunder of spring storms pleads the brilliance of the past, and the shrieking winter winds tell of the sorrows of bygone days. The sole visitors now are starving wolves.

'In the spring of 1986, I learned from looking at Tucci's *Tibetan Painted Scrolls* about the many superb wall paintings in the temples of Ali. These appeared to be outstanding examples of Tibetan art, and I felt an urgent desire to go there immediately, certain they would have been neglected and left unprotected after the Cultural Revolution.

'First I went to the village of Khorjak in Purang County, in westernmost Tibet. Khorjak Gompa, the monastery in the centre of the village, had been out of use for several years. Nowadays it mostly serves as the village storehouse or sheep pen. The wall paintings there – the oldest in Ali – were, according to folklore, drawn by a disciple of Atisha, the famous Indian scholar-monk who was invited to teach in the area. The monks in Khorjak Gompa all returned to secular life during the Cultural Revolution. The chief lama became a high government official in Purang County, but others stayed on in Khorjak and lived peacefully with grazing stock. They have wives and children, and when the weather is fine they meet up with their former fellow-monks to sit in the sun and drink, occasionally reading sutras aloud. By sunset, the sounds of voices reading have usually turned into snores.

'One day when I was there, a lama named Chamba was resting against the outer wall of Khorjak Gompa, basking in the sun as he usually did, when a woman holding a sick baby came along. Chamba intoned prayers to banish evil spirits and gave the woman some black lumps of medicine.

'Next morning, I was at the gompa gate making barley soup when I saw the woman again, looking upset and holding her baby tight; it did not even have the strength to cry. I put my hand on the baby's head; it was burning.

'"This is a terrible fever. I've got some medicine I brought from Lhasa; if you give it to the baby, he might get better," I told the woman. But she had more faith in Chamba's prayers and didn't listen to me.

'Maybe Chamba had been drinking heavily the previous night, but by midday he still hadn't made an appearance. A young man living opposite the monastery went over and whispered something to the woman holding the baby. A short while later, she came over to ask me for the medicine.

'Early the next afternoon, I was upstairs in the gompa working on a reproduction of a mural depicting the birth of the Buddha Sakyamuni when I noticed some sort of commotion outside. I looked out the window and saw a crowd of villagers coming my way. The woman to whom I'd given the medicine the day before was at the centre of the group, cradling something in her arms. I thought then that the medicine I'd given her must have been wrong and that I was in deep trouble. But it was too late to get away.

'As I sat there frozen with panic, the villagers came up the stairs. One big fellow walked towards me. I broke out in a cold sweat but forced myself to smile. The man stood right in front of me, then grabbed my hand and squeezed it.

'"Thank you! You saved my son!" he exclaimed.

'I breathed a sigh of relief even though I was furious at being given such a shock. The villagers then gave me some dried mutton and a bag of *tsampa*, that's roasted barley flour, and went on their way. I was filled with an inexpressible happiness to think that the medicine I had so casually given to the woman had produced this result! All I'd done was to imitate a doctor examining a patient. This was surely a case of that old saying "The blind cat catches a dead mouse."

'After that, many people started coming to see me every day. There was a child with boils on his head, and an old person whose gold tooth had come out. There was even an old woman whose sons carried her to see me because she had hurt her back when a yak kicked her while she was milking it. As thanks for helping her they gave me a bottle of *qingke* barley wine in a bottle that smelt of petrol. Four days later my medical kit was empty, including the supply of musk-deer ointment I had been saving so carefully. Chamba's daughter took my last remaining bandage to use as a hairband.

'Then the Purang County officials heard a rumour that a Han Chinese from Lhasa had come on horseback to Khorjak Gompa and was making copies of the wall paintings there. They were spurred on by this rumour to hold a meeting – since they always had time on their hands – at which they concluded that the wall paintings must be incredibly valuable, conveniently forgetting that they themselves had destroyed Khorjak Gompa during the Cultural Revolution. Although one Public Security official was dispatched to keep an eye on me, the villagers kept me informed of the officials' intentions.

'In that part of the country, the county officials' word is law. One night, while everyone was sleeping, I mounted my skinny horse and escaped from Purang County by moonlight with the help of Chamba's younger brother.

'Crossing several mountains, I arrived at the border of Zanda County. However, I heard that the exalted dignitaries of Zanda County were apparently just as intelligent as their counterparts in Purang, so I decided to leave well enough alone. Pulling my thin, tired horse by the reins, I walked along a ravine. For food I hunted ground squirrel and rabbits. I came across a thin, mangy-looking wolf, but it felt like looking at a reflection of myself, and I couldn't point a gun at it.

'Although it was my first visit, I had a clear idea of the geography because a friend in the military had given me satellite and aerial photographs of the region. It was just like having a view from Heaven. Eventually I came to the Guge Kingdom ruins. They rose up in front of me like a giant beehive. There were several hundred caves in the grey-brown mountains, and several temples nestled into the mountainside looked as though they were about to crumble. From a distance, one giant ruin that had fallen right at the edge of the Xiangquan River looked like the corpse of an enormous monster. The hush of death flowed through the ravine, and the only sound was my own breathing. Suddenly, I heard terrible cries erupting from the hundreds of caves. It was the sound of the wind racing through the gorge, as if lamenting past sorrows.

'Nowadays, there are very few people living around there – just a few dozen in the town of Zanda, about 20 kilometres from the ruins. This area is surrounded by the enormous Toling Gorge, and a faint vehicle track passes through the gorge continuing on to the Shiquan River. The road is more than 200 kilometres long, and the journey takes two days – if you don't break down.

'When the snow begins to fall in November, you can't see where the road is until spring comes; then Zanda is connected to the outside world again. Travellers entering and leaving in the spring witness strange scenes: the wreckage of overturned jeeps and trucks, and broken-down cars that have almost all been turned into iron skeletons. Tyres and car parts also lie scattered on the ground, with battered corpses nearby. There are even bodies of people frozen to death sitting in the seats. Ali is very much a place of death. It's like the Chinese saying "Though you can see the mountains, your horse may die before you reach them". If the weather is cloudy, there's no way of knowing which direction to go in. Sometimes people walk for days and end up in the place they started from.

'On over 90 per cent of the land in Tibet it is impossible to raise crops. The altitude is too high and the difference in temperature between night and day too extreme. It is difficult enough for plants, let alone cattle and sheep, to survive. In addition, many of the lakes contain toxic minerals. Wild horses, yaks and sheep face death when winter comes and the snow piles up high, so they frequently form groups and plunder grass from the nomads' lands. Nomads, on the other hand, kill the wild animals in order to protect their own livestock, which live on the edge of starvation. With the carcasses the nomads make soup to feed their lambs and calves, breaking the natural order by turning herbivorous animals into carnivores.

'In such an environment it is not at all strange that people too should eat one another. Cannibalism is said to have existed in Ali at times of severe natural disaster since long ago. Another reason for it is a tradition that says if by chance you encounter somebody who resembles a Tibetan deity or one of the bodhisattvas, and you secretly kill and eat that person, then you take their good fortune for yourself.

'In the village of Tsaparang on the Xiangquan River lives an old man called Wandue, who is the guardian of the Guge ruins. I'd heard that he had a weakness for drink, so I went prepared with several bottles of Xinjiang wine as a gift. On the way, the horse I was riding became excited and rutted with a young mare; two bottles got broken in the process. Nevertheless, I soon made friends with Wandue. He said to me, "Do as you like. Live in the temples if you want to." Clutching his bottles of wine close, he threw me a bunch of keys. I felt as if the emperor had granted me a gold seal and permission to become king of Guge.

'Inside the ruins I found a number of temples and four large caves, with many paintings still remaining. There is the White Temple (Lhakang Karpo), the Red Temple (Lhakang Marpo), the Yamantaka Temple, the Tangcheng Hall, Tara Hall and Samsara Hall. Each had been destroyed to different degrees, but the White, Red and Yamantaka temples at the base of the ruins were comparatively well preserved. Up above there were secret paths that wound around in every direction, continuing up to the Summer Palace and the peak itself. Catapults had been placed along the pathways, and the surviving walls had a number of holes in them; it was easy to imagine the strategies of warfare in those days, and the kinds of weapons used for taking the enemy unawares. When I peeped through the holes, I saw several more tunnels. Lying around on the ground were rusty spears, shields, halberds, broken swords, suits of armour, helmets and scattered parts of bodies so disintegrated that they had lost their original forms. Altogether this created a vivid picture of the cruelty of battle in those times.

'The Summer Palace is in the centre, at the top of the ruins. It was built on a sheer cliff that would have been perfect for repelling enemies. Part of the underground path extends halfway up the mountain, but all that is visible from the outside is a big hole like a viewing platform. Damaged shields, sword handles and rotted clothing lay scattered about inside, and there was a cloying, mouldy smell of bird droppings. In the centre of the inner wall there was a scooped-out space, shaped like a human being but about half the size of an adult, which may have contained a Buddha image. Within it was a bird's nest made of grass. When I looked out from the observation platform of the Summer Palace, I could take in at a single glance the vast ravine spread out below me. In the distance were undulating snowy mountains and a panoramic view of Ali that stretched for hundreds of kilometres.

'At the rear of the ruins, a secret pathway snaked down to the bottom of the ravine; it had been used to fetch water during battle. The Tangcheng Hall is on the peak, and behind that is the Assembly Hall, wide enough for ten carriages to enter.

'It began to get late, and the evening sun shone on the side of the castle, turning it to gold. There were birds darting about playfully, sometimes skimming past my face and twittering loudly. They made me feel that there was still some life in this castle of death. I decided that it was time to settle down for the night, so I looked through the numerous caves to find a good spot to sleep. The castle had been divided up according to social class. Lamas' residences were on the middle levels, while living quarters for the common people and slaves were in the bottommost ones. As many as several tens of thousands of people are said to have lived there. Taking my own status into consideration, I decided to settle into one of the small caves on the lower levels. Among the broken stone pots inside I found one that was relatively undamaged. It was ideal for boiling water and preparing meals.

'Next day I started to make reproductions of the wall paintings. I found murals in a comparatively good state of preservation in the White Temple, the Red Temple, the Samsara Hall, the Yamantaka Temple, the Tangcheng Hall and the hidden cave-temple below it. Many of the paintings were in a deplorable state due to weathering and the destruction of the Cultural Revolution. The paintings are unlike those in other regions of Tibet, having been influenced by Persian and Indian art. Ali is the wellspring of Bon, the native religion of Tibet; hence the fusion of

Buddhist art with primitive Bon culture is also a distinctive feature of Guge art. The wall painting in the hidden cave-temple is typically Tibetan; on the bottom right there are animals, Bon designs, and a dozen or so figures of beautiful women dancing and singing. The craftsmanship in this painting is truly marvellous, and there is no question that it is amongst the finest examples of Tibetan Buddhist art. A serving girl holding an offering is depicted on the right wall of the entrance to the 'Samsara' shrine. Her Asian elegance is exquisitely charming.

'The subject matter of the art in the ruins is also diverse in comparison with that in other regions of Tibet. In Tibetan art one often sees Buddhas, bodhisattvas, Mahayama (the mother of Prince Gautama), the Tara goddesses, celestial deities, protector-deities, exalted lamas, various sages, diagrams for worship and pictures of celebratory ceremonies, Buddhist historical events and Hell, but those in Guge also depict the royal family and charts of succession for Indian, Tubo and Guge kings.

'The *Picture of Hell* mural, painted around the perimeter of the Tangcheng Hall, makes the blood run cold. It shows the various drawn-out, miserable fates that await sinners, who are shown with heads and bodies separated, limbs severed and bones scattered about; hanging upside down from trees; drowning; being captured and killed by demons; being devoured by tigers, leopards, eagles and hawks; having their buttocks pierced with spears and burning in an inferno. These were not just pictures but actual punishments, and apparently even crueller ones used to be devised as well. Folklore has it that when people broke the law, they would be put naked into a scorpion's hole 3 metres in diameter at the rear of the 'Samsara' shrine – it was so deep that the bottom was not visible – and slowly be stung to death. These paintings are a record, if you will, that portrays both the elegance and the cruelty of life in those times.

'My routine consisted of starting work at daybreak. Time slipped by, until one day I went out searching for something to hunt in a nearby valley but found nothing. I had eaten up all the rabbits and pigeons in the vicinity and so went further afield than usual to a stream to the south, but still I found nothing. The wolf I had seen previously prowling around this area was also nowhere to be found. I had eaten my last remaining handful of *tsampa* the previous night. Finally, when the sun dropped below the mountains, I found two wild mice.

'"Buddhism teaches us that life is death and death is life," I said to the mice, "so I'll make you live."'

'That evening I drank a large pot of mouse soup, but in the middle of the night I woke up hungry. A strong wind blew outside the cave, and I was chilled to the bone with a coldness I hadn't experienced there before. My stomach growled and no matter what I did I couldn't sleep. Then suddenly the crows living at the top of the castle flashed into my mind. I painted a picture of them in my head – they were much plumper than the mice I'd eaten that day – so off I went and killed one. I cooked and ate it, then threw the bones outside the cave. Next morning when I awoke, the crow's bones were gone. Sleet was falling. Thinking that I might be next on some creature's menu myself, I left the Guge Kingdom.

'In 1988 I visited Ali again, but someone had painted

over many of the murals with paint normally used for commercial hoardings. Nor could I see any of the shields, halberds, armour and other things that had been scattered about. These had been sold in far-off tourist areas of Tibet as travel souvenirs. All I could do on that trip was to take as many photographs as possible of the wall paintings before they disappeared forever. Unfortunately, I dropped my batteries in the river, so I used the foil from cigarette packets to reflect the sunlight as a flash. But there was no hope of reliving my days as king of Guge.'

The lecture comes to an end, and the hall resounds with rising applause. Members of the audience stream up to shake Yong's hand and embrace him as he stands there wiping away rivers of sweat. The cultural attaches of the German and French embassies offer to publish a collection of his Guge photographs, and the French embassy asks about mounting an exhibition in France.

Yong came alone to Beijing from Tibet, but in just a short time he's created a stir in the capital. He'd been travelling in Ali, making reproductions and photographs; now here he is in Beijing holding an exhibition and giving lectures. But the only ones to applaud and recognize his achievements are foreigners, and now he fears that the Public Security Bureau will close his exhibition down.

5. BEIJING PUBLIC SECURITY BUREAU, XICHENG DISTRICT BRANCH

16 February. We catch a taxi from the Central Academy of Art to the Music Hall and are met by the sight of several men in suits standing on the steps up to the gallery entrance.

'Driver, take us to the Workers' Publishing Company in Liu Pukang.' Yong suddenly has the driver change direction and takes me to the home of his teacher Yu Ren. 'Aya,' he says, 'why don't you stay here today and rest?'

'What's going on?'

'It's nothing. You're sick; please rest. Teacher Yu is a good person; he's even been to Japan. It'd be best if you just take it easy here today.'

All of the unusual excitement must have gotten to me, for I've developed cystitis – I had Yong take me to a doctor – and on top of that my head is heavy from coughing fits brought on by the Beijing dust. It all brings my own fragility home to me, accustomed as I am to the sterile environment of Japan.

Yu Ren, from north-east China, was the reason Yong began to paint. His influence on Yong has been enormous, to the extent that Yong's speech is tinged with a north-eastern accent. Yu Ren was indicted during the Cultural Revolution and sent to Yong's home town for labour reform, to paint historical pictures for the Revolutionary Martyrs' Memorial Hall.

Xinxian, a county town in the mountains of southernmost Henan, is known for having produced many bandits and generals. Yong was born the fourth son in a family of five children. His mother had been born in Dangushan, the daughter of a military commander who was assassinated at a young age. Yong's father had been born in Xincai, and although he came from a family of landlords, he participated energetically in the Communist Revolution, joining the party at sixteen. Thanks to this, Yong and his family were able to escape the worst, despite the family's status as members of the landlord class. Yong nevertheless experienced countless incidents of persecution in his childhood.

At the age of eleven Yong began to study painting with Yu Ren. Yong's father had no wish to see his son become involved in politics. Other artists besides Yu Ren came to Xinxian for labour reform, but they preferred to ingratiate themselves by teaching the sons of high officials and local dignitaries. Yu Ren was the only one generous enough to teach Yong the basics of painting with any seriousness. At the time, Yong was a tough country boy; a knowledgeable, cultured person from Beijing was someone to be respected. On the day that Teacher Yu finally left Xinxian, Yong ran sobbing after the bus that carried him away. 'Young Number Four Son,' Teacher Yu had said to Yong affectionately, '"The painting reflects the artist." If you

want to paint, you must start by building your character.'
Yong took these words to heart.

Later on, whenever there was a big exhibition of
European art in Beijing, Yong would visit his old teacher
with presents. Yong was eager to show Teacher Yu the
results of his own labours this time, but when he did so Yu
Ren's reaction was not at all what Yong expected.

'Number Four! You cannot exhibit these pictures! Take
them away from Beijing immediately!' Teacher Yu roared,
his face red with anger. Having attained a position within
the Communist state, Yu Ren was no longer the teacher of
old.

'Where has my teacher gone, the one who told me that if
I wanted to paint, then I should first start by building my
character?' All those years Yong had continued to be
mindful of his teacher's advice, so it was a huge shock for
him to hear Teacher Yu's words.

The fact that Yong has now brought me to his teacher's
house in spite of this difference of opinion must be out of
consideration for me, since Yong knows that Teacher Yu is
friendly towards Japan and that I'll be able to relax here.
Yong stops the taxi and climbs the stairs inside a brick
building to a flat on the second floor where he knocks on a
door.

'Teacher Yu, *ni hao*, I've brought my girlfriend, Aya.'

'Number Four, it's been a while. Come in.'

Teacher Yu and his wife welcome me warmly. Yu Ren is a
kind-looking man with grey-streaked hair. I guess that the
reason he opposed Yong's exhibition was not out of ill-
will, but because he's learned how to live by his wits in this
country.

'Number Four, come to think of it, this telegram came for you yesterday.' Teacher Yu pulls a telegram from a drawer – the one I sent to Yong from Guangzhou! Because of the Spring Festival it has taken more than ten days to arrive in Beijing.

'The Chinese Telegraph Office is completely useless.' Yong takes the telegram and frowns. Then, leaving me to the care of Teacher Yu, he hurries off to the gallery.

I learn from Teacher Yu that he has held an exhibition in the *Ichimai no E* gallery in the exclusive Ginza area of Tokyo and has been featured in a Japanese art magazine. In his childhood he was educated in Japan and learned art from a Japanese teacher.

'Japan is a good place. It's clean. The people are well-mannered.' Teacher Yu picks up photographs taken on visits to Kyoto and Nara, smiling nostalgically.

In the afternoon Teacher Yu goes out, and so, with nothing else to do, I study my Chinese. Whenever I can, I use my Chinese–Japanese dictionary to search for the meanings of words I don't know, looking them up by pronunciation. Perhaps because I'm driven by an impatience to learn this language that quickens with each new incident I witness, I'm absorbing new vocabulary at a rate incredible even to myself.

Suddenly I remember a phrase that I haven't been able to work out by consulting the dictionary. I hear these words every time some upset occurs: '*ta ma de ge bi, cao ni ma de ge bi.*'

'What does that mean?' I've asked Yong, but whether it's because it's too difficult to explain, or just too much trouble, he's only ever answered me vaguely, saying, 'It's nothing.' It occurs to me to take the opportunity to ask Teacher Yu's wife about this phrase. But when I do, the blood drains from her face.

Just at that moment, the door opens. Teacher Yu has returned with his daughter and her husband. Teacher Yu's wife rushes over and speaks to them. What have I said?

'Um, come over here.' The daughter's husband signals to me, laughing with his eyes, to enter the study. 'You mustn't use language like that. Of course, it's because that Number Four is so uncivilized. Would you understand perhaps if I wrote it in English?' He writes something on a piece of paper and explains carefully. At last I catch on – this is coarse language indeed! It means 'Go fuck your mother!'

'Do you understand now why you can't use language like that?' Teacher Yu's wife admonishes me, having at last regained her composure.

Bang! The door opens. Yong has returned, gasping for breath, and immediately pours out the day's happenings in a rush. 'Some Tibetans living in Beijing came to protest at the exhibition. But after I explained it all carefully, they understood. Then they came back and said how impressed they were, and gave me some *maotai*. They even said it was a proud thing for Tibet.'

'Number Four! What is this? You absolutely must refrain from using foul language in front of this nice young Japanese lady.' Teacher Yu's wife, who's been lying in wait for Yong, scolds him ferociously. Yong looks embarrassed, like a naughty boy who's been found out, and glares at me.

'Teacher Yu, if you can find the time, please come and see my exhibition.' Yong expresses his thanks and grabs my hand, and we leave Teacher Yu's home as if we're making an escape.

'Those men in suits we saw this morning, were they Tibetans?'

'Yeah, they're Tibetan intellectuals living in Beijing – some of them were academics. At first they were hostile to the idea of a Han Chinese painting pictures of Tibet, but after hearing me out, they were amazed that I understood Tibetan Buddhism better than they did. Here, let's have a drink!' Yong pulls a bottle of highly alcoholic *maotai* from his backpack.

18 February. Yong's exhibition is closing. It has run for only five days, but in that time there's been a succession of articles about it in publications such as the *China Daily*, the Canadian newspaper the *Globe and Mail*, the *Beijing Review*, the *People's Daily* and *China Pictorial*. Foreigners from all over Beijing have come to see it. A German company is even planning to film in Tibet using Yong as an actor. Almost all of the paintings have been snapped up by collectors.

Yong walks slowly around the gallery in a deeply emotional state, looking at his work. It's almost as if he's talking to these paintings with whom he made the long journey from Lhasa. He doesn't look particularly happy as he points out the pictures that have been sold. He tells me that paintings are like children to an artist, and handing them over to someone else is very painful.

'Don't sell them. Keep them, then.'

Yong calls me a child and laughs. He makes his living from painting, so of course he sells his pictures.

Almost all of his buyers are embassy employees and Western collectors stationed in Beijing – Spanish and Bolivian diplomats, Americans and Germans. It turns out that the large work depicting two lamas among writhing female bodies has been bought by a successful Chinese businessman and collector in Beijing. Yong is glad that one of his paintings will be owned by a Chinese. Aside from anything else, there are financial reasons why his paintings are always bought by Westerners: Yong won't negotiate on his prices.

'This'll more than cover the last few months' expenses. I'll be able to get by without having to sell any more paintings for the next few years.'

Although plain-clothes policemen have paid several visits to the exhibition, there's no indication that the Beijing Public Security Bureau intends to do anything untoward.

The final sales contract is concluded with a German collector. Otherwise, there are very few people around. At four in the afternoon, we decide to take the paintings down. We carry them outside and put them down in the car park, then stack the 'children' onto the bicycle and fasten them with rope.

'I'm going to hold exhibitions all over China. In Shanghai and Guangdong as well. Aya, you come too!' Yong sings out in high spirits. It looks like he intends to set the whole of China on fire.

Unusually for Beijing in winter, thick clouds hang in the sky. It gets chilly as the day darkens, so we quickly prepare to leave the Music Hall behind us. Liao Hong and I ride ordinary bikes, while Yong climbs on the bicycle with the large canvases piled on top of each other. Just as we start off, we hear the urgent scream of a siren.

'What's that?'

The siren grows louder and louder. Suddenly, a dark-green jeep races to a stop inside the car park, right in front of us. The car with the siren is a Public Security jeep. Three policemen get out and stride briskly over to us. Planting themselves threateningly in front of Yong, they order him to unload all of the pictures.

Yong says nothing; he simply unfastens the rope we've just tied and begins to unload the paintings. The policemen examine them one by one, then call Yong into the gallery office and begin questioning him. Mr Fu, the owner, is also called in. Liao Hong and I can do nothing except wait outside. My uneasiness increases at the sight of him standing there with his arms crossed, staring after the security police. After a while, they come out of the office and take another look at all the paintings lined up, then grab several and roughly put them to one side. Yong stands there in silence, his face extremely pale.

'They're being confiscated,' Liao Hong whispers on his return from helping to carry the paintings.

Confiscated? What do they think art is? Anger wells up inside me.

Liao Hong's face is frozen in a frown, and Yong – where has all his usual spirit gone? – is as meek as a kitten, tamely doing what he's told.

In the end, seven paintings are taken. 'We are confiscating these paintings. Present yourself at the Public Security Bureau tomorrow. Understood?' the policeman orders, turning on his heel as if to emphasize his authority.

Since the Cultural Revolution, there hasn't been an exhibition like Yong's in which an artist has openly expressed his ideas. What's more, it's unprecedented for pictorial works to be confiscated like this. Because the exhibition received attention from every branch of the media, both domestic and international, the Public Security Bureau didn't close it down while it was running for fear of the uproar it might cause. Instead they waited until the final day to make their move.

On the night the pictures are confiscated, we move from the Central Academy of Art to the Beifang Hotel in Dongdan to stay out of reach of Public Security; Yong has told them that we are staying at the Academy of Art. We show my passport at the hotel's reception desk and convince them that we're both Japanese tourists but that the embassy is holding Yong's passport for renewal.

The tidy room, with a large window and orange curtains, has an en-suite bathroom and is far more comfortable than the studio in the Academy of Art. The bathroom is clean, and there's plenty of space for two big beds. Yong hadn't stayed in this kind of hotel, where a room costs 80 yuan in FECs per night, as he'd been economizing in anticipation of his exhibition.

But he doesn't relax. He just sits silently on one of the beds, scowling and restlessly lighting cigarettes.

'Isn't there any way you can get your pictures back? Can I do anything?' I ask, unsure of what to say, or of whether I should even speak at all when he's so upset.

'Why don't you just say you held the exhibition because of your connections with foreigners? If you say you held the exhibition with Aya, a Japanese woman, then Public Security won't be able to do anything to the paintings, will they? Public Security can't interfere in foreigners' activities in Beijing,' proposes Liao Hong, who's accompanied us to the hotel.

'No, I'll go to the Public Security Bureau and see what happens. Maybe I'll get the paintings back. I'll try to explain about my plan for an exhibition tour of China.'

'That won't work. If you go to Public Security and get locked up straight away, then it's the end of everything. I'll go first and check out the situation.'

Early the next morning, Liao Hong sets out for the Public Security Bureau. When Yong gets out of bed he vomits violently; his stomach has been badly affected by the shock of having his paintings confiscated. We wait nervously until Liao Hong returns late that night.

'Liao Hong! What happened? I was worried that something had gone wrong.'

'There're still no charges – it seems they haven't made up their minds yet. They were leaning on me to make sure you'd put in an appearance so they can ask you in person why you paint those pictures.'

'But why are you so late getting back?'

'I went to Chen Jun's party.'

'Was it to do with the demand for Wei Jingsheng's release?'

'Yeah, that's right. There was a big crowd of artists at the JJ Art Bar. They all signed a petition. There were about thirty names on it, yours too.'

'What! My name? They used it without my permission!' Yong's face blanches.

Chen Jun had asked Yong to join the movement to release political prisoners numerous times, but Yong had declined. Having his name added to a petition without his knowledge was really adding insult to injury.

'Public Security will probably start rounding up people who signed the petition soon,' Yong moans, holding his head in his hands.

20 February. Yong gets ready to present himself at the Public Security Bureau. Watching him, I recall the words of the Chengdu artist: 'I was inside for ten years ... you'd better be ready to do at least half that.' At the time I found the idea inconceivable, but now it's gradually becoming more real.

'I might get the paintings back. I have to go there for the sake of those seven paintings.'

Yong, Liao Hong and I get in a taxi and head for the Public Security Bureau. In Tiananmen Square, I look over at the portrait of Mao Zedong as we drive down Changan Avenue. As soon as we get out of the taxi, Yong throws up again, his eyes watering. The grey concrete building of the Beijing Public Security Bureau, Xicheng District Branch towers into the cloudy Beijing sky in front of us.

We enter and enquire at the office. 'Cao Yong. I was ordered to present myself.'

'Go to the second floor.'

As we're about to go up, our gazes are arrested by the sight of many wooden frames flung roughly to one side of the dust-covered stairs, some still with scraps of canvas attached. These surely are the frames from Yong's confiscated pictures. I feel the blood drain from my face.

Only Yong is summoned into the room on the second floor. When the door opens, I glimpse several policemen sitting with their legs crossed, puffing on cigarettes and drinking tea. Liao Hong and I sit on a bench near the window to wait. A jabbing pain pierces my stomach.

It seems most unlikely that Yong will be able to get through to that bunch in the room cloudy with cigarette smoke. I imagine the cold, inhuman faces of the policemen, sipping tea as they gradually turn the heat up on him. The seven confiscated paintings were all masterpieces; some had been sold, including the large work that was to be the first of Yong's owned by a Chinese collector. At the moment, though, we should be more concerned about getting Yong out of here and avoiding prison.

I suppose ninety minutes pass before the door clatters open and Yong emerges, saying 'Let's go.' We quickly leave the Public Security Bureau and hail a taxi. 'There's no chance they'll give back the paintings. I was within an inch of being put away myself,' he says with a tight smile. He describes the interrogation:

'"You probably know yourself the effect of coming to Beijing and pulling a stunt like this. Why did you hold such an exhibition?"

'"I simply wanted to have an artistic exchange in Beijing through my pictures. Since I plan to take the exhibition on tour to Shanghai and Guangdong, may I have my pictures back?"

'"Fool! You are not to take one step out of Beijing!"

'"Cao Yong, why did you paint such pictures?"

'"I lived deep in the mountains of Tibet for a long time. I

rarely ever saw a newspaper or a television. I also did research on the surviving wall paintings in Tibetan temples. The union of man and woman is the main subject of these paintings, and many of them show women's naked bodies."'

Yong showed them photographs of the wall paintings, but these too were confiscated, along with the film containing photographs taken at the exhibition.

'Apparently the branch chief wasn't there today, so they couldn't decide the charges. Until they do I'm prohibited from leaving Beijing.'

China is like one giant prison. People aren't free to choose where they live or work; the government assigns everyone a work place. Every citizen is controlled by a file that records all the details of their life, starting from birth; there are, moreover, numerous secret informers who keep close tabs on the population's every move. To leave the government's social framework is equivalent to death. Wherever you run, you're doomed to be caught. That's probably why the Public Security Bureau have said that they will judge Yong's work and decide the charges at a later date; they believe that since he has virtuously submitted to interrogation he won't try to leave Beijing. He's painted pictures regarded as 'obscene' and attracted crowds of foreigners to an exhibition – in China these acts are a 'crime'.

'Cao Yong! How awful for you!'

We're resting at the hotel when some Western friends who've heard the news come to see him. Foreigners can easily visit Yong in this hotel because he's staying here as a Japanese national.

'The news of your paintings being confiscated has been broadcast overseas by Reuters. I can arrange for you to get political asylum in the US. It's definitely not good for you to stay on in China,' says Richard, an American journalist I'd met at the Friendship Hotel, the moment he enters the room, still panting for breath.

'No, that's out. It'd bring disaster on my family. And besides, I want to go back to Tibet. If I seek asylum, I can never come back to China.' Yong shakes his head adamantly.

'So what are you going to do? Are you saying you'll just walk over the border?'

If Yong takes refuge in the American or Canadian embassy, there will probably be no difficulty in gaining recognition as a political refugee. With his paintings confiscated, if he stays on here and does nothing, he'll be charged and wind up in prison. But if he does seek asylum, there's no knowing what kind of persecution his parents, brothers and sister will be subjected to as the family of a defector. It isn't possible for Yong himself just to flee to safety.

Yong decides that he will cross the border into Burma from Yunnan. Having previously been to Nepal and Kashmir, he doesn't seem to think that crossing the border is such a big deal, but it's obvious to me that entering another country illegally on foot is fraught with danger. There's the possibility he'll be caught and forcibly returned to China as an illegal immigrant. And even if he does succeed in smuggling himself into another country, what kind of life will he have? Will he have to spend the rest of his days using a false passport?

... Marriage. That's it! If he gets married then he can go overseas without giving politics a second thought. In a situation like this, we can't be too concerned about methods.

'Yong, let's get married and you can escape to Japan.'

This, then, is the beginning of our journey of escape.

1. ESCAPE

We lose no time in going to the Japanese Embassy to enquire about a visa. I believe that we can get one can quickly if we're married, but I don't know how to go about applying.

'Visa applications are examined by the Foreign Ministry in Tokyo, so it will take some time,' we're told. 'First you'll have to get a passport. Then, if you apply for a visa to go to Japan for the purpose of getting married, that will probably be the quickest way.'

'Isn't it necessary to register our marriage in China?'

'No, you apply for a visa on the basis that you'll be going to Japan to get married.' The embassy gives us a list of the necessary documents.

'I will be returning to Japan with a great artist. Instead of a honeymoon, I'm going to Tibet now,' I write in a letter to my parents, adopting a cheerful tone to tell them the news of my decision to get married. When I was last home at New Year, I told my parents about Yong. My mother smiled and said, 'That's lovely – how romantic!' But she was probably not expecting me actually to get married. No doubt she'll worry, but I pray that she understands. I ask my parents to send an extract from my official family register to Beijing as soon as possible, so that Yong can prove he's marrying a foreigner and obtain a passport. In my letter I also give my parents a brief summary of recent events and enclose newspaper articles about his exhibition. I don't mention anything about the paintings being confiscated by Public Security because I don't want my mother and father to worry.

In order to get Yong a passport, we need to go to Lhasa, his registered place of residence. While waiting for my papers to arrive from Japan and before leaving Beijing, however, Yong must deliver the paintings he still has to their new owners, as well as return the deposits he received for some of the confiscated pictures. After Public Security took the paintings away, Mr Fu was also questioned and the Artists' Gallery was ordered to suspend business. Yong feels very bad about this, but – given his own position – there's nothing he can do about it.

Yong is on edge – a bundle of nerves – and can neither eat nor sleep properly. Apparently the police have been searching for him at the Central Academy of Art and at the homes of young artists in Beijing. A few days later we hear from one of the art students that three policemen came to the school in the middle of the night to arrest Yong. In the meantime, an investigation has begun into the activities of Chen Jun and the others who petitioned for the release of political prisoners. Artist friends involved with the petition are panicking; Yong isn't alone in feeling that Beijing has become a city of fear.

The fact that Public Security hasn't noticed that Yong's work unit is Tibet University is the only thing protecting us. While he was being questioned he described himself as 'an unemployed vagrant' because he isn't actually doing any work at the university. As a result, Public Security has apparently concluded that he's a 'wandering artist' of 'no fixed occupation'. There's therefore little chance that their investigation will reach Lhasa at this stage, so we have some time to get ourselves there and obtain a passport for Yong. It also helps that Public Security has been busy dealing with people involved in the campaign for the release of political prisoners.

It may be prudent not to leave Beijing immediately, since the police are no doubt keeping a sharp watch on all train and bus stations. It's also unlikely that they know Yong is with a Japanese national and attempting to leave the country by getting married.

'I'm going to a friend's place in Tianjin. Then I'll go to my relatives in Guangdong,' says Yong. He tells different lies to each person he meets, in case his friends are interrogated and, under duress, can't help but give away his whereabouts.

Ten days pass. In the exact time it takes for a letter to reach Japan and receive a reply, the documents I requested from my parents arrive.

'We're hoping the two of you can come to Hokkaido during Golden Week,' they write, referring to the cluster of public holidays in May. This is a generous invitation. It seems they looked at the articles about Yong's exhibition and understand that I haven't lost my mind. My parents have been through my three older sisters' marriages, and know from experience that the more opposition they show, the more problematic such situations can become.

Once we get Yong's passport, we should be able to leave for Japan, so I'll be back there well before the end of the spring break at the beginning of April. There is, of course, no knowing what lies ahead, but I'm confident that he won't have any trouble getting by wherever he is.

By 1 March, eleven days after the confiscation of Yong's paintings, we leave Beijing for Tibet. Yong has had stomach trouble all this time, vomiting every morning. His cheeks have become sunken with fatigue and worry, and there are dark circles under his eyes.

Early in the morning on the day of our departure, Yong sends a telegram to his sister Cao Qing in Luoyang, where she works in a spinning mill. Since we intend to leave the country as soon as we obtain his passport, there will be no time to visit his parents, but we'll be able to see Cao Qing. Luoyang is on the way to Tibet by train. Yong asks her to wait on the station platform for us.

Before our departure, we go to the bustling shopping street of Wangfujing to buy supplies. Warm clothes are necessary to protect against the cold in Tibet, and I have nothing but a thin overcoat, so I buy a padded jacket. Yong has been so busy with his exhibition that he hasn't had a single opportunity to come here. He stocks up on *lianhuanhua* – graphic novels – as a distraction from his worries.

We have tickets for train number 121, departing for Xining at 9.26 p.m., but end up in a hard-seat carriage because we bought them in a hurry. As usual, the carriage is crowded from wall to wall, but we count ourselves fortunate to have been able at least to get reserved seats. Although we breathe a sigh of relief to be leaving Beijing, sitting up on hard seats all night is tough. It's no exaggeration to say that Chinese hard-seat carriages are pure purgatory; people are jammed up against each other, some even sleeping on the luggage racks just beneath the ceiling; six people squash into seats intended for three, while others settle themselves on the tables next to the windows or in gaps between people on the floor. You cannot go to the toilet. 'At last!' you think, after almost treading on people's heads to get there, only to find that someone is occupying it forever with the door locked. The water supply is erratic, and you can't even wash your hands. And, even though you may be utterly exhausted and barely able to stay awake, you must be vigilant against thieves. The carriages reek of body odour, excrement and food, but if you open the window, it's too cold to sleep.

I doze a little, but the seat next to the window is cold, and day breaks before I've had even a wink of real sleep. Yong has spent the night reading and hasn't slept at all. Cao Qing should be waiting for us at Luoyang, but around midday the train stops for a long time, apparently because of an accident up ahead. In the cold rain, hawkers rush to the stalled train and stand beneath the windows, loudly touting tea, eggs, stuffed buns, cigarettes and drinks.

'Those train hawkers are the worst. The buns have nothing but leeks in them.' Yong is indignant.

I have to agree that the hawkers I've met on my train travels have seldom had anything delicious to offer. They sell poor-quality goods at high prices, which is why Chinese people travelling by train carry huge amounts of food with them, including dried noodles, dried sunflower and pumpkin seeds, chicken cooked in soya sauce and bottled fruit. They munch and crunch on these, undaunted by the human crush around them, for a tenacious grip is essential to stay alive here, and people have to be vigilant about replenishing energy.

When we finally arrive in Luoyang, three hours late, Cao Qing and her husband, Chen Zhiqiang, are still waiting on the platform as planned. Cao Qing is wrapped in a blue coat, her cheeks tinted pink from the cold.

'Mama made this for you at Spring Festival, Fourth Brother.' Cao Qing addresses Yong affectionately and passes a brown-paper-wrapped bundle up through the train window with a worried look on her face. Yong hands her his slide films of the Guge Kingdom for safekeeping – there's no knowing what will happen on our journey of escape. We plan to call in on Cao Qing again on our return from Tibet.

'This is Aya. We're going to Lhasa together to get a passport so we can get married. After Lhasa, we plan to go to Japan. The police confiscated my paintings at my exhibition in Beijing. Our parents mustn't worry. Tell them from me to take care of their health. We'll be going straight on to Japan, so I don't know when we'll see them.' Yong speaks quickly but enunciates every word carefully.

Fifteen minutes later, the train is moving off, heading west again. The hard-seat journey takes its toll. It's extremely tiring to sit contorted and squeezed up against other people. And you must be constantly alert to make sure you don't fall off the seat, otherwise you'll lose your place. I experienced this hard-seat hell before – for five days straight – when I had to get to Hong Kong to catch a plane. I remember finally just collapsing on the filthy floor and falling asleep.

When I tell Yong about this, he replies that it's weird for foreigners to put themselves through that sort of thing. Maybe, but my life in Japan is so soft that I really wanted to put myself to the test. A main topic of conversation, and even of boastful talk, amongst Japanese backpackers in China is how far they can travel on tickets at the prices reserved for ordinary Chinese. I suppose this is incomprehensible to people who actually live in the country.

'I'll see if I can negotiate a soft sleeper,' Yong offers, standing up.

The first-class soft-sleeper carriages are for the likes of high-ranking Communist Party officials and military officers, as well as foreigners, so there are usually some tickets available. Even so, ordinary citizens cannot buy them. However, on this particular afternoon, Yong miraculously obtains tickets by convincing the conductor that his 'wife' is not well. Feeling like we've been rescued from hell, we leave the hard-seat carriage.

The soft-sleeper carriage has individual compartments that contain two sets of bunks to accommodate four people altogether. There are white sheets covering the bunks, curtains at the window and even a thermos of hot water for personal use. I sit down on this bed sent from Heaven, and Yong opens the parcel Cao Qing handed him.

'It's some of my mother's sausage!' Inside is a homemade sausage and some round fried bread, all still warm. Yong is tearful as he bites into the sausage. He offers me some, and it really is delicious, stuffed with finely chopped, seasoned pork. Yong has been unable to eat much since leaving Beijing, but after filling his stomach with his mother's cooking, the tension seems to melt away at last.

'I went home on the way from Lhasa to Beijing,' he tells me. 'I had to do stuff like make wooden stretchers for my canvases and frame them. There was a bit of an incident. One day, my father and his neighbour started quarrelling. My father's retired, and this guy is the upstart who took over his job. They've been on bad terms for a long time. I went over to see what was happening, and this jerk went and shoved my father and sent him flying. I got angry and punched the guy, which broke his nose, so he got taken off to hospital. Soon after the police came, and I ended up being taken to the police station. There I met a former People's Liberation Army soldier who'd been in the west, and we started chatting about Xinjiang and Tibet. The police told me I'd be in detention for fifteen days to a month, so I should bring in some bedding. "I see, I'll go and get ready," I told them, pretending to give in, and shot out of there. When I got home I was ready to bolt, but my father stopped me, "Don't run – it won't look good. If you have to stay in for a month, then so be it." It was no joke, I tell you – there I was, trying to get ready for my exhibition, with no time to waste on crap like that. But my mother quickly packed my things. "Young Number Four Son," she said, "hurry! Escape through the back." So I grabbed my gear, climbed over the back fence and ran for dear life. I went to Liao Hong's house and hid out there. Then I asked my brother, who has a car, to help me escape in the middle of the night, and eventually I managed to get my paintings to Beijing. Mama never says much, but she's always there for me.'

I notice Yong's eyes glistening as he tells me this, and for a moment I see the face of an ordinary young man in his twenties. Be that as it may, he really does seem to find trouble wherever he goes, and the way he threw off the police with his supposedly compliant attitude isn't something he just learned yesterday.

We arrive in Xining some time after four in the afternoon on 3 March. Once we change trains and get to Golmud, Lhasa is straight ahead. Yong's spirits improve on reaching this remote town beneath a sky filled with sombre clouds. He's like a different person.

In the square in front of the station are a few food stalls. Yong finds one selling tripe soup and whoops for joy before tucking in. His hearty appetite is a sign that he's well again. The old women working the stalls seem amazed by the sight of him ecstatically putting away the tripe soup. He eats serving after serving until six, then seven empty bowls are stacked up in front of him, at which point he stands up at last and says composedly, 'Right, let's go.'

The following morning at half past seven we board a slow train to Golmud, once again on hard seats. The train feels as if it is crawling along. Yong becomes engrossed in his books. The windows are dirty, so I can't enjoy the scenery. And, what's more, the water taps are dry. When we stop at Haergai Station on Qinghai Lake, Yong informs me that the fish from the lake are delicious and buys several from a hawker on the platform. I see what he means: deep-fried and about the size of a mackerel, they are rather good.

While we're nibbling on our fish, the conductor comes over and asks if we want a sleeper. Yong looks up and arranges his face into a smile to begin negotiating. In addition to the price of the sleeper, he gives the conductor a stack of the graphic novels he's finished reading, and cigarettes on top of that, and then pours on the compliments so heavily that I think his nose will start growing.

'Why should you have to do all this? You humour the conductor, give him presents, flatter him, pay money, and even then we don't get to shift to a sleeper straight away. This is a joke!'

Yong looks at me fuming in wide-eyed wonder. 'You're tired, so we're better off in a soft sleeper, aren't we?'

When I was travelling as a foreigner, I'd show my passport and obtain a sleeper, albeit at three times the price Chinese citizens would have to pay. But is this what Chinese people have to do if they want one?

We finally shift to a sleeper around eight in the evening, but right up until we get off the train, we have to continue humouring the conductor.

On 5 March we arrive in Golmud, in the middle of the Gobi Desert. We go directly to the bus station and buy tickets for the next bus to Lhasa, which departs the following morning at nine.

'The boiled mutton here is the best. I'm a regular,' Yong tells me as we enter a Muslim restaurant: a humble, flat-roofed building made of sun-dried bricks. Inside, a large pot of simmering mutton on the bone gives off a wonderful smell. A Hui man wearing a white hat greets us hospitably. We order 3 kilos of meat, which we eat with our fingers along with a high-country feast of freshly baked nan bread, tripe soup and Wanzi tea.

Afterwards, our bodies warmed by the meat, we set out to do some shopping in preparation for Tibet. The town is very quiet, and the inhabitants look utterly bored. People play billiards on roadside tables, the elderly sit puffing on their pipes and women wrapped in Hui ethnic dress come and go. Stray dogs sprawl motionless on the ground, and sandy winds off the Gobi blow through the town. Yet somehow I find myself liking this remote place with seemingly nothing to recommend it.

'Aya, you're going to Lhasa for the first time, so you're bound to get altitude sickness,' Yong informs me while stocking up on a canteen and some medicine. But I'm too excited to listen.

Next morning, we get on the bus for Lhasa. There are three other foreigners on board: a first-year Japanese student from the Hokkaido University Faculty of Fisheries, an American and an Englishman. Most of the other passengers are Chinese and Tibetans, and there are several young PLA soldiers being dispatched to Tibet. The long-haul bus departs with overflowing luggage roped to the roof. After a while, the desert comes to an end and the Tibetan landscape begins to take its place.

'There's freedom in Tibet. I really love it here,' Yong says.

In fact Tibet is a place of exile, several thousand kilometres from the meddling interference of the strict Beijing government, whose influence barely extends this far. It is possible to find freedom – albeit limited freedom –

in exchange for a hard life in a harsh environment. The closer we get to Tibet, the brighter Yong's expression becomes.

Intense sunlight, thin air, snow-clad mountains that pierce the deep cerulean sky, cobalt lakes nestled in the sere wilderness, clusters of black yaks ... time flows ever more slowly the further west we go. Stone houses stand out white against the landscape. Sleeping dogs, sheep, Tibetans wearing *chupas* ... The bus continues steadily towards the sky, while the scenery – spare, clear and beautiful – flows by the window like a fondly recalled painting.

'When I went to Lhasa from Henan in 1983, it took as long as two weeks to get there from Golmud. Now with the Qinghai–Tibet Highway you can get to Lhasa in twenty-six hours – things have really changed.' Yong may well say this, but it seems an extremely long journey to me.

As time passes, I start to feel dazed, as if I've become anaemic, and soon I have a pounding headache. I feel nauseous, and my start ears ringing.

'This is Wudaoliang. Maybe it's got something to do with geography, because we're only at 4000 metres – which isn't that high – but when you reach here the air suddenly gets thinner. It's as if the air dies. Here, drink lots of tea.' Yong passes me the canteen as I sit there limply. More time passes, then suddenly the young PLA soldiers abruptly start dancing in the gloom. No – I'm mistaken – they aren't dancing. They're writhing in pain!

'*Wo de ma ya! Wo de ma ya!*' 'Oh my mother!' In unison they shriek their woe and rage around the bus, hands tearing at the air, as if seeking an escape from terrible pain. I witness this bad dream from the depths of my own daze.

At dusk the bus reaches Amdo, at an altitude of more than 4000 metres, and parks at a hotel.

'We're stopping here for the night. Six-o'clock departure tomorrow morning. Don't be late!' the driver barks and promptly gets off the bus. I'm not amused – spending a night at this altitude is more like torture than rest.

People swarm around the reception area. There's a blackout in the hotel and it's pitch dark. By the light of a candle, I follow Yong unsteadily to our room. I become nauseous and vomit in the dark. Moaning from my headache, I stretch out on the dusty, damp-smelling bed under a heavy quilt.

'I suppose this is the famous altitude sickness, then,' I groan.

'I hate it that the bus driver and this hotel are in each other's pockets. If the driver brings guests here, he gets something out of it. It's always like that. Anyway, you must drink lots of tea.' Yong has been away from Tibet for several months, and he too appears to be suffering from headache, but he staggers up to fill the canteen for me.

Time passes painfully slowly. Whether I lie down or get up or walk around, there's no escaping the anguish. I spend the night groaning, and all the while, through the window, a beautiful sky filled with glittering stars watches over me. In this night I glimpse both Heaven and Hell. This sacred high land imposes a baptism of fire on its new pilgrims.

2. MARTIAL LAW

'Driver, could you let us off in front of the Bank School?'

On 7 March, some time after four in the afternoon, Yong gets the bus driver to stop along the Qinghai–Tibet Highway, and we get off without going into Lhasa. My headache and nausea have improved as the altitude is only 3700 metres.

'My brother Cao Gang lives here.' Yong clambers up onto the roof of the bus to unload our luggage, then we walk over to the Bank School.

'Bank School is a strange name, isn't it?'

The Bank School apparently teaches finance and economics to bank workers. Cao Gang is a teacher there and lives with his wife, Li Qingli, in the dormitory block. We pass through the main entrance and knock on the door of a second-floor flat.

'Hey, it's Number Four, you're back!'

'I brought my girlfriend. This is Aya.'

'*Ni hao!* Welcome, welcome!'

Despite our unexpected visit, Cao Gang, Li Qingli and their big German shepherd welcome us warmly. I immediately notice a large sheep's skull on display in the living room: the one Yong found last summer in Kashgar.

'You really did bring it all the way to Lhasa!'

'You remember it? When I cleaned out my room, I asked Cao Gang if I could leave it here.'

Over a cup of tea, Yong tells the others the Beijing story. Relaxing at long last, I play with the dog. Now if Yong can just get his passport, we can get to Japan safely.

Around dusk, there's a sudden sharp knock on the door and the sound of shouting.

'It's the students. I wonder what's up?'

Cao Gang answers the door, and several rather agitated students burst into the room.

'There's a riot in the city! Martial law's been declared!' one student yells.

'We saw foreigners on the bus that just arrived being rounded up and taken to a petrol station. They've been sent straight back to Golmud!' adds another.

The students had gone into town to buy some fruit for us. They tell us how, on the way back, they'd seen troops and tanks deployed to quell the protests started by Tibetans two days ago, as well as PLA soldiers lining the roads who were checking the identity papers of all passers-by. The students' faces shine with excitement as they hand over the apples and mandarins.

'It's because the anniversary of the Dalai Lama's flight into exile in India is coming up. Some Tibetans started an independence movement to commemorate that event, which occurred in March 1959. The first uprising occurred thirty years ago. Also, the Panchen Lama died this year.

He's the most important Tibetan spiritual leader after the Dalai Lama.' Yong is used to riots and explains all this matter-of-factly, but I'm completely taken aback. I've heard about the Tibetan independence movement but never thought that I'd actually encounter it. Just as we're finally escaping from Beijing, it seems that Tibet isn't going to welcome us either.

'Nevertheless, I'll go to the university tomorrow, where my official register is held, and try to apply for a passport,' Yong says glumly.

Early in the morning Yong gathers up the documents he needs and sets off for the university. Since I can't go out because of martial law, I play with the dog and gaze out the window. Suddenly, on the Qinghai–Tibet Highway outside, right in front of me, a long column of tanks and big PLA trucks passes by, headed for the city, with several dozen armed soldiers riding in each truck. The situation in Lhasa must be really serious.

'Here you are, Aya, eat these and you'll feel better.' Li Qingli offers me a bowl of sweet white dumplings filled with sesame paste. The Chengdu-born Li Qingli is an attractive, dainty and slightly built woman. A huge photograph of her in a white wedding dress and Cao Gang in a tuxedo adorns the wall of their flat. Yong pointed it out to me and made fun of Cao Gang, saying, 'He's actually quite ugly', but I think that they're a really lovely couple.

'Thank you, Li Qingli.' As I eat the dumplings, several wooden boxes in a corner of the room catch my eye. They contain a number of what appear to be art books. 'Are those Cao Yong's?'

'Yes, he brought all those boxes here before he went to Beijing.'

'May I have a look?'

'Of course you can, silly, you're not a stranger here!'

Immediately I start browsing through the boxes and find a book of paintings by Robert Rauschenberg. The inside cover is autographed. Has Yong met him? It must be ROCI – yes, that's it! This maestro of American contemporary art travelled around Asia, including Tibet, as part of his Rauschenberg Overseas Culture Interchange project, creating 'action art' by making works out of rubbish found at each location. Besides this book, there are other autographed books sent by artists in Australia, France and Germany. I also find several dozen photographs, including some of Yong with Westerners. One of them shows the New York photographer Don Carroll who visited Lhasa and bought Yong's work, clasping Yong's hand in front of one of his paintings. I guess this was taken last October. I remember seeing Yong wearing the T-shirt Don gave him in Beijing – hugging his hopes for the future to his chest.

When I overturn the box, a gold fountain pen and paper knife signed by the West German Chancellor Helmut Kohl spill out.

'Li Qingli, what's this? Are these from Chancellor Kohl?'

'That's right. Umm, I think it was in the summer two years ago, Chancellor Kohl visited Tibet, and apparently Yong was given them then. Kohl bought one of his paintings.'

Tibet, and Lhasa in particular, is a special place within China because of the interaction with the rest of the world that is possible here. Their reasons for coming may vary – political visits, travelling and climbing in the Himalayas – but it is to Lhasa that European leaders, politicians, scholars, artists and journalists come. Given the restriction of information and strict control over contact with foreigners that exist in the rest of China, it was only because Yong was here that he was able to meet people from around the world.

Yong returns in the evening, utterly worn out. 'Martial law's in force – there's not a single tourist in Lhasa. They were all shut up in the petrol station and then put on buses, sent back to where they'd come from,' he gasps.

Things have taken a serious turn. Yong has managed to obtain an extract of his official register from the university. However, if he goes to Public Security to apply for a passport so that he can leave the country to get married, they will know that he has a foreigner with him. No doubt I'll be deported and Yong will be charged with concealing a foreigner. To add to our woes, various government offices aren't functioning as usual owing to the riots.

The situation couldn't be worse. The PLA is suppressing the rioting Tibetans who've destroyed post and telegraph offices and shops run by Han Chinese. Along the Barkhor, the circular market street around the Jokhang Temple, soldiers are meting out punishment with their machine guns, firing indiscriminately at anybody who looks Tibetan – even children and the elderly. If they see even so much as a shadow in a window, they rake it with machine-gun fire. Soldiers have surrounded temples and turned them into prisons, and all lamas are being kept under strict surveillance, while security police and soldiers line all of the roads, conducting identity checks so stringent that even a mouse couldn't get around them.

'I finally made it back, with my ID in one hand and being stopped for checks every ten steps,' Yong tells me.

In Beijing, Public Security was chasing Yong because of his exhibition; now we've finally reached Lhasa, and martial law has been proclaimed. Just our luck!

'There's nothing we can do; we'll just have to wait.' Cold comfort indeed.

Still unaccustomed to the altitude, I catch a cold on the evening of our second day in Lhasa and experience difficulty breathing. At first I think it's an ordinary cold, but I'm racked by an awful cough that won't stop. Yong stays up all night watching over me and worrying, and when dawn comes, he rushes out of the house, saying, 'I'm going to get some oxygen from the university.' A short time later he returns holding a puffy green-brown plastic bag like a large pillow, filled with oxygen. Clinics in Tibetan work units always have a supply of oxygen on hand. Breathing difficulties are nothing out of the ordinary here.

'You have to be extremely careful about colds in Tibet, especially in winter. I know a few foreign travellers who came to Lhasa in winter, caught colds and ended up dying of pneumonia. No more washing yourself all over.' Yong scolds me for washing myself, including my hair, last night. 'There're fewer checkpoints in Lhasa today than yesterday,' he says. 'I think the riots will peak today or tomorrow, then probably die down gradually.'

If we wait a week, perhaps martial law will be lifted. We cling to this thread of hope.

Yong explains the history of the Tibetan independence movement to me.

'Ever since the mountains were formed, the Himalaya snow has never melted, and the Tibetans who lived among these peaks led a life secluded from the rest of the world. They didn't accept modern civilization, nor did they welcome visitors from the outside.

'However, in the middle of the twentieth century, a shocking change occurred. In 1951, the fourteenth Dalai Lama convened a meeting of shamans from all over Tibet who were believed to be able to summon the wind and rain, control the thunder and make demons obey them. He held a great ceremony in Jokhang Temple Square in order to drive out the Communist Chinese, who were moving into the country to take it over. The crowd of shamans kneaded *tsampa* flour and yak butter into dolls shaped like PLA soldiers, which they placed in the centre of the square. Then they began to dance. Tongues hanging out, they brandished swords and ferociously hacked the dolls to pieces. At the finish of this mad dance, scraps of *tsampa* were scattered all over the ground; the dolls had been mutilated beyond recognition. In an atmosphere of growing excitement, the people of Tibet looked up at the heavens, eagerly awaiting the arrival of the gods who would save them. White clouds drifted calmly in the blue sky above.

'Suddenly, an earth-shattering sound broke the hush. But it was not the battle cry of the guardian deities, nor was it a Buddha's voice of salvation; rather, it was the sound of gunfire from the PLA, smashing the last temple gate on their approach to Lhasa.

'A messenger brought the news that the Chinese army had already subdued the town of Linzhi. For the first time, the gate to this snowy world – never before opened – had been breached by the Chinese government.

'Eight years later, on 10 March 1959, the people of Lhasa began their first armed uprising against the PLA. On 17 March, the Dalai Lama fled to India, where the Tibetan government-in-exile was established at Dharamsala in 1960.

'Then, in 1966, China began a wholesale eradication of rights and culture unprecedented in the history of humankind: the Cultural Revolution. Tibet was, of course, not exempt. Overnight the greater part of several thousand temples was totally destroyed, golden Buddhas were melted down, and anything with the name of a god or Buddha attached to it was reduced to ashes. Buddhist monks were forced to return to secular life, and those who even then refused to abandon their old gods were promptly incarcerated.

'The Communist government called this policy "destroy the old, establish the new" and "eliminate superstition".

'Afterwards, all that remained were empty temples. Images of Mao Zedong were hung on the altars before the dust had even had time to settle. The people of Tibet began to venerate him as a new god. Their custom of faith was so strong, developed over aeons, that they couldn't suffer its loss for even a day.

'In October 1987, the lamas led the people in armed protests. Demonstrations demanding independence have occurred every year since, and there is constant friction with the Chinese government. The seventh Panchen Lama stayed on in China as a pipeline representing the voice of Tibet to the Chinese authorities, but his sudden death has greatly shaken the Tibetan people. Along with the thirtieth anniversary of the 1959 revolt, it has inspired an independence campaign on an unprecedented scale.'

Ever since we arrived in Lhasa, I've been cooped up in the Bank School because of the identity checks being conducted by the army, so Yong decides he will 'do something about getting a *jieshaoxin*' for me. This flimsy piece of paper is a letter of introduction, issued by a work unit, that functions as an ID.

On 12 March, he somehow manages to obtain a letter for me. Written on it is this description: 'Fiancée visiting from the interior'.

'It's okay. Just show the police this casually and keep walking; they won't ask you anything,' Yong tells me.

Given the mixture of Han Chinese, Tibetans, Hui and other ethnic groups in Lhasa, it's enough to be Asian to pass through the checkpoints without suspicion. In fact, on the way here, I'd been asked numerous times if I was Yong's younger sister.

We go out through the gates of the Bank School and I can see that there are still dozens of PLA soldiers conducting identity checks at the roadside. Yong goes in front on a bicycle, while I walk behind with Cao Gang and

Li Qingli. It's true that I'm slightly nervous but certainly happy to get a breath of fresh air.

With his shoulder-length hair, Yong catches the attention of the guards, who stop him for questioning.

'What's that? Hey you! Wait! You're not Tibetan? Show me your ID.' While the guards' attention is focused on Yong, I pass through the checkpoints without difficulty.

At the sight of the Potala Palace soaring into the blue sky, I feel as if I've finally arrived in Tibet. We reach the bustling free-enterprise market at the foot of the Potala – looking at it you'd never think there'd been any riots and massacres.

'Everyone seems very laid back, don't they?'

'Around here, there are riots all year round. People are all too used to it.'

We buy a slab of pork, eggs and lots of fruit and vegetables so that we can at least eat some decent food to keep our spirits up. On the way back from the market, a friendly-looking dog runs over to us, wagging its tail.

'Ahuang! Ahuang!' Yong calls out to her. He's often spoken of this dog. With her curly brown coat and amber-coloured eyes like a wolf's, you couldn't say that she's beautiful, but it seems she hasn't lost any affection for her wandering owner and greets Yong joyfully.

'Ahuang suddenly appeared one day when I was having a shit out in a field,' he explains. 'At first I thought she'd come to eat it, but apparently that wasn't the case. I said to her, if she was on her own, then she should come with me, and she followed right away – didn't take so much as a sniff. That's the difference between her and other dogs in Lhasa. Anyway, that's how Ahuang and I got together.

When times were good, we'd both stuff ourselves until we couldn't move. The day I went to Beijing, she left the pups she'd just had and chased after the bus for several kilometres. I was yelling at her from the window, and before I knew it, I was crying.'

'While you were away, this one got on the right side of the butcher and managed to stay alive. And several times she stole chickens from people's houses – what on earth did you teach her?' Cao Gang asks with a weary expression. In Yong's absence, Cao Gang had had to rescue Ahuang after she'd been caught stealing those chickens. A proud dog and fussy about her food, Ahuang prefers to eat meat like her master.

Next day we venture out to the Lhasa River; the farmland scene is tranquil. Yong loads an air gun with lead pellets. He's extremely sharp-sighted and shoots a succession of small birds in the shade of the trees. Although these are supposed to be for our dinner, Ahuang opens her mouth to catch the sparrows and other small birds as they plummet, promptly chomping them down.

While watching this and musing over the fact that this is one beast that would never be any good as a hunting dog, I find myself almost drooling: what a pleasant feeling it must be to have fresh warm sparrow's blood flow down into one's empty stomach! Since coming to Tibet, I've felt a growing, irresistible desire to eat meat. In this land of strong sun, cold nights and climatic extremes, you could become ill if you didn't eat enough meat. I take the gun and bring down three birds.

Our catch is small because of Ahuang. Yong has thirteen

birds in hand, but this is still not enough for a meal, so we also buy a duck from a farmer.

'Ahuang had a good feed today for the first time in a long while. Usually, I'd shoot fifty sparrows for a meal. I couldn't live without my gun.'

'Guns are prohibited in Japan. What will you do there?'

'Really?!' Yong is at a loss.

Catch in hand, we visit Yong's friend Lao Peng, who lives at the School of Post and Telecommunications alongside the river. It's a quiet place with a sunlit garden. Lao Peng, a small, plump man, greets us with a smile.

'A duck and some sparrows! Let's cook them straight away.'

Yong and Lao Peng set about preparing the birds. They wring the duck's neck, pluck it clean of feathers, chop it into pieces and put it into a pressure cooker with garlic, ginger, scallions and red pepper. At this altitude, water boils at a temperature of 70 degrees, hence a pressure cooker is an indispensable item. The small birds are plucked and stir-fried whole in a wok with soy sauce for flavouring.

In no time the two men have prepared a veritable feast of red-cooked duck and stir-fried bird. This is a good life indeed: to catch something yourself and then be able to cook and eat it immediately!

'I think Lhasa's a wonderful place. Much more enjoyable than Japan.'

'Do you think so, Aya? I've been bewitched by Tibet since the first time I came here. I still am. If I go anywhere else, I always feel like I can't see the real sky. But try living here and you'll find it's really tough. There's a heap of hassles you don't know about.'

'When did you first come to Lhasa?'

'It must've been August 1983. At the time I was a university student, very serious ... bookish and burning with ideals.'

'You? Bookish?' I look at Yong in astonishment.

'That's right. Thinking back, I can see that Tibet changed me. When I first arrived, my work unit still hadn't been assigned, and I stayed in a guest house with others who'd come from the lowland provinces. My third day here was 15 August, the Mid-Autumn Festival – the season for eating moon-cakes. We lit a bonfire near the river and were drinking rice wine and beer. At that time there was only one restaurant in Lhasa, so the riverbank was about the only place where we could hang out. The moon was really bright, and while we were looking at it, the others started getting homesick. It was the first time they'd been so far from home, so they were probably feeling lonely. But I was happy to have come to Tibet and excited to be here.

'Later that night, a guy called Tang and I decided to take our drunken friends back to the guest house. Just as we passed the bank on East Yanhe Road, we ran into some police conducting identity checks. As we hadn't been assigned work units yet, I showed them my letter of introduction from Henan University. But the police said it wasn't enough.

'Tang got angry and yelled at them, "Of course we haven't got a work-unit ID, we've only just arrived!"

"Watch your attitude, kid!" they said. "We'll run you out of here." They swore at Tang and then hit him without warning. "Don't get cheeky with us! Shit of a kid!"

'I was young and stupid then, so I protested. "What are you doing?! The police shouldn't be hitting citizens. Such violence is unforgivable!"

'"What's that? Do you want me to hit you too? It seems you won't be satisfied unless I thump you as well," the policeman said, and hit me. Unfortunately, my reflex was to hit him back. That wasn't a good move. He turned red with anger and tried to grab me, so I took to my heels and got out of there as fast as I could. I hid in the trees at the side of the road. I thought I'd be able to get away, but I was surrounded.

'I waited, because I thought that even though the first policeman was a bit strange, if I explained properly this time, they'd understand and everything would be all right. But that same policeman came at me with an electric baton and hit me without warning. Apparently I went flying. I don't remember it clearly, but it seems I grabbed the baton he was swinging at me and was knocked out by the electric shock.

'When I came to, I was slumped against a wall. My trousers were wet. Around me were Tibetan beggars who'd also been caught. They were squatting with their hands against the wall. Of course they didn't know what the reason was – if any – that they were being held there. When the policeman noticed me, he hit me again and ordered me to squat with my hands against the wall without moving. I bent forward like I was told to do, and stayed like that for hours. It was freezing and I was numb with cold, but there was nothing I could do except wait for morning. I was drunk, I'd been shocked by an electric baton and I'd been thoroughly beaten up, so naturally I was in a foul mood. After hours of squatting, chilled to the bone, I fell into a doze.

'When it got light, I turned around nervously to look – my eyes were all swollen – but the police weren't there anymore! I felt so deeply humiliated. Nobody protects you here. Even telling the truth doesn't cut it. After that I was depressed for days. Shit!' Yong bites his lip; talking of these memories seems to have rekindled his bitterness.

'And from then on,' Lao Peng says with a meaningful smile, Cao Yong became the biggest hoodlum in Lhasa.'

'Hoodlum?'

Yong screws up his face in embarrassment. 'Nah, it wasn't like that.'

Lao Peng is a novelist. Before coming to Lhasa, he worked at a meteorological observatory in Ali. That's where he met Yong. Three years ago, when Yong was researching sites in Ali, he collapsed on Lao Peng's doorstep late one night, nearly dead from starvation. Lao Peng nursed him, making him rice gruel from his own meagre supplies. Yong has felt deeply in his debt ever since.

Lao Peng knows Ali's inhospitable environment well and tells me how astonished he was that Yong had stayed there so long. He became interested in Yong and occasionally wrote about him in magazines and newspapers in Lhasa.

'Hey, Cao Yong, in Tibet University, at least, they think you're a hoodlum, don't they? In Lhasa, Yong's famous for his shooting and his quarrelling. The only things everyone agrees on about him are that he never misses a target with his gun, and that he's always ready for a fight. But nobody knows about Cao Yong the artist, do they?' Lao Peng asks teasingly.

'Hey, quit it!'

Lao Peng ignores Yong's embarrassment and continues with amusement. 'Well, then, doesn't everyone know the story of your bravery on the Barkhor a few years back? Wasn't the whole of Lhasa talking about nothing else at the time?' Paying no attention to Yong's attempts to stop him, Lao Peng tells me the story.

'Next to the Jokhang Temple on the Barkhor is the Uighur Huis' territory. You have to understand that the Hui and the Tibetans are always mistreating the Han Chinese here. Hans are in a bad position because they seem unable to present a united front. The Hui sell all sorts of things, knives and so on, at street stalls and … hey, Cao Yong, didn't you go to buy a plastic tote bag? That's right, Cao Yong asked how much a bag was at one of those Hui stalls selling odds and ends. The Hui told him it was 2 yuan. "All right," says Cao Yong, "I'll have one, then", and he paid 2 yuan. But these Hui always talk down to us Han like we're shit, so right away the man started getting insolent and said, "It's 4 yuan, hand over 4 yuan, you idiot!" So Cao Yong answered, "But you said it was 2 yuan", and started to leave with the bag. The Hui got even more insistent and began abusing him: "Idiot! It's 4 yuan! Don't take that, you snot! If I said it's 4 yuan, then it's 4 yuan!"

'A crowd of Hui had gathered, and they were all fired up, itching to give the Han a hard time. The mob began to cheer the stall-holder on loudly: "Get him! Beat the Han dog to death! Kill him!" Generally, it would be suicide for a Han to defy a Hui in that particular place, and they knew it, so they were waiting to see Cao Yong look pathetic as he paid the money and grovelled in apology. But Cao Yong finally saw red – and spun around to kick that Hui in the face. In those days Cao Yong was training at boxing every day, so he was fast with his fists – and feet – in a fight. Anyway, this guy fell backwards with his face covered in blood. Everyone was dumbstruck. They couldn't believe that a single Han – on his own – had declared war like this. The hot-blooded young Hui toughs all jumped up. One of them aimed a thick iron pipe at Cao Yong's head from behind and swung it. Cao Yong got a vicious blow on the back.

'These Hui are also quick to start a fight. They began picking up whatever weapons they could find on their stalls: steel pipes, swords, knives. Several dozen men armed with weapons surrounded Cao Yong, and the old people all had rocks in their hands, while he was unarmed and empty-handed. On the spur of the moment he ran into a Hui restaurant across the way – and by great good fortune found a huge axe there. That was it. He rushed out brandishing the axe over his head and screaming like a madman, "I'll kill you all!"

'The Hui thugs were convinced he'd curled up his tail and run away, so this really gave them a fright. Once this guy gets angry, he goes crazy. The crowd at the stalls, who'd been cheering and getting excited, ran in all directions. "Kill the Hui! Kill! I'm coming after you!" he yelled.

'Then the Tibetans and Khampas who were watching started cheering loudly for Cao Yong. Khampas are natural-born fighters, and Tibetans worship heroes. They all love a strong, courageous guy. Cao Yong ignored the frightened Hui and brought his axe down, smashing up the goods on the stalls. The young Hui thugs who were always swaggering about ran away – all of them! It was the first time a Han had ever run amok on the Barkhor – on his own, what's more!

'The tale of Cao Yong's bravery spread throughout Lhasa. Children started to worship him, and it got so that people could be one up on each other just by saying they knew "Brother Cao". So you see, he's the biggest hoodlum in Lhasa.'

Lao Peng looks as if he greatly enjoyed telling this tale, but Yong appears embarrassed, like a child who's been caught doing mischief. While listening to the story, however, I'd begun to worry. Protests apart, the free-wheeling lifestyle here in Lhasa is wonderful. I wonder if Yong could really be happy in Japan? People can sit drinking tea in the sun until it gets dark here, and even the dogs aren't chained up but run around freely. Japanese dogs, on the other hand, spend their whole lives tied up, have almost no opportunity to run free, and then die neurotic and frustrated. Even when I say there are lots of ridiculous rules and petty restrictions in Japan, no-one believes me. Everyone thinks Japan is a place like Heaven, filled with freedom and pleasure.

16 March. We've decided to move from the Bank School to Tibet University. I'm very much looking forward to going to this place where Yong lived for so long.

'In Lhasa, teachers have as much status as dogs on the Barkhor,' he tells me on the way.

'Why?'

'It's the law of the jungle here. The likes of teachers

don't do any harm, or any good either, so no-one pays them any mind. Other than being a Communist Party official, it's much better to be a truck driver or something. And it's far better to be a peasant selling vegetables in the free market. In Lhasa, there's a terrible shortage of goods. Everyone's jealous of truck drivers and tries to suck up to them because they can get hold of petrol. Peasants can get free yak dung to use as fuel, and they have lots of things to eat. But teachers? They don't have anything.

'The university bans the use of electrical equipment other than 60-watt bulbs so they can save on electricity. It's also forbidden to prepare meals on electric hot plates. That's as good as murder! To stop people using electricity when they can't get hold of petrol or kerosene, or even firewood and yak dung? If I'd obeyed those rules, I don't know how many times over I'd have died of hunger. Everyone secretly runs wires from the university's electricity lines for their stoves. But sometimes they do spot-checks. Suddenly they kick down the door and barge in. They don't give a damn about what people might be doing inside. But if you only ever did what you were told, it wouldn't matter how many lives you had; they wouldn't be enough. That's why it's always a cat-and-mouse game.'

Tibet University, near the Lhasa Bridge, is the largest university in Tibet. As many as a thousand teachers and students are housed in dormitories in the large modern buildings made of reinforced concrete that line the river. This is the centre of Tibetan culture and education, an elite place where only the best could get a post. It is, so to speak, the Tokyo University of Tibet. When the senior art teacher at Tibet University, Zashi Tseren, saw Yong's work, he was immediately offered a job there.

'Li Qinpu! Li Qinpu!' Yong yells, his voice carrying up from the bottom of a three-storey building. Presently, a window opens on the second floor and a youth wearing spectacles looks out. We go up to his room.

Li Qinpu greets us, his narrow eyes creased into a big smile behind lenses like Coke-bottle bottoms. Tall, with the appearance of a philosopher, he lives surrounded by piles of books, and spends nearly every day reading. He's Yong's great friend; the two were always talking philosophy and politics, and for a while, apparently, a rumour even went round that they were gay because they were so close. Sometimes, though, their debates became heated, and there were occasions when they didn't speak for days. Li Qinpu is like a resigned hermit steeped in pessimism.

With him is a tall, thin woman, Pei Danfeng. Later Yong tells me that since her husband, an abstract painter, went off to Vienna, she's heard nothing from him. She's been strong, living alone, but recently has become close to Li Qinpu. I hear that in addition to teaching music she has a business selling mushrooms she brings in from Linzhi.

I also meet Zhang Husheng, a history scholar, thin and slightly built yet brimming with energy and always thinking up new business ideas, because it's nearly impossible to lead a decent life on the low salaries they all receive from the university. After Husheng married the round, plump, Beijing-born Xiao Mei, he started a business by turning the rooms they'd been assigned into a coffee shop and billiard parlour for students. This unconventional scholar also sometimes goes into the town to sell the ink paintings that Yong taught him to do.

Yong's friends are open and generous – they seem quite different from Han Chinese in the lowland provinces – but they're also strong and resilient, surviving in tough conditions by helping each other. In this environment, getting anything done is inconvenient in the extreme, and there's also the constant friction with the Tibetans to contend with, but there's no doubting the free rein the Han have up here.

While his friends start to prepare food in Li Qinpu's room, Yong finally relaxes, as if back on his own territory at last.

'When I first came here, Lhasa was completely undeveloped,' he recalls. 'The single People's Restaurant didn't serve food fit for human consumption. It had razor blades and stuff like that in it! When the canteen was open, we could always get light meals of cold rice and steamed buns there, but during the university holidays, it would close, and that was hell. I had no money, no food or fuel either. I wasn't ready for my first winter in Lhasa. I was hungry and cold – it was hopeless! Yak dung was going for 5 yuan a bag, but back then I couldn't afford to pay that much. One day I was so hungry and desperate, I remembered a leftover steamed bun I'd thrown out my window several weeks before. So in the middle of the night I crept outside with a candle and went looking for it. Pitiful, isn't it? There's a fence outside my room that stops people and dogs coming in, so it was still there. I picked up the scattered pieces of bun from amongst the leaves, but the climate is so dry and the sun so strong that it'd turned hard as rock. I went back to my room and did my best to crush it and knead it with saliva, then swallowed it down. But even then my hunger was barely satisfied. That's when I began to think about stealing food.

'It's not a sin to steal things from people who're better off than you are – that's what Tibetans think. Because Li Qinpu was really straight in those days, he made himself out to be all proper, saying stuff like "You mustn't steal other people's possessions." But if your stomach's empty, you can't be too concerned with niceties like that. So anyway, we went out looking for food in the middle of the night. Didn't have to worry about anyone seeing us, because there weren't any other fools walking around in the dark except stray dogs with the same idea. Li Qinpu couldn't see anything, so he hung onto my clothes and followed me. Eventually we found some dried beef hanging in the window of a rich Tibetan's house and borrowed it with the help of a long stick. I cried with happiness when I bit into that dried beef. Remember, Li Qinpu?' Yong speaks with deep feeling. 'Back then, we were jealous of any houses with fires. Any place we found with smoke rising – didn't matter if it was black or white – we'd go and procure food supplies immediately.'

Yong and his friends had arrived in Lhasa as 'Youth Assisting Tibet'. The Communist government needed lots of Han Chinese to work there and encouraged young people to 'support Tibet' by offering them various perks. In 1983, up to eight hundred young graduates had arrived here from the lowland provinces. They'd been promised the status of high government officials and paid a salary higher than anywhere else in China, but despite the special treatment, many of them fled because they couldn't endure the rigorous environment. After a little over a year, only a few dozen of the toughest remained, Yong amongst them.

'Look, I bet you could read a newspaper!'

'You're right. I had no idea it was this bright here.'

The moonlit Tibetan night is as light as an arctic night of the midnight sun. We leave Li Qinpu's room and gaze at the moon, exhaling white clouds of breath. Impoverished scholars in their attics wouldn't need candles to read by here.

The university is deserted because of the Spring Festival break; a dog howling in the distance makes the only sound. We head for Pei Danfeng's room, where we will stay, in a block of teachers' dormitories made of sun-dried bricks and concrete.

'This teachers' dormitory is called the "poor man's district" of the university,' Yong tells me. 'See those big Tibetan-style houses over there? That's where the Party officials live. People who attend the work-unit political-study sessions don't have to put up with the poor living conditions me and my friends do.'

'What's political study?'

'Stuff like studying documents from the central government, reflecting on our own thoughts, and other crap. It's more important to participate in that stuff than it is to work! You can skive off work, but if you don't attend political study, you're finished. No chance of promotion, that's for sure. I didn't usually go. You can waste your life on it.'

'Didn't you get into trouble?'

'I'd always ask the work-unit leader if it really was his intention to sack one of the "Youth Assisting Tibet". I'd threaten him by saying that this would create a political problem. When you say that, they can't do anything. My file is filled with bad reports, and I'm also well and truly on the university blacklist. That's why I had to live in the poor man's district.'

'Where's your old room?'

Yong guides me to a corner of the dormitory block. His room is surrounded by a wall made out of scraps of wood. At the entrance is a door that locks from the inside and an ingeniously crafted secret hole enabling it to be locked from the outside as well.

'See, this way it looks like I'm in, even if I've gone out. That way nobody can just wander in. I put a lot of thought into making this.'

There's nothing at all left in the room, let alone bedding.

'Aya, you'll catch cold. Quick, let's go back and get into bed.' At Yong's urging we return to Pei Danfeng's room. There's no heater, just a big bed. Since there's not much vegetation in Tibet, there's very little that can be used as heating fuel. Yong searches the room and pulls out an electric hot plate from a corner; he connects it to a cord hanging from the ceiling. At night the communal water supply is cut off, and we can't even wash our faces.

'Even this is unbelievably luxurious compared to how it used to be. The university turns a blind eye to electric stoves, and we have water piped up to the dormitories. We used to have to go down to the river to fetch water.' While Yong talks, I dive into bed, still wearing all my clothes.

*

Next morning, after a long sleep, we go for a walk with Ahuang and Husheng's dog, Huazi, along the river. Tibetan women squat on the banks, chatting as they do their laundry.

The sky here is too blue. There are sere, ochre-yellow mountains and, behind them, snow-capped peaks that pierce the sky. I feel as if I'm on a completely different planet. As on the surface of the moon, the difference in temperature between night and day is extreme: summer in the daytime and winter at night. The people who live in this land of arrows of sunlight that fall from heaven, of thin air and freezing nights, are robust and sturdy.

'How interesting! There's absolutely no perspective, is there?!' Yong laughs at the sight of me turning around to take in the scenery.

'Remember the saying "Though you can see the mountain, your horse may die before you reach it"? It means that you can see even distant mountains clearly. I often had that notion brought home to me on my travels. Even though the mountain you're headed for looks very close, you can walk for kilometres and kilometres and the distance doesn't decrease. It can be really frustrating.'

We walk along the riverbank and light cigarettes. To our left a large bridge spans the river. 'Across this bridge, the road goes to Linzhi. It connects to the highway that passes through Sichuan. The road along the river in the other direction goes to Gongkar, Lhasa's airport.'

The area around the university's rear entrance is a dry riverbed with small, round pebbles, but when we walk a little further we come to an empty plot of land covered with grass.

'This is a slaughter site. The Hui mob are always killing their sheep here.'

Presently, we hear the sound of dogs barking. Strays have gathered on the riverbank and are fighting over something that has washed up there, which they proceed to devour.

'What's that?'

'Oh, it's a baby!' Moving closer, we see something that looks like a lump of meat wrapped in a cloth. It's the corpse of a newborn child, the face already unrecognizable. The dogs are chewing it to pieces, eating up the scraps of flesh. Yet somehow this sight blends perfectly with the scene – it's as completely natural here as any other everyday event.

'Bodies requiring water burial are always being thrown into the Lhasa River. After I found that out, I decided never to eat fish from Lhasa, because they get fat on corpses. Stay!' Yong restrains Ahuang from joining the other dogs.

4. THE SICHUAN–TIBET HIGHWAY

It's now two weeks since we arrived in Lhasa. Martial law is still in force.

'This is the longest period of martial law I've ever experienced,' Yong sighs.

Then one day a friend hears a rumour that the Public Security police are looking for Yong.

'What's it about, do you think?'

'I dunno, but I heard they wanna get hold of you. Something about you hiding a foreigner.'

'Damn! Aya, we've got to get out of Lhasa. I remember when the Danish husband of a language student at Tibet University was taken into custody in Beijing. They treated him as a spy and wouldn't let him leave the country. If you're caught, Aya, you could be accused of spying or worse.' Yong looks grim.

'But how can we get out of here without the police seeing us?'

The Qinghai–Tibet Highway out of Lhasa is under tight surveillance by the army. If I'm discovered, I could also be mistaken for a journalist, which would probably get me into all sorts of trouble. Yong would be charged with the serious offence of sheltering a foreigner, and could be imprisoned for years on suspicion of being a spy and sending information overseas about the protests in Tibet. It's also quite possible that by now the police in Lhasa have been informed about his exhibition in Beijing.

The atmosphere is tense, with security police searching the Barkhor every day, intent on crushing the independence movement. They also keep a close watch for overseas supporters of the movement, spies sent by the Dalai Lama, and politicians from India and elsewhere. Checkpoints are everywhere, and a constant watch is even kept on foreigners staying legally in the city. We hear that the British teacher of English at Tibet University couldn't stand it anymore and has fled to her own country. Yet despite the strict surveillance, to the government's annoyance, news of events in Tibet is broadcast over Voice of America as soon as they happen. And there are also Tibetans from overseas in hiding here. The government has begun searching the Barkhor in the middle of the night.

Yong isn't sleeping well. One night he awakes with a violent start, panting heavily, sweat running down his face.

'What's the matter?'

'I dreamt that the police suddenly kicked the door down and barged in.'

Distant sirens echo through the night. The police intensify their search for spies. We hear that the foreign manager of the international Holiday Inn Lhasa is under surveillance. The way things are escalating, snowballing before our eyes, is bewildering.

The sole escape route we could use is the Sichuan–Tibet

Highway, which descends through south-east Tibet, crossing the mountains and continuing on to Chengdu. Compared to the closely monitored Qinghai–Tibet Highway, there's only one checkpoint, at Dazi. Yong guesses that if we pass through this checkpoint, there will be no more inspections and we can slip out of Tibet more easily.

'The Sichuan–Tibet Highway is the most dangerous road in the whole of China. It was built by the PLA in order to invade Tibet. They started from Sichuan, clearing the forests, crossing the mountains and fighting as they went – it's a road steeped in blood – and there are numerous trucks and corpses buried at the bottom of the cliffs. It used to be an important road into Tibet, but these days the shorter, well-paved Qinghai–Tibet Highway is the main route up. As a result, the Sichuan–Tibet Highway isn't kept in good repair. But it's much quicker to go that way. Nowadays it's used for transporting freight or travelling to Sichuan and Yunnan. I often went that way to Chengdu when I was smuggling. On those mountain roads the rainy season is the worst time. There are steep cliffs that collapse suddenly, and often there are terrible disasters.'

I hold my breath as Yong speaks, but, having come this far with him, I can't turn back. I have to admit, too, that a part of me is looking forward to this thrill-packed highway journey.

'Are you scared?'

'No, death is the same wherever you are. This way is at least more interesting than trying to avoid danger so you can live longer. I'll be all right. Let's give this Sichuan–Tibet Highway a go.'

'We'll be fine. I know the road well, and I've been on the brink of death many times. Guess I've managed to stay alive this long because I've got the devil's own luck.'

Yong immediately goes out to buy bus tickets. Since there are no direct buses from Lhasa to Chengdu along the Sichuan–Tibet Highway, we have to go by bus to Linzhi, about 200 kilometres away, and then trust to luck to hitch a lift on a truck.

26 March. It's still dark when we catch the bus bound for Linzhi. At Dazi, a sleepy inspector boards the darkened bus and checks our IDs. I show him my fake ones, and we get through without difficulty. I can now speak everyday Chinese and am posing as a Chinese citizen, but there's always the danger that, if I'm questioned, my speech will give me away. Yong's on edge. If we're discovered now, I'll get away with deportation or a fine, but as for Yong ... his fate will definitely be imprisonment. With the business of the exhibition as well, he's skating on thin ice.

We arrive at Linzhi in the evening. As the Chinese character in its name suggests, Linzhi is a town surrounded by forests. It's the timber-production centre of Tibet, and there are many wooden houses in the town, something I hadn't seen at all in Lhasa. Shouldering our luggage, we set off from the bus station for the town centre, searching for somewhere to stay. We spot several men in dark-green uniforms coming towards us.

'It's Public Security,' Yong mutters, his face strained. We exchange glances and continue to walk calmly down the street past them, since it would look unnatural to try to avoid them.

'Oy, wait there!' A voice brings us up short just as we've walked by and are breathing a sigh of relief.

'Show us your ID!' the police order, grinning.

Dismayed, we come to a halt, and Yong quickly pulls out his Tibet University work-card and personal ID with shaking hands. I do my best to conceal myself behind him and be as inconspicuous as possible. But the police merely give the IDs a fleeting glance and thrust them back at him as if they are of no interest.

'What's this? Oh, we thought you were a foreigner. You know martial law's in force, don't you, because of the protests?'

'Nah, we're proper Han Chinese. She's got identity papers too.' Yong laughs and shows them my papers.

'We thought you were a foreigner, with that really long hair, even though you're a bloke!'

We breathe another sigh of relief as we watch them depart laughing.

'Let's find a truck headed for Chengdu and get out of here right away,' Yong says in a low voice and quickens his pace. We find a rundown hotel built on crooked stilts above the river. I burst out laughing at its ungainly appearance. Where on earth does this building style come from? The building is a confused circular construction. We cross a narrow bridge through to a spacious interior apparently separated into private rooms on all sides. It's just like being on a boat. The floor squeaks as we walk on it, and our room appears to be in imminent danger of collapse. Its round windows are also reminiscent of a boat, and the walls are a dreadful mess of pasted-on magazine and newspaper pages. We sit down on the bed and sigh yet again with relief.

'Linzhi Tibetans have very strange customs,' says Yong.

'Like what?'

'They believe that people with big ear lobes are lucky, and if they kill such a person, then that luck will come to them. My ear lobes are big, so whenever I come here people are always looking at them and drooling. It's really creepy. Tibetans are also very skilful at killing with poison … putting some terrible poison under their fingernails and then slipping it into your cup when you're not looking, that kind of thing.' Yong strokes his ear lobes as he speaks.

'Oh, they're huge, aren't they?' I take a good look at them and am amazed by their size.

'Yeah, they're so big because I was a naughty boy when I was a kid and was always getting them pulled.'

We've had such a fright with the security police today that we climb into bed early rather than going out into the town again.

27 March. Since early morning we've been standing by the side of the Sichuan–Tibet Highway. Yong yells out to every truck that passes by, asking their destinations. Eventually he finds one transporting fertilizer to the next town of Bomi.

'I'll give you a lift for 40 yuan,' the driver says, and we climb aboard immediately. Not long after leaving Linzhi, a vista of blossom-covered mountains unrolls before us. It's a nostalgic reminder of a countryside scene in Japan –

wooden houses, spring mountains bursting with green shoots and apricot blossom. Tibetan men carrying hunting guns walk along the road. I put my head out the window and take deep breaths of the sweet-smelling air.

When the sun is low in the sky, the driver stops at a restaurant in a small village on the grass-covered plain. Farm women lit by the evening sun herd sheep across the grassland while swinging their rope slings, and innocent-looking sheep wander aimlessly around the shabby wooden restaurant. The whole scene entrances me – it could be straight out of a painting of medieval Europe! To think that the world of Barbizon School landscapes exists in the East too, here in the Himalayas.

'The area around here is so beautiful. I'd like to live in a place like this forever,' Yong sighs.

'If that ever happened, the peace would probably evaporate by the third day!' I laugh mockingly, looking him in the eye.

'*Tashi delek.*' Some bored-looking men drinking tea greet us immediately we enter the restaurant. They are Khampas: strong, large-boned sturdy people who live in this region of Tibet. They wear stiff fur-lined *chupas*, and their hair, probably uncut since the day they were born, is wound around their heads and tied with red bands. Adorned with ornaments and with large swords hanging from their waists, the men look truly stylish. Their eyes glitter like those of carnivorous animals, and each one, standing magnificently with one arm hanging out of his coat, oozes a wild, masculine appeal. When I ask them to show me the shell-covered cloth bags slung over their shoulders, I'm captivated by the exquisite craftsmanship.

I'd heard that Tibet resembled medieval Europe. Under the rule of the aristocracy and lamas before the Chinese invasion, strict religious teachings were widespread, but it was also a time of celebratory feasts, ceremonies, wandering minstrels, martial-arts competitions, mounted parades, pilgrims, bandits, hermits, fanatical believers and soothsayers. Under Chinese rule, however, Tibet has become increasingly Sinocized and the old culture's been lost, yet a whiff of times past lingers in the villages along this highway. I see how Yong's persistent use of classic Western techniques in his paintings is perfectly suited to expressing the atmosphere that endures in Tibet.

'Bomi. We've arrived. This is where you get off.'

It's well into the night when the driver stops the truck. A sigh escapes me as I look at the map. 'From Linzhi to Bomi is not even a twentieth of the Sichuan–Tibet Highway! When will we arrive in Chengdu?'

'The journey from here on will be rough going.'

We pick up our belongings and get down from the truck.

Night has closed in and cold rain falls on Bomi. It's pitch black and completely deserted, without a single human being in sight. We find lodgings at the government-run PLA guest house on the highway and sit on our bed eating biscuits and tinned food by candlelight, since there's a blackout in the hostel. No restaurants are open, and the hostel too is silent as the grave.

28 March. In the morning, we walk the streets, looking for a truck to Chengdu. But the only responses we get are negative headshakes. 'There haven't been any trucks at

all recently,' an old man smoking a pipe tells us.

'First thing to do is get something to eat. Then we can think about it.'

We enter a small roadside eatery – the only one open. The food served by an old Tibetan couple is so awful I put my chopsticks down. 'I suppose they're Bomi farmers turned restaurant owners. Well, this food isn't fit to eat!'

Yong angrily barges into the kitchen and begins to lecture the old couple on the basics of cooking. They fold their arms and listen with interest, then prepare our meal again. When our stomachs are eventually satisfied, we go for a stroll and stop to look at a Tibetan house we notice at the foot of a mountain. The large wooden building is a lovely sight, surrounded by trees, with cows and chickens in the garden. While we stand there gazing at it, the owner comes out in response to the barking of his dog.

He greets us in a friendly manner despite the fact that we're strangers, and invites us into his house. Inside, he shows us to a bench covered with a Tibetan-style rug, and his wife offers us some yak-butter tea. The tea is poured into cups from a long, narrow copper teapot with a small spout and has a distinctive sour smell. I have great difficulty in swallowing it. At last I manage to drink a little, but to my dismay the hostess hospitably fills my cup to the brim again. As I sit there feeling nauseous, Yong composedly drinks several cups.

'You should drink it, it's good for you,' he says with suppressed laughter.

A fire burns brightly in this pleasant, comfortable living room generously furnished with woollen carpets. Warmth and affection permeate every corner.

'This is a lovely house, isn't it?'

'We built it last year. It cost 10,000 yuan,' the husband informs us, smiling with pride.

Ten thousand yuan is unbelievably cheap! Converted into Japanese currency it would come to about 200,000 yen, a sum for which you couldn't possibly hope to build a house. The couple's children pick apples of various sizes and bring them to me while the husband sits cross-legged by the fire, smiling contentedly and slowly puffing on a pipe.

5. OLD LI

After three days we're utterly bored with waiting around in Bomi, so when a convoy of three lumber trucks bound for Chengdu arrives, we immediately rush out to try and negotiate a lift. The trucks are stopped at the side of the highway, and people wanting to travel to Chengdu soon collect around them.

'Can you take us? There're two of us.' The driver we approach looks to be the oldest of the three. He's called Old Li. His face, deeply engraved with wrinkles, takes on a sly look.

'Chengdu, eh? Well, that'll be 120 yuan per person.' He demands a price higher than the going rate.

'We'll have to take it.' Our lift secured, we're able to relax. We can't depart immediately because of the paperwork the drivers need to complete first. That evening we go back to the small farmers' restaurant for a meal before embarking on our long journey. Thanks to Yong's culinary advice, the old couple have succeeded in learning to serve up decent food.

*

31 March. We put our luggage on the back of the truck and squeeze into the passenger seat – it's a tight fit. At 11.20 a.m., we depart for Chengdu. My heart beats faster when I think about travelling the Sichuan–Tibet Highway at last. Old Li is also travelling on this highway for the first time. Although he looks closer to seventy, he tells us that he's just over fifty.

Soon after leaving Bomi, Old Li's truck, which is travelling last in the convoy, gets left further and further behind the other two. We get the impression that he's a hindrance to the other drivers, not just because of his age, but because, we soon realize, his truck is badly worn out and stalls every half hour. Whenever this happens, Old Li tut-tuts and climbs down to look under the bonnet.

'All you've got is my truck,' he says arrogantly. He's taken advantage of our position and his manner is rather insolent, but Yong still takes it upon himself to help with the repairs; he's accustomed to fixing trucks.

There are no guard rails – no protection at all – on the road, which follows the steep cliffs, weaving through the mountains. After some time, we reach a spot where an endless stream of stones is tumbling down the steep slope onto the road. Just like in an American Western.

'Truth be told, there're four trucks at the bottom of this cliff from when my friends and I were smuggling before,' Yong murmurs with a grave look. 'There are rock falls all the way along this mountain. The unlucky ones get hit and die. Two friends died that way along here.'

I wish he'd waited until after we'd gotten through this section to tell us that.

Yong tells us how in 1985 he went into business in order to make some money to support his painting. He hired a driver and sent a large quantity of Indian woollen cloth to Chengdu, but the four trucks got caught in a landslide. That year, eighty transport trucks were buried at the base of these cliffs! The following year, a novelist acquaintance of Yong's in Lhasa was visiting here in search of material when she too was killed when a boulder fell on her car. A year later one of her friends, another woman, died the same way.

By now Old Li is scared. He stops the truck just before the slide and sits there, frozen.

'We'll run to the other side and then help you over, Old Li. Wait here,' we tell him. At least this way we'll be taking the smallest risk and saving ourselves. We get down from the truck and sprint across while keeping an eye on the falling rocks. Old Li steels himself while Yong watches the slope and signals him on. Fortunately, no large rocks fall on the truck, and it gets safely through the worst bit.

We continue along the highway in the twilight, with Old Li's truck stalling repeatedly, until we reach the next town of Basu, late at night and long after the other trucks. There are no restaurants open at this hour, and we can find nothing to eat. The other drivers invite us to their hotel room and give us some fruit because they feel sorry for us. I relax and eat some mandarin.

'Your Chinese is strange,' one driver says, looking hard at me. I spit the mandarin out in alarm. Quickly Yong says, 'Her pronunciation is strange because she's a Korean from the north-east.'

'Oh, is that so?'

China is a vast country full of ethnic groups. Not everyone speaks standard Chinese, and there are many regional dialects. In Shanghai dialect, for example, the word for 'Japanese' is *Sapuning*, while in Cantonese it is *Yapunyan* and in standard speech it is *Ribenren*.

'That's right,' I tell them, 'I'm a Korean from the northeast', and force a smile.

'Where's your home town?' they ask me next.

'Er, ho ... home town?'

'Her home town is in Jilin.'

'I suppose it's cold there.'

'Yes, yes. It's very cold. There's lots of snow!'

And that's how I become a Korean from the province of Jilin.

Next morning the drivers decide to leave Basu first thing, still without us having had a meal. 'Hurry it up just a bit!' The other drivers goad Old Li before going on ahead.

'Try and find us a restaurant at the next town, will you?' Yong asks him.

We've been going for two hours or more when the truck suddenly stops on an upward slope.

'Shit! It's stalled again.'

Yong and Old Li check under the bonnet, but this time nothing works. 'Ah, this is hopeless,' Old Li grumbles from underneath the truck. Just at that moment, a bus comes down the hill. Old Li waves it down and promptly jumps aboard. 'I'm going to get a mechanic. Look after the truck; I'll be back tomorrow,' he calls out and is taken back along the road we've just come on. There's no time to offer even a word of protest. I'm dumbfounded by this turn of events:

now we're stuck on this desolate mountain road without any food.

'This kind of thing often happens in Tibet – we call it "*dang tuan zhang*". It means having to wait around like this in a broken-down truck or car for a mechanic to come and save you. If you're not riding in a Japanese vehicle, then you're bound to experience *dang tuan zhang* in Tibet.' Yong looks around at the landscape as he speaks. On one side of the road a stream flows along the bottom of a ravine, beyond which is mountain with a few Tibetan houses at its foot.

'I'll go over there and see if I can get us some food,' he says and disappears. Left alone, I sit myself on top of the logs in the back of the truck and bask in the sun, but my stomach is empty and I feel dizzy. Not many vehicles pass along this road; I can see why Old Li jumped onto that bus so quickly. The midday sun is pleasant, and I nearly doze off.

A little while later, Yong comes back with a black chicken dangling from one hand. 'Look, I traded this for that broken digital clock from the bus accident when I left Lhasa.'

'Wow, are we going to cook it here?'

We begin to prepare our meal immediately. Yong shuts the chicken up in the truck with its legs bound and starts to collect firewood, while I fetch water from the stream. Yong then slits the chicken's throat, collects the blood in an enamel mug and adds salt so that it congeals. Inside the body he finds one nearly perfect egg and three small, partially developed ones. We skewer the chicken meat on twigs and cook it over the fire. Thus one live chicken is turned into a feast of savoury-smelling meat grilled to perfection, with soup made from blood, offal and eggs. We consume it in a trice. But unfortunately it's barely enough, so when we spot a PLA jeep coming along the road, Yong flags it down.

'Can you give us something to eat, please? We're *dang tuan zhang*!' he yells, upon which the army guys drop something onto the road and disappear. It's a pack of dry provisions. I immediately take a bite and discover that the flavour is similar to the Japanese energy-supplement bars called 'Calorie Mate', which I find quite agreeable. After that Yong stops every vehicle that goes by, and in this fashion we get a stream of biscuits, dried noodles and even cigarettes thrown at us. In no time we've stocked up on supplies.

'We could open a shop out here!' If this is *dang tuan zhang*, it's nothing to be afraid of.

'Being on the highway helps. If this had happened somewhere in Ali, we'd be in serious trouble. I was stuck there and went for eleven days eating only black-bean horse feed. In the end I couldn't shit I was so constipated.' Apparently our current situation doesn't qualify as an adventure for Yong.

Presently, two young Tibetans come by, having climbed up from the houses below, and from the way they're staring at us, they appear to want something. Yong offers them cigarettes and says something in Tibetan which produces looks of delight. They turn back the way they came.

'We agreed to trade eggs for petrol,' Yong says and laughs like a naughty boy.

The two youths return towards sunset, carrying a

misshapen iron bucket. One of them pulls a bundle of straw from the folds of his *chupa* containing nine carefully packed, small, round eggs. Chicken eggs are a precious commodity in Tibet. In Lhasa they're cheap at 3 jiao each because large quantities are transported from lowland China, but on the Sichuan–Tibet Highway the cost of chicken eggs is unbelievable, an astronomical 1 yuan or more! Much more expensive than in Japan.

Yong checks the eggs, then pokes a plastic hose into the petrol tank and sucks the petrol out. The misshapen bucket is soon full, and the two youths happily turn back, taking care not to spill any petrol on the way. The temperature drops rapidly as darkness descends while we cook a meal of boiled eggs. After eating we wrap ourselves up in sleeping bags and a green army-style greatcoat, and settle down to sleep in the truck.

2 April. Close to noon, just as we're finishing our roadside breakfast of eggs and noodles, Old Li returns in a mechanic's car. 'Hey, sorry about that,' he apologizes, throwing some biscuits over to us. After the mechanic crawls under the truck and replaces some round metal parts, the engine starts immediately. Maybe Old Li's feeling a bit guilty about making us wait all night, for he makes conversation in a much friendlier manner than previously.

'I work for a transport company in Xining and have been driving a truck for more than thirty years. But whenever I got married, my wives would die on me! So I've been married five times now. The current wife is young enough to be my daughter – she brought a kid with her when we married. That makes four kids I have to look after, counting the ones from my wives who died. This year my oldest son's getting married, so I've got to get some money together for that. That's why I took this job, because I could make 600 yuan at one go.'

'What an awful son! Making his father slave like this,' Yong, the devoted son, exclaims indignantly.

'Have to keep my nose to the grindstone for Her sake,' Li says with a wry smile. Apparently his young wife had a difficult time getting by after divorcing her previous husband.

Suddenly we smell burning. I crane my head out the window and see thick black smoke billowing out from a rear wheel. Old Li gets down from the truck and urinates on it.

'Oy, is that enough, just to piss on it? Are your sure it's all right?' Yong asks worriedly, but Old Li simply climbs into the truck again, saying, 'Aw, it'll probably be okay,' and continues driving.

I enjoy gazing at the changing landscape; scenery from all four seasons unfolds as we ascend each mountain. Just when it seems that the blossom-filled valleys and thick forests of giant trees will continue forever, grasslands open out, and then suddenly we're crossing a rocky peak covered with snow. Tibetan herders swing their slings at twilight. A stream brimming with clear water flows along the side of the road, and hills, tinted many hues by the light, stretch on forever.

Boom! A loud explosion shatters this reverie, and the truck tilts over. It's a puncture. Just as Yong feared, urinating on the burning tyre wasn't enough. Both tut-tutting, he and Old Li set about changing the tyre in the middle of the grasslands. I get out and breathe deeply, appreciating the cold, clear air. It's unbelievably beautiful here, like a dream world, with the rolling hills mysteriously metamorphosing into all the colours of the rainbow.

'Let's hurry. The other trucks'll be waiting for us in Chamdo for sure.'

The last rays of the sun soon fade away, and the worn-out truck continues doggedly along the dark road, but at its fastest it can't reach even 30 kilometres per hour. Suddenly there's complete darkness and our vision is totally obscured! The bonnet's flown open. Yong and Li both sigh and go to investigate the metal catch. Of course it's broken. All we can do is tie the bonnet down with rope wound round and round and set off again.

The truck, a pitiful sight with its lips clamped shut and stalling every half hour, finally reaches Chamdo at midnight. There we find the other two trucks in the car park of a hotel. Stray dogs set up a commotion when we get down from Old Li's vehicle. Shooing the dogs away in the dark, we get ourselves over to reception and take a room. Li's fellow convoy-drivers and others going to Chengdu are in the hotel, where they've all been waiting impatiently for our arrival.

'Oy, where the hell've you been? We've been waiting the whole day!'

Old Li explains, but the other drivers just smile bitterly and look exasperated. It appears they've run out of patience, and there's a deep sadness in Old Li's tired, dejected face.

It's decided that we'll stay in Chamdo for a day to get the truck fixed. I'm relieved to hear that it will be serviced, since all these breakdowns have been making me nervous about what lies ahead. We sleep soundly until the afternoon, then go out to visit a monastery on a hill in the town.

When we enter the monastery grounds, the faces of lamas peer out at us one by one from the gates and windows of a stone building we thought must be deserted. An old lama followed by a group of young ones walks over to us.

'You two, what are you doing?'

'*Tashi delek.* We are Japanese tourists. May we see inside, please?' Yong greets the lamas in Tibetan with a smile. Since Tibetans feel animosity towards Han Chinese, we've both suddenly become Japanese. In the presence of Chinese people I pretend to be one of them, and in the presence of Tibetans I turn Japanese. Adding my Korean identity into the mix, I'm having trouble keeping it all straight in my head.

The temple murals have all been newly repainted and are of scant interest.

'What on earth's happened to the Tibetans' values? Do they think it's all right to paint over something just because it's old? That's what they do, you know. Valuable pictures painted hundreds of years ago get splashed over with paint like you'd use for signboards. The murals in the temples at Ali are being repainted beyond recognition. Magnificent, breathtaking pictures painted by highly skilled artist-monks in ancient times get covered over by the lousy artist-monks of today with amateur work that looks like cartoons.' Yong can't contain his anger. I can understand his feelings – after all, he went to the ends of the earth to make reproductions and take photographs because he felt a sense of responsibility for the vanishing ancient paintings of Ali.

Nevertheless, some of the stone Buddhas lined up in the temple garden are probably very old, and several have interesting designs, so it's worthwhile taking a look. As we walk along, the number of lamas following behind us keeps increasing, the older ones watching us constantly with worried expressions. We feel uncomfortable, so we say our thanks and go outside.

We sit on a rock gazing at the scenery and light cigarettes. It's getting late, and the mountain peaks glitter in the evening sun as if they've been scattered with gold dust.

Presently, several dozen lamas stream out from the monastery onto the hill. Lining up along its edge in a position commanding a good view and with their backs to us, they squat in unison. What ceremony could this be?

Fascinated, we observe as liquid flows from beneath the hems of the lamas' robes and stains the ground. I simply stare, forgetting all about politely turning away. Illuminated by the evening sun, the lamas' crimson robes are beautiful, glowing against a backdrop of glittering rocky peaks.

4 April. Morning. We're leaving Chamdo.

'I made sure it had a good going-over. We'll be right now.' Old Li sits confidently in the driver's seat. The repairs yesterday were worth it – the engine hardly stalls at all. Travelling last in the convoy as usual, we once again set off resolutely along the Sichuan–Tibet Highway.

Every time we cross a mountain, the scenery changes dramatically. We emerge in a place where large, wonderfully coloured butterflies dance and strange birds warble in a dense wood of giant trees. Suddenly, a black animal leaps across the road.

'That was a musk deer. There're lots of them in this area. I've tried to catch them. The balls of the musk deer are stuffed with tiny insects, which are really good medicine – incredibly potent. So much so that a pregnant woman can miscarry just from a whiff of it.'

Ah, so that was a musk deer! The musk made famous by perfume and Indian incense comes from this animal. I think about the lithe black creature the size of a dog that we've just glimpsed.

We pass through the primeval forest to find treeless, grassless, snow-covered peaks stretching ahead of us. I look down and see a verdant valley floor below; then we pass through a tunnel of natural ice pillars, and the stark white mountains continue. Without chains on the tyres there's no way we can proceed any further, so we stop in the middle of the road and set about fitting them. Conditions are completely different from what they were two hours ago; a cold wind blows, and permanent snow lies in heaps along the roadside.

'Hey, if you've got a camera, how about taking a picture?' suggests Old Li, but unfortunately my auto-focus camera has stopped working. It too has succumbed to altitude sickness.

When the chains have been fitted, the convoy cautiously sets off into the driving snow. The road is steep, with no guard rails – one false move and we'll find ourselves upside down on the valley floor. Several broken-down trucks are stopped in the vicinity of the peak. Averting our eyes as we pass several people who are *dang tuan zhang*, we pray that we'll be spared a breakdown in this place at least.

Once we're safely across the snow-capped peak, a magnificent lake hidden amongst the ice-covered trees comes into view. Reflecting the azure sky on its surface, it's like a precious piece of jasper. The frozen air is motionless, and the scene resembles a still-life painting: it's a masterpiece amongst God's creations that, like a virgin spirit of the earth unsullied by human touch, captivates those who look upon its remote beauty. The scene is so bewitching that I want to burn it into my retina forever.

We pass the lake in the twinkling of an eye, and the tawny crags stretch on. I see lovely Tibetan houses built from unhewn rocks stacked one on top of the other, blending with the natural hues of the scenery.

Large vultures circle above the wilderness dyed yellow by the setting sun. Rolling on their great wings wider than a person's outstretched arms, they fight over a yak's corpse in a haughty dance. Elderly Tibetan pilgrims with faces like ancient tree trunks make full-body prostrations on their cold, precipitous journey towards Lhasa.

'Sichuanese Tibetans make incredible pilgrimages. They wrap a strong thread tightly around their ring finger to stop the circulation. Then they start doing their prostrations. The journey of more than 2000 kilometres to Lhasa takes one or even two years. By the time they finally reach the Potala, their ring fingers are all dried and shrivelled up. They smear their shrivelled-up fingers with yak butter and burn them on a temple altar in the Potala to give thanks for the completion of their pilgrimage. I met lots of pilgrims doing prostrations at Mt Kailas who were perfectly content to offer all they owned to the mountain. They think that if you haven't got any money, then tomorrow you can beg. It's much more important to earn their passage to Heaven,' Yong tells me with an expression of deep emotion.

As evening falls, we arrive in a town called Jomda. The three trucks stop in front of the PLA soldiers' guest house.

'Where's reception?' Yong asks some soldiers sitting on the guest-house fence.

'Shut up! There's no room for the likes of you two. Piss off!' they yell at us out of the blue.

'Shit! Here of all places we get turned away. Arseholes!' Yong scowls fiercely. At any other time he probably would start a fight, but we can't afford any trouble. We're now in a region off limits to foreigners at any time. So he swallows his anger and we leave the guest house behind us.

Carrying our luggage on our backs, we begin looking for another place to stay. For some reason, Old Li and the others seem to be able to stay at the PLA guest house.

'Why was it only us that got turned away?'

'When soldiers see a couple together, they feel so jealous and frustrated that they give them a hard time for no reason at all.' Yong tells me that PLA soldiers who get stationed out here can't return to China for years at a time. 'You have to feel sorry for those soldiers. When I was in Purang, out in Ali, I met some border guards. There's nothing at all out there, the wilderness just goes on and on, and you never set eyes on a woman or anything. I knew how they felt because I lived in Ali for ages too. You just can't help wanting a woman. If I found even a flea, I had to see if it was male or female. Then when I finally went to Xinjiang, there was this calendar with a picture of an actress on it pinned to the wall of a restaurant, and I was completely overcome. Pictures like that usually disgust me, so I don't look at them. But that time I was staring at it and drooling, licking my lips and stroking it with my hands. I truly thought that she was just so beautiful.

'Young soldiers in the frontier wilderness regions don't see a woman for three or four years at a stretch. What's more, they're in a place with no material goods of any kind and only ever eat crap from old tins. The army outposts still have tins of food left over from when China was at war with India in the sixties. As for information – well, there's only year-old newspapers, or at best six-month-old ones. So the soldiers have this really tough life forced on them.

'One day, the wife of a troop commander came to visit one of those army posts, because officers are permitted visits from relatives. Anyway, a few nights later, the commander left his tent for a bit, and in that time a soldier came in and raped the wife. When the commander came back and saw his wife in a deranged state, he realized what'd happened. She told him she'd scratched the left arm of the soldier who'd attacked her, so the commander immediately ordered all the men to assemble. He inspected each one without saying why, and soon found the soldier with the scratched arm. The offender was a guy who was usually very quiet and serious – someone who looked after the pigs, and things like that. The commander didn't take any action. If he'd wanted to, he could've charged the guy and had him sent to prison. All he did was to have the soldier transferred to a different post two years later. He didn't say anything about it to any of the other soldiers either. That commander well and truly understood the young soldier's suffering. What do you think? Wasn't he a good leader?'

It's as though these remote western regions are a lawless man's world – just like the American West. Such a world should be appealing, I suppose, but on encountering the reality I'm not sure how far I can go along with it.

While walking we've been surrounded by the children of Jomda. They look completely bored and stare at us curiously – these strangers in different clothes – pestering us so much that it's hard to make any progress. A little further on we find a small, dirty-looking guest house and dive into the reception area. No-one is inside, but seeing as the wood-burning stove is lit, it seems likely someone will come soon. We sit by the stove and wait. The children push their faces up against the glass door and windows, watching us intently.

Soon an old Tibetan woman comes along and, making a show of it being great trouble, arranges a room for us. The room is covered with a thick layer of dust and looks as if it has been a stranger to cleaning for decades. Frowning, I gently turn the quilt over on the bed, taking care not to raise any dust, and sit down. Unexpectedly, Old Li's face appears at the door.

'I decided to stay here too,' he says, looking embarrassed. It seems the other drivers have given him the cold shoulder. We eat dinner with Old Li and then retire for the night to the dust-covered bed in which we fall asleep while being plagued by ticks.

5 April. Today we expect to pass out of the Tibetan Autonomous Region and into Sichuan Province. My back aches from sitting in the truck all day every day, so I'm delighted to be reaching Sichuan at last. About three hours out of Jomda, a huge river comes into view.

'The Jinsha River! Cross it and we're in Sichuan!' Yong exclaims joyfully.

'Thank goodness, Sichuan at last.' Old Li is also beaming.

In last position as usual, we follow the other trucks to cross the bridge.

'Idiots! Stop!' An angry voice yells at us.

Old Li stops the truck at the approach to the bridge, and we put our heads out the window to see about ten Tibetans and Chinese surrounding a Public Security type, all standing with arms folded and looking at us threateningly.

'The rules state that two trucks cannot cross this bridge at once. You're fined!' the Public Security official barks at us. A flustered Old Li, not knowing what this is all about, is dragged down from the truck by the mob and surrounded. They begin forcing him to kowtow.

'That lot are always like this, setting on outsiders. They're like bandits.' Sighing, Yong stuffs his pockets with all the cigarettes we have and gets down from the truck.

The men have forced Old Li to kneel and are shouting angrily, demanding that he 'apologize'. But the pathetic sight of his head scraping against the ground – face pale from this unforeseen disaster – doesn't seem to satisfy them. Far from it, in fact, for they laugh sadistically, appearing to be enjoying his torment.

'Let's shut him up in the fort next to the bridge and see how he likes a bit of rough stuff.' Their excitement builds as they repeatedly force Old Li to kowtow and his wrinkled face becomes covered with dirt.

At this point, Yong breaks nimbly into the circle of men and, while apologizing on Old Li's behalf, offers cigarettes to the ringleaders. The tension eases after an exchange of conversation mixed with jokes. Still smiling, Yong returns to the truck and pulls out several books which he takes back and hands to the men. The effect is immediate: their eyes fasten on the volumes as they scramble to get hold of these rarities – kung-fu novels by the hugely popular Hong Kong writer Jin Yong. Rescued from the circle of bandits, a pale-faced Old Li stumbles back to the truck.

'Come on, let's get out of here fast,' Yong urges.

The remote western regions of China are lawless places. On fine days, the biggest amusement for these men is to laze around in the sun, waiting for some prey to come along that they can pick off. Anything will do as a distraction from the boredom.

'Foreigners seem to think that Tibetans are all pure and good, but the peasants are all just like that bunch,' Yong mutters angrily.

Lagging behind the other two trucks once again, we hurry to Dege. Travelling along the cliff-lined road, we see many richly coloured Buddhas painted on the mountainside in front of us. They appear to be floating as they're thrown into relief by the last rays of the setting sun.

'What are they?' I ask Yong.

'They were painted to console the spirits of the dead in all the trucks buried at the bottom of these cliffs.'

The dark mountain road is frightening. A chill runs down my spine as I stare at the bottom of the valley. I can't help feeling that the spirits of people who met mournful deaths there are calling up from the darkness of the ravines for us to join them.

Old Li says little and appears to be getting drowsy from accumulated fatigue. I pull out the vitamin-C tablets I brought from Japan and push one into his mouth. These are really supposed to be taken dissolved in water, but they release a strong tart fizz if you put them straight into your mouth. Old Li makes a startled sound and looks bewildered.

'Oy, Old Li, have you ever given a foreigner a lift in your truck?' Yong asks abruptly.

'Nah, I've never met, or even seen, a foreigner.'

'So this is the first time, then. Don't tell anyone. The fact is, she's Japanese.' Drawing me close, Yong finally reveals my identity.

'You're kidding, I wouldn't have known! That country where Hondas come from? She's not that different, is she?!' Old Li exclaims wildly, the drowsiness completely shaken off. Now that Yong has revealed my true identity to Old Li, I understand how much they've come to trust each other.

Next day, going from Dege towards Ganzi, the truck starts to play up again, stalling every half hour. Yong is livid. 'This is because you're stingy and only ever do stop-gap repairs,' he accuses Old Li. 'When we get to Ganzi, get a mechanic to have a proper look!'

At Ganzi, tranquil rolling grasslands stretch into the distance. We take rooms in a lovely small Tibetan-run guest house. The wooden building, decorated in the Tibetan style and with handmade wooden beds and window frames, is well cared for – vastly different from the bland government-run guest house. The old Tibetan lady who runs it points across the grasslands to indicate something.

'Aya, it seems there's a hot spring over there.'

'Really? Let's go!' I haven't had a bath since we left Lhasa.

Yong, who can't understand the Japanese love of baths, is always grumbling, 'Why do you have to wash yourself all over so often? Do you want to catch cold and die of pneumonia?'

Like the Tibetans, Yong thinks it's perfectly natural to have only one all-over wash each year. To be sure, that isn't such a hardship in the dry Tibetan climate. Grime and oil secreted from the body function as the ideal protective covering for the skin and hair against the strong sunlight and dry air. It would be wrong to dismiss this as just being dirty. However, even though I didn't especially like having baths in Japan, I still have one every week or so, and I've been forcing Yong to do the same. So he's become fed up with my constant demands for him to bathe.

On this occasion, though, it's Yong who takes the initiative and leads me to the hot springs. A chorus of frogs serenades us as we make our way along the narrow track through the grassland in the dusk. We join up with a Tibetan family – a heart-warming scene such as I haven't witnessed in a long time. The spring is in a five-roomed shack, each room containing a large, square concrete bath filled to the brim with hot water. We pay 5 yuan at a tiny booth and rent a room all to ourselves. A continuous stream of hot, cloudy water fills the bath to overflowing. Thrilled at finding a hot spring in a place like this, I sleep well that night.

7 April. We leave Ganzi for Kangding. However, it turns out that the truck has in fact not been repaired properly. Yong discovers this after grilling Old Li when the engine stalls again – a long way from Ganzi. He learns that Old Li only ever has the bare minimum of repairs done because the company in Xining won't cover the cost.

'I took it to the garage, but they told me it would cost 600 yuan! That's no joke. My earnings from this job would all be blown away.'

'Money's worth nothing if you're dead!' Yong yells,

loudly rebuking Old Li for his excuses, but it's too late now.

On the mountain heading towards Kangding, the mist gradually thickens. After a while, we near the entrance to the pass.

'Oy, wait! Stop!' A traffic policeman standing at the roadside loudly orders us to halt. Old Li gets down from the truck and listens to what he has to say.

'Your right-hand light is not on. That's a 50-yuan fine.' This time the situation doesn't improve even when Yong gets down to intercede. Paying a fine won't make the light come on. This fine won't prevent any accidents. It will do nothing more than line the policeman's pocket.

'I'm never driving the Sichuan–Tibet Highway again!' Li shouts hoarsely.

The other two trucks will probably arrive in Chengdu tomorrow. But in this state – Old Li flogging his clapped-out truck along with his tired old body – who knows when we'll arrive? Many times we've thought about looking for another truck, but we worry about Old Li, whose face reveals his complete dependence on Yong.

7. XINDUQIAO PRISON

Old Li hurries on towards Kangding, bent on getting to
Chengdu quickly and finishing this job. Chengdu is not far
from Kangding, and there's also a good chance that the
road from there will be paved and in much better
condition. The truck struggles up the steep mountain.

Late afternoon and it's becoming dark. Yong and Old Li
are both silent as we drive along the cliff-lined road.
Suddenly, the truck lurches over to one side. In disbelief I
see Yong push Old Li out of the way, then grab the steering
wheel and turn it desperately while simultaneously
thrusting his leg under the driver's seat and slamming on
the brake pedal. The truck doesn't stop. It shudders
precariously along the edge of a precipice until – still
shaking violently – it runs into the mountain at the side of
the road with a great thud, and the engine stops. In the
silence I hear rocks tumbling over the cliff behind us.

'Hey, look where you're going! Do you want to die?!'
Pouring with sweat, Yong roars at Old Li. I look out the
window at the deep, deep ravine below, and goose pimples
rise on my skin. Old Li failed to take the curve on the

mountain road and has driven us straight along the edge of a precipice.

Old Li looks strange; saliva trickles from his twisted mouth, and his eyes are dim and unfocused. His left arm hangs loosely, and it looks as if he can't move it. 'I'm all right, let's go. Let me drive,' he mutters in spite of his condition.

Between us, Yong and I pick him up and move him into the passenger seat, then Yong shifts to the driver's seat. Once installed on the passenger side and wrapped in sleeping bags and every item of clothing we can find, Old Li resigns himself to the situation and closes his eyes. The poor old man has been paralysed by shock and fatigue.

'I'll try and drive to the nearest town.' Sitting in the unfamiliar driver's seat, Yong starts up the ignition and moves off slowly and cautiously, but his face instantly blanches. 'I can't believe he managed to come this far in this truck.'

The truck is just as knocked about as Li; the brakes don't work, the steering wheel doesn't respond as it should and the gears are no use at all. Even so, Yong's able to coax it slowly along the now gently sloping road. Directly ahead, a small town comes into view. The road sign says 'Xinduqiao Prison'.

'This is where criminal offenders are kept.'

Of all the places to arrive at! I suppose the highway stretching between Sichuan and Tibet is the perfect place for keeping prisoners – if they escaped, they'd just die along the mountain road.

'A prison town. Are there prisoners here?'

'Oh, everyone who lives here is one.'

We stop the truck at the edge of the road and are about to go and find a doctor when Old Li forces himself up and crawls over to sit in the driver's seat.

'I'm all right, let's go. Let's get to Chengdu. Quick, off we go!' His left hand hangs limp and unmoving. 'Buy me some liquor, would you? If I have a drink, I'll soon get better. It's all right! Come on, let's go straight away,' he pleads, gripping the steering wheel with his right hand, a dazed expression on his face. Is getting this job finished quickly and getting home safely all he can think about, I wonder. He keeps repeating himself as if he's delirious and has taken leave of his senses.

We ask the townspeople who've gathered round where we can find a doctor and immediately head for the small clinic, some prisoners kindly helping us to carry Old Li. The clinic is in a corner of a concrete building near the side of the road. Inside there's a doctor reading a book. This man is about fifty, composed and intelligent-looking. He too is an inmate of Xinduqiao Prison, although he doesn't look at all like a criminal; there's integrity in his face.

The doctor looks up from his book and then politely examines Old Li. He gives him an injection and prescribes some medicine. I'm able to get some medicine for my cystitis, which has flared up again. Since there was no medicine in the towns along this highway, I'd thought there was nothing I could do about it until we reached Chengdu.

'Apparently he's been living in this town for ten years already. I don't know what his crime was exactly, but I bet it was something to do with politics,' Yong informs me in a low voice after a chat with the doctor.

We help Old Li to a hotel, where the receptionist quickly

arranges rooms for us. In one of them there's a washbasin which I fill with hot water; then I massage Li's body and immobile left arm with a hot towel.

'Your wife's a good person.' Tears rise in his eyes.

'Old Li, have a good sleep. Later we'll bring you some rice gruel,' Yong says to comfort him.

'You two really are good people.' Old Li's face twitches into a smile. The medicine takes effect, and he falls asleep.

At the hotel restaurant we order some rice gruel to take to Old Li and a meal for ourselves. The young man in the kitchen is glad to see visitors from the outside and talks non-stop. He cooks us a remarkably delicious meal of stir-fried bean-curd skin; we hadn't expected to find food this good out here where there's such a scarcity of ingredients.

'This is fantastic, really delicious! You're a genius of a cook!'

Upon receiving Yong's praise, the young man grins, picks up his pan and heaps the leftovers onto our plates. How ironic this all is – that the inmates of this prison town should be the most congenial people we've met on the Sichuan–Tibet Highway!

We take the rice gruel to Old Li and make him eat it in bed, then go to our room to rest. The room is spick and span, comfortable and – most surprising of all – has clean, pure white sheets on the bed.

'Let's make Old Li rest up here. It's quite impossible for him to drive to Chengdu in his condition. We'll look for another truck to take us there.'

To get to Chengdu, we must cross a precipitous mountain called Mt Erlang.

'Old Li and his truck can't cross that mountain. I'll try

and persuade him to stay and get the truck fixed properly,' says Yong.

You never know what will happen on journeys in Tibet, which is why trucks always travel in convoys of three or more. But the two young drivers in our convoy have abandoned Old Li and sped off to Chengdu.

Although we realize that Old Li has been knocked about in both body and spirit, there's nothing more we can do about the misfortune that burdens him. We too are anxious about our own fate. It seems like all the suffering Yong has experienced in his life has made him sensitive to the pain of others, and even now he's still worrying about Old Li. He decides to give the exhausted man an extra hundred yuan to persuade him to stay here for a while. Yong's kindness impresses me.

While resting in our room and listening to Yong's small shortwave radio, we unexpectedly hear news about Chen Jun, whom we had met in Beijing: 'Chen Jun, who submitted a petition to the Beijing Public Security Bureau with twenty-four thousand signatures calling for the release of Wei Jingsheng and other political prisoners was punished with deportation and fled to the United States via Hong Kong.'

'It's Chen Jun! I'll be damned! I never thought I'd be hearing news of him out here.' Yong's eyes shine with happiness; perhaps the news that he has a fellow-fugitive has given him heart. An image of the small, fair-complexioned Chen Jun floats into my mind. I wonder how that delicate Shanghai-born young man could have found such courage? Every one of the young artists we met in Beijing possessed more than average talent. If their potential could just be fulfilled, this whole country would become a much better place.

I think of the handful of Chinese people I've met in this brief period, and of how things stand with them: Chen Jun in exile; Yong with charges against him and his paintings confiscated; the prisoner doctor who's a skilled physician; the people running this hotel who keep a clean establishment that couldn't be surpassed anywhere; the culinary genius in the restaurant. These are only a few; how many other talented people must there be whose abilities are being suppressed.

8 April. It's early morning. We stand at the side of the Sichuan–Tibet Highway waiting for a truck bound for Chengdu. But nothing stirs in the distance, not even dust on the dry ochre-yellow road. Only the strong Tibetan sun blazes down on the desolate Xinduqiao Prison.

'Hey, let's get going! Hop in.' We turn around at this sudden summons to see Old Li about to get into his truck. Open-mouthed, we race over to him.

'Don't you worry, I had a good rest last night. I'm all right now. Get in, quick!' Old Li insists and sits himself firmly in the driver's seat.

'I don't believe it! For Chrissake, you couldn't move your left arm yesterday! Stay here a few more days and let the doctor look at you. And get your truck fixed properly!' Yong thunders furiously, but stubborn Old Li won't be beaten.

'I'm all better now,' he replies. Then he drives the truck once around the wide hotel car-park and moves his left arm to prove it. It's true his condition has improved unbelievably. That prisoner doctor certainly is competent; my cystitis has gotten much better. To celebrate Li's recovery, we go to the hotel restaurant and eat more of the most delicious food on the Sichuan–Tibet Highway.

The road to Kangding is apparently not so hazardous, so if we take it slowly, there might not be any problems. And since Kangding is also a big town, when we arrive there we can probably find mechanics, as well as buses going to Chengdu. Even if we waited here, there's no knowing when we could find another ride, so in the end we climb into Old Li's truck again. Yong yells instructions into his ear as we go, making sure he drives carefully.

'Did you try and drive yesterday? I bet you found it tough – I'm the only one who can drive it,' Li boasts. He can say that for sure. It would be difficult for anyone else to handle the quirks of this clapped-out old truck.

The road descending to Kangding slopes like the sides of a deep pot, and we slither down, down, down to the bottom. The blue Tibetan sky and ochre earth disappear to be replaced by high peaks straight out of a Chinese landscape painting of mountains and water. Finally it's farewell to Tibet, a land close to the heavens.

Since both Old Li and the truck seem to be in good shape, we pass through Kangding and keep going. Late in the afternoon we arrive at Luding, at the start of the Mt Erlang ascent. But Old Li doesn't stop here either, continuing towards Mt Erlang. This is the last barrier; once across that mountain, the most dangerous sections of the road will be behind us and Chengdu just a stone's throw away.

'We're okay, it's still early. Let's cross the mountain during the night and get to Chengdu.'

'Old Li, if you think you can climb Mt Erlang in this truck, you've got another think coming. If you don't believe me, just try it.' Yong folds his arms in exasperation.

We begin the steep ascent, but part way up the truck comes to a stop and starts slipping back. Yong makes Old Li turn the steering wheel to stop the truck by running it into the slope at the roadside. Yong has been tense ever since we left Xinduqiao, and now it shows; he's utterly exhausted and soaked with sweat. He makes Old Li turn the truck around slowly and head back to find a hotel in Luding.

'Do you get it now? If you don't get a really, really good repair job done on this truck, then it's useless. It can't cross Mt Erlang. Old Li, have a good rest, then you'll think of something. Send a telegram to your company in Xining, or contact the other drivers in Chengdu. Just take care of yourself a bit, will you?' Yong repeats what he's said to Old Li a hundred times already and – as if shaking himself free – bids him farewell.

9 April. Morning. We board a bus bound for Chengdu and travel up the Mt Erlang pass to an altitude of 3400 metres. The road is just as steep as I'd been led to expect it would be, with poor visibility due to fog. During this last leg of our journey along the 2500-kilometre Sichuan–Tibet Highway, I think about what the prospects are for an old man called Li.

8. SANYA

9 April. Evening. We arrive at Chengdu.

'That chicken at Mt Erlang was fantastic! But two bowls of it barely touched the sides of my stomach. What a pity we couldn't have more!'

After crossing the mountain from Luding, the bus had stopped for a meal break. The restaurant had been a shabby wooden affair nestled against the side of the mountain. Inside, white clouds rose from a stack of steamers containing unglazed ceramic pots in which a sublimely delicious dish called '*guanguanji* chicken soup' had been slowly simmering away for hours. The chicken was being cooked by the steam – with not a single drop of water added – and flavoured only with salt and pepper. A layer of rich yellow fat floated on top of the soup. The bus passengers bought it in droves, and sadly it was soon sold out. Afterwards we couldn't stop talking about it.

'You'll be wanting to send a telegram, I suppose.' Yong searches Chengdu to find a telegraph office for me. I've been worried about my parents all the time we've been on the Sichuan–Tibet Highway; they've heard about the uprising in Tibet and are probably anxious about me, but there were no decent communications facilities along the way. I've been having endless nightmares in which I've seen my mother's anxious face.

Naturally, Chinese telegrams are written only in Chinese characters, so I can't add Japanese characters to form a grammatical message in Japanese. I just write 'Aya well not worry', and breathe a little easier.

Yong is gaunt, with dark circles under his eyes; he's been taking care of both me in my sickly state and the worn-out Old Li, and now the strain shows. But he has the capacity to recover his strength quickly if only he can eat, and there's so much delicious food to be had in Chengdu: roast duck, savoury stuffed buns, steamed dumplings, roasted rabbits' heads and hotpot.

'I really love hotpot! Aya, you have to try it,' Yong tells me and leads me to a restaurant so I can sample this dish. Hotpot, a Sichuan specialty, consists of simmering reddish-black oil containing chillies, garlic and lots of other spices, into which duck's blood, pork and chicken entrails, meat and mushrooms are dipped. A pungent fragrance rises from the oil gently bubbling in the pot attached to the centre of our table.

'Good, isn't it?' Yong gulps down large mouthfuls as if it's really delicious, but I recoil after one bite.

'I'll get diarrhoea if I eat this stuff.'

Yong really loves hot, spicy food and would be satisfied with a meal of just chillies and meat. He can quite easily put away a few dozen extremely hot stir-fried fresh chillies. And with meat, it's not just the flesh that he likes, but the offal and fatty parts as well. Steaming hot, fiery food full of nutrition – the pictures he paints are much like the food he eats.

The roasted rabbit's head is delicious. As grotesque as the pile of them may look in front of the shop, their brains do taste fabulous – just like cheese. Yong also buys a roast duck and a roast goose to take away, polishing off a whole bird on his own back in our hotel room. In fact, after the privations of the Sichuan–Tibet Highway, we spend the whole day eating.

17 April. We board a soft-sleeper carriage in train number 251 bound for Guangzhou. From there I plan to go to Hong Kong to get another visa for mainland China, since the three-month one I obtained in February will expire soon.

'How long will it take to get another visa?'

'You collect it the day after applying, so I should be back within three days.'

'Aya, now you know what it's like in China – how difficult and all, what a nightmare it can be. Will you just keep on and go back to Japan?' A resigned smile hovers on Yong's face.

'It's all right. We're together. Anyway, I'm *amanojaku*.'

'What do you mean, "*amanojaku*"?'

'Somebody who's contrary – who'll say "left" when everyone else says "right". And if you tell them not to do something, they want it even more.'

'That's me to a T,' Yong laughs. 'An *amanojaku* person has nothing on me.'

'Hmm, you're right there.'

Yong's breath becomes deep and regular as he falls

asleep. I watch his slumbering face, glad to be able to be of help to a man such as this, one whose spirit blazes like fire. The fact of his paintings being confiscated is proof of the strength of that spiritual energy: his exhibition was simply electrifying. Barely two months have passed since I left Japan, but to the person I am now, Japan seems like a distant dream. So much has happened; the events taking place around me are so intense that I feel as if several years have passed. This spring I should have entered my fourth year of university, but spring break finished long ago without my having returned. What use is art school anyway? Hasn't Yong already taught and shown me so much more than I could learn there?

If we can get a passport once martial law has been lifted in Tibet, then we can escape the reach of Public Security and go openly to Japan. I won't go back until I can leave China with Yong. There's no other choice.

19 April. After two nights and three days we arrive in Guangzhou.

'I've never been here before. I can't make sense of Cantonese. It's like a foreign country here.'

'Let's go to the Shamian youth hostel. It's cheap and comfortable.'

Whenever I've travelled to China, I've always come via Hong Kong, so I know my way around here a little. Shamian was a foreigners' enclave until the People's Republic of China was founded, and traces of the former residents linger in the many European-style buildings, while the streets are orderly and attractive.

*

20 April. I board the night ferry to Hong Kong alone. Yong sees me off at the pier.

'It's okay. I'll be back the day after tomorrow when I get the visa, and I'll phone the hostel too.'

'If you've got time, would you get me some painting materials, and summer clothes, and shoes as well? I thought I'd do some paintings and sell them if we run short of money.' Yong hands me 300 Hong Kong dollars.

'After I've got the visa, let's go to Hainan Island,' I suggest.

Hainan Island is the southernmost province of China, a special economic zone run along capitalist lines. It's unlikely that the long arm of the law could reach there from Beijing. I've been there before and feel sure that if we go to that island with its blue sea, white beaches and bamboo bungalows, we'll recover from our exhaustion, and Yong's stomach will get better. Although he puts on a bold front, stress affects him badly, and he's always vomiting. Besides, he was born in the mountains and hasn't ever seen the sea in his twenty-six years.

In the ferry's large second-class sleeper room, I find my bunk and flop down. I recall how Yong and I dreamt up such plans last summer at Heaven Lake, to travel the world and paint ... But now we can't even leave China together, let alone travel the world.

Several Japanese travellers laugh loudly. Looking at them is like seeing a recent picture of myself. I used to enjoy carefree travel in China, and whenever I met other Japanese, we'd chat, criticize the Chinese and exchange jokes. Back then, I had no desire even to learn the language. But now, posing as a Chinese and travelling with a Chinese man, a completely different picture is unfolding before my eyes. China is a world where vitality and manoeuvring – and chance too – call the shots. For its citizens to live with dignity, they must travel a hard road. Any young Japanese can paint pictures and, of course, exhibit them, but these are activities for which you have to risk your life in China.

When I arrive in Hong Kong the next morning, I go straight to Wanchai to get my visa extended at an office with the long-winded name 'The Visa Office of the People's Republic of China, Ministry of Foreign Affairs in Hong Kong'.

'I am going to marry a Chinese national, and my fiancé is waiting for me on the mainland. Is it possible to receive my visa a little faster, please?' I ask in Chinese.

'Yes, come back in the afternoon' is the reply. It's incredible how much my Chinese has progressed!

Outside, I buy a telephone card to call home from a public phone box. In Hong Kong it's possible to make international calls from public telephones. I wonder if the telegram I sent from Chengdu has arrived.

'Aya! Where are you?' My older sister answers the phone.

'I'm in Hong Kong now. How's Mum?'

'In hospital. She collapsed and was hospitalized when she heard the news about the riots in Tibet. Oh, I'm so glad you're safe.'

My sister's words stun me. So my forebodings had been right!

'Everyone rushed to get passports so they could be ready

to leave Japan if they had to. When can you come back?'

I can't go back yet.

'Tell everyone it's probably going to take a while before I can get back to Japan, but I'll return safely – I'm sure of it – so please be patient and don't worry.' I hang up, but it's some time before I can move from the spot.

Next, I go shopping for paints. Acrylics are best, seeing as we'll be on the road, so I buy Newton acrylics, several illustration boards and a sketchbook as well. Now for shoes. I have only winter shoes, and Yong has been wearing his climbing boots, so I buy some grey sports shoes. Then I set out to buy some summer clothes in a back street of Tsimshatsui lined with clothing stalls. I pick up a short-sleeved shirt for 20 Hong Kong dollars and try my hand at bargaining in Chinese.

'Ten yuan, how about it?'

'No sale!' The man at the stall shoots a look at me and snatches the shirt out of my hand. He seems completely convinced that I'm a mainland Chinese. My temper rises and the slang slips out of my mouth before I know it: '*Cao ni ma de ge bi!*'

Upon hearing this, the stall-holder turns red and shakes with anger. I hadn't fully realized the power of these words before. Then I lose my nerve and turn to leave. The sound of the man's voice, still abusing me loudly, brings home to me how different things are now. When I was in Hong Kong before as a Japanese, everyone treated me in a friendly fashion, even when I haggled a bit. In my Chinese-speaking guise, however, I seem to have acquired the smell of the mainland.

But this way is far more interesting than just being

treated with amiable smiles. I continue with my shopping, bargaining with relish in Chinese.

Blue, transparent sea; beaches of white, squeaky sand; metallic-blue fragments of tropical fish swimming in the water; firework-bursts of coconut palms soaring like large birds; scattered flowers in startling hues. We've arrived in the southern paradise of Sanya, on Hainan Island.

26 April. After I obtained my tourist visa in Hong Kong and met up with Yong again, we crossed over to Hainan Island by boat from Guangzhou. This special economic zone is crowded with shops run privately by people from all over China. Hence the hospitality and service at the hotels and restaurants are beyond comparison with that on the mainland, but prices are also higher, not much different from Hong Kong.

We're staying at the little-known Seaside Hotel in the Dadonghai Beach area, a hotel that stands alone on the shore, apart from the crowd. With its peaceful and friendly atmosphere, it's becoming quietly popular amongst travellers. In addition to the main concrete building, five or six simple bamboo-and-thatch huts surround an open space furnished with tables and chairs made from tree stumps. We rent a hut and set about enjoying the lifestyle in Sanya. Our hut has two wooden beds covered with mosquito nets – accommodation very fitting for this liberated southern land. Travellers sit around the tree-stump tables decorated with large bottles filled with beautiful shells to chat, play music and enjoy the carefree life.

But Yong appears to feel keenly the huge gap between his own situation and the easygoing atmosphere of this island.

'Students have started demonstrating for democracy.' He's agitated to hear news reports of incidents in Beijing on the hotel television. The former general secretary of the Communist Party, Hu Yaobang, passed away on 15 April. Students, who had overwhelmingly supported him, flocked to Tiananmen Square to mourn along with other citizens. As many as fifty thousand people have begun demonstrating for democracy – demonstrations that are increasing in strength every day.

Yong takes out his portable radio to listen to Voice of America and the BBC. 'I bet all the guys we met in Beijing are in on this.' His tone suggests that he's ashamed about running away to this place.

'Have you forgotten about your paintings being confiscated?' I take him down to the sea, far away from the radio.

As well as attracting foreigners, Sanya's other main groups of visitors are traders and merchants, so the atmosphere isn't tainted by government brutality. The moment we arrived, all tension left my body and I felt completely relaxed; it requires a huge effort to get out anywhere. Yong and I swim in the sea and paint. All sense of time slips away, and we realize how it's possible to experience – at least once in a lifetime – precious freedom. Such days spent floating in the sea gazing at the endless sky can jeopardize a traveller's return to society.

The travellers staying in the other huts are pleasant companions. Various nationalities are represented amongst the people who gather around the tree-stump tables, but all have settled in here as if held captive by Sanya. Matheau, a powerfully built Canadian with a dense beard, used to be a salmon fisherman in Alaska, then taught English in Taiwan before coming to China, where he's travelling around by bicycle.

'Apparently they're not letting people into Tibet right now, but I'll get around the checkpoints by bicycle at night,' he says. He's always talking about how determined he is to go to Tibet, but he's come to a halt in Sanya and continues to dally by the sea.

Then there's Jack, a cheerful American always with guitar in hand, who sits at the table and invites everyone to join him in relaxed, impromptu performances.

I also meet several Japanese with whom I can speak my mother tongue for the first time in a long while. Yukisuke is a film director from Kyoto. He's travelling around with his wife scouting for film locations. Tanaka is a young guy journeying through Asia who's good with cameras and fixes mine for me. Miyashita, who's researching the architecture of Guizhou Province, revels in the freedom of floating in the sea and doesn't appear keen to return to Japan.

At night, we hear Latin American music performed by two young Brazilians. In the evenings the sound of a flute also echoes through the twilight, played by Eric, a Frenchman. Eric protectively caresses a baby doll fashioned from coconut shells and has decorated the entrance to his hut with a mobile made from seashells. It seems as if everyone here has regressed to their childhoods.

'I didn't know such a delicious drink existed.' Yong's

fascinated by coconuts and takes advantage of the covering sound provided by the evening showers to clamber stealthily up the hotel palms and shake down the fruit, which he then shares with the other travellers. Recently the staff have been giving him dirty looks.

I collect seashells that I use to form a big butterfly, and Yong makes bowls from coconuts after eating the flesh.

A short distance from Dadonghai Beach is Yalong Bay, a beach of fine white sand that makes a sound like powdered snow when you walk on it. Blue butterflies dance over the open sea as if crazed by the heat of the tropical sun. Purple-red berries ripen on cacti that grow along the shore and turn the mouth bright red when eaten. When the tide is low, we gather washing bowls full of turban shells. At night, we drink brandy out of coconuts with the others and dream hashish-inspired dreams. Cries from the squid-fishing boats echo in the distance, and we hear the geckos clicking, a sound that resembles small birds chirping. These engaging lizards are flesh-coloured with innocent black pupils.

The clamour of the mainland seems far away now. Under the soothing influence of Sanya, the savageness in Yong's spirit gradually calms down. In less than two weeks he puts on more than 10 kilos, developing a pot belly as soon as his gaunt body starts to fill out.

Mid-May. The travellers with whom we've enjoyed such pleasant times begin to leave Sanya one by one. We too think it's time to move on and are on the point of making enquiries about the martial-law situation in Tibet when the television delivers some shocking news.

'Martial law has been declared in Beijing!' Yong fixes agitated eyes on the television. 'The news on Chinese TV is useless,' he snorts and pulls out his radio to tune in to the BBC and Voice of America. In Tibet we were able to hear these stations clearly because there's little interference from other transmissions up there, but here the reception's intermittent and mixed with static. Yong strains his ears to follow the news.

He hears that martial law has been declared because of a hunger strike begun by students in Tiananmen Square. Several hundred tanks have been positioned inside Beijing, and the government is becoming impatient. Ordinary citizens support the students' desire to overthrow the Communist Party.

I recall the extraordinary atmosphere surrounding the artists we met in the capital, like turbulent magma surging up to find an outlet …

From the radio reports we learn that students clashed with armed police at the Xinhuamen, a gate to the central government compound on 20 April. They began a hunger strike on 13 May, and six thousand of them signed a petition demanding a lecture from Mikhail Gorbachev. On 15 May a command post was set up for the strikers. And on 20 May the government finally declared martial law, though promising that it didn't intend events to turn violent.

Yong holds the radio to his ear; he won't be separated from it. I've wondered before why Chinese people show such an enormous interest in politics, but now I understand: it's because the government touches the lives of its citizens so deeply.

But it's impossible for me to conceive of the tremendous weight of feeling that Chinese people must carry in their hearts. Yong too, from the day he was born, has been engulfed by the waves of this angry sea.

III. THE MAVERICK CHILD

1. A CHILD OF THE LANDLORD CLASS

Yong was born in the county town of Xinxian on 9 June 1962. Xinxian is at the foot of the Dabie mountains, above the Yangtze and below the Yellow rivers. It was an area known for its tea production but perhaps more so for its many bandits and generals, eighteen of whom were said to have come from a single hamlet at the beginning of the twentieth century. Xinxian may have been a poor, mountainous area, but it was also a Communist Party stronghold and the birthplace of such leaders and high officials as Xu Shiyou, Li Desheng and Wu Huanxian.

In the summer of 1966, the upheavals of the Cultural Revolution closed in. Everyone became involved – adults in their seventies and eighties, children as young as five and six – in the demonstrations, struggle meetings and parades of people engaged in the public denouncements and executions that went on day after day. One day somebody's star would rise, the next day it would fall, and so on. Rebels, 'capitalist roaders', conservatives – factions were rife.

'I didn't have the faintest idea what the purpose of Mao

Zedong's Cultural Revolution was,' said Yong. 'Maybe the orders that came from Beijing had changed a lot by the time they reached Henan.' Ever since he could remember, he'd known only the squabbling, ugly side of county-town life.

Despite his landlord status, Yong's father plunged willingly into the turbulence of the Cultural Revolution, dragging his wife and children with him.

Although he was a member of a Party Planning Committee, a 'study team' took him away for thought reform in isolation when Yong was five. Yong had no idea what being in a study team meant; all he knew was that his father didn't return home for several months. During that period his father's wages were stopped, and on the rare occasions that he was permitted to visit home, he was escorted by a militiaman.

With their father away, the family couldn't survive on the wages Yong's mother received from working in the local department store. There were nine of them, including Yong's grandmother and a girl cousin. So Yong's mother and cousin went to the market at dusk every day to scavenge for vegetable scraps, and the older boys worked hard gathering gravel and firewood in the mountains for meagre sums. At the time, a kilo of wood sold for a few pennies, while gravel, which was used in construction and roadworks, would also fetch a little money. From the age of five Yong helped his brothers collect gravel. In those days, adults who supplemented their incomes in such ways were considered 'capitalist tails' and therefore couldn't do it openly, but eyebrows weren't raised too much if children did the same things.

One evening, Yong's brothers didn't return from gathering firewood. His mother went out alone to look for them, leaving little Yong and his younger sister at home. It was close to daybreak by the time she returned, accompanied by his brothers and cousin, who were all soaking wet. They'd been caught in a sudden downpour and had not only lost the wood they'd spent all day collecting but had also been in danger of being swept away by the heavy rain.

Every day, people hammered away in the mountains digging out rubble, creating lots of small caves in the process. There was one cave that extended back as much as 3 or 4 metres from the entrance. One summer's day, Yong went into a deep cave by himself to hammer out gravel while his brothers were in a neighbouring one, absorbed in their task.

Suddenly, there was a tremendous roar. Yong's brothers raced over and found that Yong's cave had collapsed, burying him under the rubble with only his head poking out. Frantically they dug away the rocks and boulders, but by the time they'd finally cleared them, Yong had stopped breathing. The brothers carried him home covered in blood, his hideously twisted right leg hanging from his hip.

When his mother saw him, she broke down in tears. His father rushed home from the study team and, cradling Yong in his arms, sobbed as though his heart would break. Funeral preparations began.

Then Yong's father put his ear to his son's chest and shouted, 'His body's still warm! His heart's starting to beat again!'

They took Yong to the Xinxian People's Hospital, where

he regained consciousness after a day. Although he was in pain, his life wasn't in danger. But nothing was done to treat his crushed leg, apart from putting it in plaster with a metal support. After many X-rays and several attempts to set the bones under anaesthetic, the doctors concluded that the bone was too badly fractured and that further treatment would be useless. They recommended that the leg be amputated at the White Horse Temple Bone Clinic in Luoyang. Yong's family, however, had no money to take him there, so he spent several weeks in hospital without receiving any treatment at all. In the humid summer heat, his leg became septic and began to give off an awful smell. His mother tended him constantly, cradling him to sleep in her arms and pleading for treatment repeatedly, but the doctors only told her to take the boy to Luoyang as soon as she could.

One day, after Yong had been in hospital for more than a month, a peddler in his forties by the name of Sheng happened by. Sheng was a familiar sight in the county town as he went about selling his wares; whenever he appeared balancing a pole hung with bamboo baskets across his shoulders and beating his drum, children would bring scrap metal and bottles to exchange for sweets. They never knew when he'd turn up, but they waited for him eagerly.

'The little one has a broken leg,' Yong's mother told Sheng through the hospital window. She pulled the bed covers down to show him.

Sheng grimaced when he smelt the rotting flesh. 'Ah, there's nothing to be done. It's rotting.'

Yong's mother looked at Sheng sorrowfully.

'I know a remarkable healer – if anyone could've helped, it would've been him. If it'd been a bit sooner, he could've fixed the leg easily,' he said in a low voice, looking around to check that nobody was watching.

'Where is there such a person?' Yong's mother asked in surprise.

'He's a blind old man called Zhu Xiazi. Maybe there's a chance he could still do something. If you really want Young Number Four Son to get better, you have to get him out of the hospital. He'll only deteriorate while he's in there,' Sheng whispered.

Since Yong's father was back in the study team, his mother made the difficult decision to take Yong home. That night, she had his older brothers help load Yong onto a cart and slip him out of the hospital. If the hospital had learned what they were doing, there would've been big trouble: not only had Yong's family taken it upon themselves to discharge him, but Sheng had shown distrust in the hospital by recommending Blind Zhu. Both these acts would've caused a great scandal, and everyone's loyalty to the Party would've been put in doubt.

Without delay, Sheng discovered where Blind Zhu lived and arranged for him to visit Yong. Blind Zhu arrived with his grandson leading him by the hand. Walking unsteadily with the help of a bamboo cane, he wore an old-fashioned robe of faded steel-blue. His bald head wobbled on his thin, doddery body and his hands trembled feebly. His eyes were two black holes in his head.

He touched Yong's leg and said, 'What's this strange thing stuck on here? Get it off at once!' Decayed flesh stuck to the cast that Yong had been wearing for more than a month. He nearly fainted from the pain as he was held down and the cast was removed.

Blind Zhu then poured some white spirit into a bowl and set it alight. He immersed his hand in the blue flame and, with it still burning, carefully began to stroke and knead Yong's leg.

'The bone buds have already begun to grow. It's a bit tricky.' Blind Zhu had his grandson bring him a black bag from which he removed four pieces of bamboo, a black herb, some other dried herbs and a dirty piece of cloth.

'Go and get me some leaves from the paulownia trees at the foot of the mountains,' he said to his grandson. To Yong he said, 'You'd be better by now if I'd seen you earlier. But now you're this bad, I'm going to have to do something that will hurt a bit.'

Blind Zhu asked for Yong to be held down. Then, with steady hands and amazing speed, the old man began to put the bone fragments back together, one by one, meticulously rearranging them to form the leg's original shape. Yong cried out in agony. Next, with astonishing dexterity and unbelievable strength, Blind Zhu returned the leg to its original alignment. Then he put some dried medicinal herbs in his mouth and chewed them to a paste. He spat the black, sticky mixture out, spread it on the leg and placed the paulownia leaves on top. Finally, he wound the old cloth around the lot and secured it with the bamboo pieces.

Yong's mother gave Blind Zhu a precious bundle of dried noodles to thank him and he returned home, taking care not to be seen. Ordinarily he made a living from grinding grain into flour, and if it got about that he was also administering this kind of treatment, he would've been accused of being a 'capitalist tail'.

Blind Zhu had been sightless since birth. He'd learned the skill of healing at the age of twelve from a beggar to whom, by chance, he'd given alms. He'd honed his abilities by reassembling ceramic fragments inside a hemp bag. After the Cultural Revolution began, there was no opportunity to use his talent.

After that first treatment, Blind Zhu came to Yong's house several times and examined the leg thoroughly, until one day he counted on his fingers and announced, 'Tomorrow at noon, the boy will yell loudly. Then the leg will be completely healed.' And just as Blind Zhu had predicted, the next day at noon Yong found himself crying out. Eventually he went onto crutches, and his leg gradually got better.

'My right leg wasn't saved by the great Communist Party's People's Hospital. It was saved by an old man, little better than a beggar, who'd learned traditional healing arts,' Yong says when he shows me the deep scars still visible on his leg.

Yong's father came home from the study team at last, yet the family was only able to enjoy normal life for a short time. In the winter of 1969, they were sent away to the country to undergo *xiafang*, or thought reform. They left Xinxian on an old truck sent by the county which they loaded up with their few possessions. Yong's parents, cousin and three older brothers sat outside in a raging wind laced with snow, while Yong, his grandmother and his sister huddled in the passenger seat. Yong had no idea what was going on.

Their destination was a border area of Henan Province,

the poorest part of the county known as a place of banishment for criminals. The truck stopped in the middle of a village called Budian, which was controlled by the Shawo Commune. Yong and his family were bundled out into a fierce snowstorm. His mother hugged Yong and his little sister close while his grandmother, cousin and brothers stood next to them, freezing.

Budian was a village of about a hundred dwellings; farmhouses with mud walls and tiled roofs lined the road. Yong's father immediately went to meet the Party Secretary, as first of all they needed somewhere to live. In the end they were allocated one of the tiled-roof houses that was already sheltering a family of four sent by the Shawo Commune for *xiafang*. Yong and his family were assigned to one room – far too small for a family of nine.

They carried their bedding, boxes of clothes and everything else they'd brought with them inside before stopping to rest. They'd been travelling since morning, and, on top of their fatigue, their stomachs were growling. Night had closed in, and the village was silent. When Yong's mother went over to the communal stove – meant for everyone's use – the other family became enraged and refused to let her have any food or even use a single pot to cook in.

'There's nothing for it. Let's kill the chicken and eat it.' Amongst the luggage was a chicken Yong's family had brought to use as an alarm clock. This was all the food they had. Yong's mother broke up the clothes boxes to use for firewood, and the eldest son, Cao Zhi, went outside to search for bricks with which he built a simple stove. They put the chicken in a pot of water to boil, since they had no other ingredients. But the pot was large – large enough to cook for everyone – and there wasn't enough firewood to keep it heated. So Yong's mother pulled some books from their luggage, intending to burn them.

'You can't burn those!' Yong's father indignantly snatched the books from her hand. He was blazing with anger that she'd try to burn these volumes, their covers printed with pictures of a strange-looking moustached foreigner whom Yong had often seen pictured next to Chairman Mao.

Yong's mother asked Cao Zhi to go and fetch some more water so they could make the chicken soup stretch a bit further. A short while later he returned carrying an iron bucket with both hands. But his steps were unsteady, and his face was deathly pale. He put the bucket down, took two or three steps into the room and collapsed with exhaustion.

It was unfortunate that, of all the places he could have chosen, Cao Zhi fell onto the cooking pot with the chicken in it. The brick stove collapsed and the pot was overturned, covering Cao Zhi in hot chicken soup and smouldering cinders. Yong's father rushed to pick Cao Zhi up and cool his burns with water. Cao Zhi had forced himself to work like a slave for his family during the preparations for their move, and this was the result. Their grandmother washed the chicken and fed it just to the children.

The next day, Yong's father went into the mountains to cut firewood. Cao Zhi didn't rest either, instead going out with his father; he was used to the mountains from having to cut firewood himself every day while his father was away in the study team. It was snowing heavily when father and son returned in the evening, their faces stiff with cold. In winter the trees became frozen, making the task of cutting firewood even more arduous than usual. Moreover, the snowfalls that year were particularly heavy.

The local peasants viewed these 'landlords' coldly, so their children never made any moves to approach Yong and his siblings. Yong's parents became utterly worn out from labouring in the fields with the peasants every day; his mother, whose health had long been bad, collapsed frequently. She was often unable to sleep due to toothache, moaning in agony every night, and the herbal remedy she tried to relieve the pain didn't seem to have any effect.

Whenever Yong's mother couldn't sleep, she saw ghosts. There were in fact strange noises in the night; the family heard people's voices and footsteps in the darkness. They were alone in the house now because a few days after their arrival, the other family had disappeared. When Yong's family were finally leaving Budian themselves, they heard for the first time that their tumbledown house had been used as a hospital mortuary. Yong deeply resented the callousness of allotting such a house to people sent for *xiafang*.

One day during the evening meal, the house began making queer sounds, creaking all over, and the roof boards began to groan.

'It's going to collapse!'

The family jumped to their feet and ran to huddle in a corner. The next instant there was a great crash and the roof fell in. Yong's younger sister, Cao Qing, would've been crushed if her father hadn't grabbed her. The roof had collapsed under the heavy weight of accumulated snow, and half of the house was destroyed. Despite the unprecedented levels of snowfall during the period around Spring Festival, Yong's house was the only one in Budian to collapse. His father – who was under serious investigation – had deliberately been assigned the worst house in the village.

In spite of the collapse of their house, the village wouldn't give the family anywhere else to live. Yong's father appealed to the work brigade and the commune, saying, 'If we freeze to death, it's your responsibility!'

Finally they were permitted to move to a storehouse that stank of agricultural chemicals and contained a jumbled mess of farm implements. There the family prepared for a gloomy Spring Festival. Yong's father sought to create a bit of festival spirit by writing two traditional New Year's couplets on paper strips to hang at the entrance: 'I raised my eyebrows and looked contemptuously at the person censured by the public and yet, lowering my head, submitted willingly as a cow to the wishes of a boy' and 'Only heroes can quell tigers and leopards / And wild bears never daunt the brave'. These were perfectly respectable poems by Lu Xun and Mao Zedong. Hearing of them, however, the Public Security agent from the Shawo Commune stealthily made copies, thinking that this was perfect material with which to incriminate Yong's father.

'These characters written by Cao Hongshan are undoubtedly a problem. We must keep an eye on his actions,' said the Budian production-unit leaders. 'He's the subject of a serious investigation by the county.' People unanimously raised their voices in criticism. These ignorant peasants didn't know that the couplets included words written by their great leader. After Yong's father attended a commune meeting to explain that one of the verses was by Mao Zedong and to criticize their blasphemous behaviour, the furore eventually subsided.

The Cao children put all their efforts into picking wild mountain vegetables, catching frogs and shooting sparrows with catapults to provide some variety at mealtimes. One day an older brother caught lots of frogs. Since they would only be eating the back legs, the brother cut those off and told Yong to throw the bodies away. Yong put the bodies of more than forty frogs into a bamboo basket and threw them into a ditch at the front of the house where the family disposed of rubbish. That night they feasted on stir-fried frogs' legs.

The next morning, Yong went out to the rubbish ditch and found a cloud of flies buzzing around. A dozen or so of the frogs he'd thrown out were still moving; although they didn't have the strength to shake off the flies that were settling all over their bodies, they were alive and their front legs twitched as they snapped their mouths and puffed out their cheeks. Yong didn't need his crutches anymore, but his leg was still weak and the frogs reminded him of what might have become of him if his family had been able to raise the money for an operation the previous summer. His leg would've been leg cut off, and he'd look just like the frogs. Yong was never able to eat frogs' legs again.

More than a year passed, *xiafang* came to an end, and the family returned to Xinxian. Yong turned ten. The family was living a quiet life in a tiled-roof brick house at the foot of the mountains.

One hot, humid summer's night, everyone was sitting outside in the cool air. Xinxian was a small place; you could walk from one end of it to the other in no more time than it took to smoke two cigarettes. It was dark and still; only insects' calls echoed in the darkness. The family was preparing for bed when a loud explosion ripped through the quiet. Next they heard people running out from the centre of the town, yelling, 'A class enemy has thrown a bomb!'

The following morning when Yong went to school, he noticed that the girl next to him, Zhang, was very subdued and had red, swollen eyes.

'Zhang's father was badly hurt in the blast last night. He's in hospital.' Her classmates were discussing the rumours. Her father, Zhang Xiaoqian, was the secretary of the town's Party Committee.

'Ceng Qingcheng did it. He bombed the town meeting hall last night.' The incident was the talk of the school.

Later the son of the Public Security bureau chief, Xie Wei, came into the classroom. 'They caught him! My father's trying him right now,' he called out triumphantly.

Ceng Qingcheng was around thirty years old, a graduate of the Huan Chuan Teacher Training School. Being both an intellectual and a member of the landlord class, his status was extremely low, and he had a miserable life with his old father. During the Cultural Revolution, he'd been sent to a village for *xiafang* and had spent endless days in labour reform. The heartless peasants refused to give him a house, so father and son had no choice but to make themselves a sleeping shelter out of straw and wood. But every time they built it, the peasants would knock it down. Thus they weren't even allowed to have a place to live – let alone land to work – and were forced to perform the hardest of tasks while being kicked and punched into the bargain.

The two found it impossible to eke out a living and ran away to their home town of Xinxian. When they arrived, however, they were sent back to the village. This happened repeatedly until, unable to endure such a harsh life anymore, the old man died.

After his father's death, the villagers continued to treat Ceng Qingcheng cruelly. He dragged his exhausted body back to Xinxian but once again was immediately returned to the village. Finally, he began living secretly in a mountain cave in Xinxian and made a living selling firewood in the town. Yong and his friends saw him on two occasions fetching water from the river when they were fishing. The former teacher's health was obviously poor and he spoke little; he was as thin as a scarecrow and his face was yellow.

The news of Ceng Qingcheng's whereabouts finally reached the ears of Secretary Zhang, who led a militia group to the cave. They caught the teacher and destroyed his sole possessions: a dirty quilt and a large pot. Then Secretary Zhang ordered the militiamen to drag the teacher back to the village. This took place about a week before the bomb incident.

Ceng Qingcheng promptly returned to Xinxian again, but his demeanour had changed – this time he'd brought with him a bag of chemical fertilizer that could be used to make explosives. At his cave he gathered up the broken pieces of his pot and crunched them to create even smaller fragments, which he then combined with the fertilizer. The bomb was finally ready.

Under cover of darkness, Ceng Qingcheng stole into the town night after night and hung around Secretary Zhang's house waiting for an opportunity to take his revenge. One evening, a meeting of the town's Party members was being held in a hall. Peeking in at the entrance, Ceng Qingcheng saw that Zhang was there along with the hated Party officials and militiamen who always sent him back to the village.

Immediately he lit the fuse and threw the bomb inside. It fell directly at the feet of Secretary Zhang, who was standing near the podium. There was a hush before the hall erupted in confusion. However, the fuse was a fraction too long. Secretary Zhang kicked the bomb away so that it landed in the middle of the hall near some mothers and children, whereupon some militiamen, who were standing alongside them, grabbed it and threw it outside. Secretary Zhang hid under a desk. Ceng Qingcheng quickly snatched up the bomb and threw it back into the hall, but in his haste he failed to throw it accurately. The next instant there was a fearful explosion, and Ceng Qingcheng fled for his life.

One child and three adults died, and a dozen or so people were injured. Secretary Zhang sustained head injuries and lost his left eye. Ceng Qingcheng tried to escape along the river, but close to daybreak he was caught by the militiamen. On being captured, he apparently asked them whether Secretary Zhang was dead.

'No, he's in hospital, injured.'

When Ceng Qingcheng heard this, all of his strength drained away and he collapsed. From then on he refused to speak a word.

The sentencing rally was held several days later in the square opposite the train station, where a temporary platform had been constructed from bamboo. Ordinarily, sentencing rallies were held in the town Assembly Hall, but this time it was being conducted in the square so a large crowd could watch the proceedings.

Yong raced over to the square with his friend and classmate Xie Wei, son of the Public Security chief. People from all work units were obliged to attend public struggle sessions and sentencing rallies, and students were also encouraged to attend. As many as ten thousand onlookers filled the square.

Several large banners hung over the podium, emblazoned with proclamations written in large characters: 'Execute Ceng Qingcheng by firing squad to satisfy everyone!'; 'Down with the counter-revolutionary element Ceng Qingcheng!'; 'Never forget the class struggle!'; and 'Political power grows out of the barrel of a gun!'

Ceng Qingcheng was bound in the so-called 'jetliner' position, with his hands raised and bound behind his back. Tied to his back was a long pole with 'The firing squad for Ceng Qingcheng!' written on a piece of cloth. Public Security Bureau Chief Xie sat in the centre of the platform, flanked on either side by a dozen or so high officials and soldiers. Ceng Qingcheng was sandwiched between two soldiers, already too exhausted to support himself, forced to stand where people could see him easily.

Chief Xie stood up and shouted, 'Down with the counter-revolutionary element Ceng Qingcheng!'

'Down with the counter-revolutionary element Ceng Qingcheng!' the crowd responded, and continued, 'Long live the dictatorship of the proletariat! Long live the Communist Party of China! Hurrah!' The ear-splitting cries surged up like angry waves.

A threadbare, ragged yellow silk shirt hung off Ceng Qingcheng's emaciated body, and his dark trousers were torn. Occasionally he'd raise his head and look around with the pale, drawn face of a man already dead. He'd evidently received a terrible beating, for his face was distorted and covered in blood. When his larynx twitched, blood flowed afresh from his mouth and neck. It looked like he was trying to say something, but this action only pulled awkwardly at the bleeding flesh around his throat, and no sound emerged.

'A doctor operated on his throat with wire. It's so he can't yell counter-revolutionary slogans,' Xie Wei informed Yong.

The soldiers roughly jerked Ceng Qingcheng down and forced him to bow his head, a sight that burned itself into Yong's memory, for he was close enough to be splashed by Ceng Qingcheng's sweat. When the sentencing rally was over, Ceng Qingcheng was thrown onto the back of a truck and driven around the streets. Everyone knew that he'd be executed and wanted to know where it would happen so they could go and watch. But nobody knew the location.

'Hey, I know because I asked my father,' said Xie Wei. 'It's going to be on the waste ground at the foot of that mountain over there.'

Yong followed Xie Wei, going ahead of the crowd to the area of vacant ground. An event like this was nothing unusual – there were plenty of opportunities to watch firing squads – but it was always difficult to get close enough to see anything much because of the dense crowds. This time, however, there'd be no wall of people so thick that a child couldn't squeeze through! Yong's heart beat fast with excitement.

'Let's wait here.' Xie Wei and Yong climbed up a slope near the site and looked out over the town. The tan-coloured mountain had been denuded during the Great Leap Forward – Yong had never seen green mountains covered with trees. A truck was driving towards the execution site with a dozen soldiers standing in the back. Ceng Qingcheng was tied to the rails and forced to stand. When the truck reached the road leading to the foot of the mountain where there were no houses, it accelerated, quickly arriving at the execution site. Several hundred people following it ran to keep up.

The truck and a jeep stopped at the side of the road next to the waste ground. Several Public Security officials and Chief Xie got out of the jeep. A dozen or so armed soldiers and some more Public Security police lined up with Chief Xie in the middle. Ceng Qingcheng was dragged roughly down from the truck and pulled over to the execution site by three armed soldiers who threw him to the ground. One soldier held his semi-automatic ready, pushed Ceng Qingcheng's head down and trained the gun at the back of it.

Bang! He pulled the trigger, and Ceng Qingcheng slumped over on the spot.

An army doctor standing by turned him over and examined his pupils to confirm that he was dead. The doctor turned round and said something; then a Public Security official pulled out a pistol, aimed point-blank at

Ceng Qingcheng's head and fired another shot. The Public Security police and soldiers left the site immediately. It was all over in the blink of an eye. But Yong, who'd seen everything from beginning to end, went on standing there, too stunned to move.

Ceng Qingcheng was landlord class. I'm landlord class too!

Presently, the large crowd that had been following the truck reached the spot. They tut-tutted in disappointment when they learned that the execution was already over. Children prodded the body with stones and twigs. Adults lifted it with their feet and peered at it. Ceng Qingcheng's penis was erect in his ragged trousers.

'The stiff's dick faces Heaven, ha ha ha!' the adults joked, mocking Ceng Qingcheng's corpse. The children used sticks to poke and swat at his penis.

Then an old man wearing shorts broke through the wall of people around the body. 'Hey, don't hit him. Stop it! Don't mess with the dead!'

Yong was impressed. *There're still some decent people around after all.*

The old man crouched over the body and began to loosen the ropes that bound it, then put his hands on the silk shirt – dyed bright red with blood – and peeled it off Ceng Qingcheng's corpse.

So that's it – he only wanted the shirt.

The old man hurried away, holding the blood-soaked shirt under his arm.

The Cao brothers were well known as ringleaders amongst the children in their town. They were tough fighters and widely feared. Having landlord-class status, they couldn't hope to go on to higher education, no matter how much effort they might put into studying, so Yong spent most of his time fighting and getting into mischief instead of going to school. When he did go, more often than not he'd be caught out in some misdemeanour and forced to sit in the front row or stand in the corridor as punishment. Whenever the latter happened, he'd wait for an opportunity to escape, then pass the time drinking starfruit wine stolen from a brewery warehouse near a friend's house, or stealing apples from orchards and fruit from the market, or shooting small birds with a catapult.

This is how the eleven-year-old Yong was spending his days when a group of artists arrived in Xinxian. They'd been sent from Beijing for *xiafang* and to paint historical pictures for the Revolutionary Martyrs' Memorial Hall.

One day Cao Gang came home with some news: 'I heard Hu Damao is learning to paint. You know, the headmaster's son.' The fact that the artists were teaching some local children to paint became a topic of discussion.

Then Yong's father, who'd been worried about Yong's behaviour, decided that he should go off and learn painting too, instead of getting into trouble all the time. Going to see one of Yong's teachers, a young woman called Zhang Mei, he requested an introduction to the artists.

The artists were staying in the grounds of the Memorial Hall, grounds that also enclosed a quiet and beautiful wooded park with large trees. Yong didn't know what 'learning to paint' entailed, but he went off to the Memorial Hall when his father told him to. He'd heard that the lessons were conducted in the artists' rooms and upon arriving saw three children painting pictures: Hu Damao, the son of the headmaster of the advanced middle school, and the Li brothers, the two sons of the Culture Hall superintendent. They were all older, so-called 'good boys', not delinquents like Yong. To Yong these children were from another world; he'd never spoken to them before and, of course, never played with them.

So he ignored them and said to Zhang Mei, 'I think my father already told you about me. I'm Young Number Four Son and I've come to learn painting.'

Zhang Mei introduced Yong to an artist called Zhang Bu, who looked up from his work and said condescendingly, 'Oy, you're a strong-looking lad. Hold this stick, will you, and stand here.'

Zhang Bu made Yong stand with his legs apart and stretch his arms out awkwardly to hold the stick. Once in this pose, Yong became the model for a child revolutionary in a picture called *Beating Local Tyrants and Distributing the Land* that the group was working on. Having supposedly gone there to study art, he instead ended up standing in an uncomfortable pose all day holding a stick.

Shit! So learning to paint is just this boring stuff!

'Don't move!' the teacher scolded him. Yong became fed up with standing in this tortuous position. Hu Damao, the headmaster's son, was painting with a self-satisfied expression on his face. He and the others had been studying with Zhang Bu for more than six months and had made great progress. Zhang Bu's favouritism towards him and the Li brothers was plain.

Next day, Yong went reluctantly to the Memorial Hall and again spent the whole day as a model. His pals were astonished to hear about the painting lessons, since this was the first time Yong had done anything that smacked of being a 'good boy', and they raced over to see for themselves. They glued their faces to the window, sticking their tongues out and making fun of Yong as he stood there uncomfortably.

That day, however, Zhang Bu told Yong that he could start painting the following morning and that he should do a practice picture at home. Yong made a friend act as his model and drew a human face on paper for the very first time. He excitedly showed this picture to Zhang Bu the next day.

'What's this! The face you've drawn looks like a gourd,' Zhang Bu scoffed and cuffed Yong on the head. Yong had drawn the face so large that it crowded off the paper.

'Oy, Young Number Four Son, go and look at Damao's picture!' Zhang Bu ordered, but Yong just hung his head and stood there silently.

After lunch, Zhang Bu ordered the children to go outside so he could have a nap.

'Yah! Gourd! Gourd! Ha ha ha!' Hu Damao and the others jeered at Yong, teasing him to pass the time. After a while Yong's patience ran out, and he began returning the insults and hitting out at Hu Damao, even though the other boy was four years older.

'Shut up! Don't be such a smart-arse! Jerk!'

The Li brothers then joined forces with Hu Damao. Yong, recognizing that the odds were against him, ran along the desks in the meeting room to escape the stick they were swinging at him. Zhang Bu was awakened by the commotion and came out to see what was going on. He took one look and – without asking any questions – slapped the small boy who was being ganged up on by three bigger boys. Yong ran off, biting his lips in mortification.

That night, Yong told his father, 'I don't want to learn painting anymore. It's more boring than school. If I go to school the teacher makes me stand and if I go to the Memorial Hall I also have to stand. That stuff is useless.'

'I see, you're a quitter! You're the kind of lazy no-hoper that fishes for two days, then hangs up your net for three! You run away from school, and you run away from art class! At this rate there's no hope of any kind of success for you!'

When Yong heard this, his mood suddenly deflated. He gritted his teeth, went to his room and began to concentrate with all his might on drawing another picture. He had no idea how you were supposed to study painting, but he tried to draw by following the example of the Revolutionary pictures he'd seen at Zhang Bu's lesson. He shut himself up in the house and drew constantly for several days, thinking that this wasn't too bad after all. When he'd completed a stack of sketches, he went back to the Memorial Hall. He'd remembered that there was another artist in residence with Zhang Bu by the name of Yu Ren.

Yong walked into the artists' quarters with his pictures hidden under his clothes because he didn't want Hu Damao and the others to know that he'd been drawing. He found Yu Ren's room and struggled to climb up the outside wall so he could peek through the window. Yu Ren was sitting at a desk writing. When he looked up and his eyes met those of the boy with close-cropped hair who'd clambered up to his window like a frog, he laughed and Yong slid back down in a fright.

Yu Ren put his head out the window and called, 'Hello there, what are you up to?' Instead of being angry, he was laughing kindly.

'Er … I want you to teach me to paint.'

'Come inside.'

Yong nervously entered the room and pulled out the sketches secreted under his clothes.

'Well now, you've drawn quite a lot here, haven't you?' Yu Ren said, complimenting Yong and examined the drawings one by one. Yong was amazed at not being reprimanded or yelled at.

'The shape of this face is different. Most people's noses are shaped like this,' Yu Ren explained seriously as he corrected the pictures. Yong was so moved that he shook. Almost all of the explanations flew right over his head, but he watched Yu Ren's face eagerly. From then on Yong began to study painting under Yu Ren. They climbed together in the mountains and sketched the scenery, and at home Yong would do still-life drawings just as he'd been taught to do them. When his father's acquaintances visited the house, Yong would ask them to model for him and sketch their faces. Sometimes he even had his own rascally friends act as models for sketching practice. Under Yu Ren's tuition, he made rapid progress, and his pictures advanced far beyond those of Hu Damao and the Li brothers.

Once, Yong overheard Yu Ren muttering, 'I'd like to do an owl', and promptly made his gang go with him deep into the mountains to search for one. They caught several, to Yu Ren's great surprise.

After eight months, the paintings of the Revolution were complete, and it was time for Yu Ren and the other artists to leave Xinxian. This was a great blow to Yong, for Yu Ren had come to occupy a sacred place in his heart.

'"The painting reflects the artist", Young Number Four Son. If you want to paint, you must start by building your character. Paintings are the artist's soul. If a person has no soul, then his paintings will be worth nothing, no matter how good his technique may be.'

Yong reflected on these words as he ran sobbing after the bus that carried Yu Ren away.

Yong continued to paint enthusiastically, thirsting for another teacher to instruct him. Then, one day, some artists came to draw more Revolutionary pictures, since Xinxian was a stronghold of the Revolution in those days. They were given a reception at the Culture Hall. When Yong heard that they'd arrived, he raced over to meet them, but when Superintendent Li saw Yong in the Culture Hall, he yelled, 'Get out of here!' Turning to the artists, he said, 'Don't mind him. He's a well-known troublemaker.'

After that, Yong lay in wait on the road for the superintendent's sons. When they came along, he grabbed the two of them and thumped them, then dragged them into a field and stuffed raw eggplants into their mouths, forcing them to eat until they were full. 'You tell your father this. If he kicks me out of the Culture Hall again, I'll make the pair of you drink river water until your stomachs burst!' he threatened. The superintendent never threw Yong out again when he went to meet visiting artists at the Culture Hall.

In 1978, classes in the advanced middle school in Xinxian were separated into science and liberal-arts courses, and streamed according to ability. Yong was put into the lower stream for liberal arts. His classroom was rowdier than any of the others. One morning when the bell stopped ringing and the school had begun to quiet down, Yong's classmates started whispering.

'Hey, there's that war criminal people have been talking about. I heard he was a Kuomintang officer who just got released.'

'Who's that?'

'The new geography teacher. A war criminal recently released from Beijing.'

When Hua Guofeng had become Chairman on the death of Mao Zedong, former Kuomintang officers had been released from prison and a number of them had returned to Xinxian.

A man in his sixties entered the classroom. He was of

medium height and rather thin, but his back was ramrod straight. His face was rugged, and a few strands of white hair fluttered behind his ears on his nearly bald head. A calm smile played mysteriously around his lips; the students couldn't tell if he was laughing or not. He mounted the platform at the front of the classroom, promptly uttered a loud 'Pah!', then clicked his heels.

'Greetings, students. My name is Shen,' he said with a military-style salute. The students laughed and jeered, but he merely smiled at them, entirely unperturbed. Later everyone came to call him 'Bald Shen'.

Bald Shen spoke about the importance of studying geography: 'If a soldier does not understand geography, it is like fighting blind. Everyone should know his position clearly at all times.'

When he heard this, Yong instantly grasped the significance of geography for his own situation.

Bald Shen's voice wasn't loud, but he had the ability to command attention. None of the teachers Yong had encountered before were as fascinating as this character. Bald Shen wore old shoes, a grey Sun Yat-sen jacket dotted with holes, and threadbare, faded indigo trousers. From top to bottom, everything he wore was old and flimsy, yet clean and neat.

During their first class, Bald Shen set the students to work by themselves, then went around the classroom. He stopped in front of Yong and looked hard at him. 'You're interested in geography, aren't you?' he said.

'Nah, it's because your lesson is different from the other teachers. I got interested in geography for the first time ever today,' Yong replied.

'You're Cao Yong!' Bald Shen laughed.

Not again! That class teacher has been tattling about me as usual. Shit. He plans to label me a bad boy forever.

'I heard that you paint. I'd very much like to see your work,' Bald Shen continued. Yong saw a warm light in his eyes.

Yong was drawn to Bald Shen from the moment they met. He'd order all the rowdy kids to be quiet when Bald Shen entered the classroom, which was a first for him and astonished everyone. Upon receiving a warning look from Yong, the other students would promptly cease chattering and sit meekly.

Bald Shen had graduated from the Huangpu Officers' Academy and fought against the Communist army in the early days of Liberation until he was defeated and captured. Since then he'd spent decades in prison, and had lost his wife and his children. In class he often digressed from the topic of geography to thrilling tales of war and his own experiences: Bald Shen jauntily leading cavalry troops in the vast wilderness of the north-west; Tibet, Xinjiang and their magnificent rugged environments; the wide horizon and the sand rising around the troops as they advanced. From these reminiscences Yong learned about north-west China; meeting Bald Shen became the spark that would point him in the direction of far-off Tibet.

3. HENAN UNIVERSITY

Political changes in China are directly reflected in the lives of individual citizens. So it was that as Deng Xiaoping's status rose, it became possible for people to modify their own destinies in accordance with their abilities.

Since the age of eleven, Yong had devoted himself to painting, hoping that he'd be able to go to art school eventually. Recent changes in the academic system made it possible for him to sit the entrance examinations for university while he was still in advanced middle school, at the age of fifteen. He sent his work to one of China's leading art schools, the Guangzhou Academy of Fine Arts, and on this basis qualified to take the entrance exams.

Immediately he became eligible, Yong went to Xinyang to take the first round of exams, which he passed easily. He then went to sit the second round at the Children's Palace in Zhengzhou. Hu Damao and the Li brothers had also sent in their work but didn't qualify to take the exams.

Yong's father was at home around this time, having been suspended from work. Yong's brothers had been sent away to do *xiafang*, so all his father's hopes were focused on him. His father went with Yong to Zhengzhou and all through the exam peered in at the window, keeping an eye on him. During the lunch break they went to the People's Park to eat a huge meal of pig's-head meat which his father had prepared. Yong was amazed when he saw it.

'Papa, where did all this meat come from? You haven't got the money!'

'It was cheap because the pig died of sickness. But there's nothing wrong with it – it's been thoroughly cooked in the pressure cooker. It tastes rather good.' He had Yong eat all the meat and only nibbled on some steamed buns himself.

'Young Number Four Son, I was watching you in there. You're better than the others – the best in fact! "Strategically, with regard to the whole, though we should take the enemy lightly, we must never underestimate our opponents in any struggle!" Do you understand?' his father shouted agitatedly.

Yong listened with his mouth crammed full of meat. *What does that mean? Why the heck is he bringing up military strategy at a time like this? I don't understand strategy, but basically this is about me beating that bunch in there. I get that much.*

Even today Yong paints the way some people would engage in a kung-fu match; there's an underlying aggression in his work that reaches out to people and that very likely dates from this competitive attitude at the beginning of his painting life.

Most hopeful applicants in Henan Province studied under a master painter called Cao Xinlin, who taught children in the Zhengzhou Children's Palace. He had graduated from the Guangzhou Academy of Fine Arts and had many connections; his word could decide who entered university to study art in Henan. In fact, it was said to be virtually impossible to get into art school without going through him.

Cao Xinlin's pupils were at the second round of examinations. At first they made fun of Yong for being a hick, but when he began to sketch, they and the teachers from Guangzhou all gathered around to watch.

When the results came out, Yong was awarded first place for creativity and drawing out of the five southern provinces of China. This achievement entitled him to enter the Guangzhou Academy of Fine Arts. Both he and his family were very proud. Shortly afterwards, however, an official notification was delivered saying that he'd been rejected. The reason given was the political investigation into his family. Undeterred, Yong put even more effort into his painting, to the point of fainting one summer day as he was sketching in his room.

Yong's mischievous friends would steal paper and pencils from school or their parents' workplaces for him, since he had no money to buy them for himself. One day, his companions came and reported that they'd found a storehouse with a load of paint that looked like toothpaste. Yong was delighted, and that night they raided the theatre-troupe storehouse where they'd found this treasure trove.

'Yippee! This looks like oil paint. I'll be able to do oils now!'

In high spirits they took the box away with them and

opened it, but the paint inside was all brown and peach. Yong immediately tried it out, but oddly it didn't dry, even after several days. They'd pinched the theatre troupe's make-up!

In 1979, the year of Yong's second attempt at the entrance exams, the only universities with art courses accepting students were Kaifeng Teachers College (later known as Henan University) and Jingdezhen Institute of Ceramic Art. Yong decided to try for the Department of Art at Henan University. He passed the first round of exams easily and again had to sit for the second round, this time in Kaifeng. His father scraped together the necessary money by selling the pig the family had been raising to eat at Spring Festival. It wasn't possible to borrow money, so there was no other way. With great effort he managed to scrape together 40 yuan.

An acquaintance took Yong and his father to Xinyang by truck so Yong could catch a train. After treating the driver to a meal to show his gratitude, Yong's father returned to the truck to fetch the money he'd left under the passenger seat to pay the bill. But the truck door had been forced open, and his bag and coat were gone. As well as the money, the bag had contained Yong's easel and his certificate of eligibility to take the exam.

Yong and his father ran around the area asking people if they'd seen anything, but of course nobody admitted they had. His father then hurried to the Xinyang Higher Education Admissions Office. The staff there remembered Yong because of his excellent results in the exams the previous year and swiftly reissued the certificate.

'But we don't have any money,' said Yong. 'What shall we do?'

Yong's father pleaded with the truck driver and eventually was able to borrow a little more than a yuan, but it wasn't nearly enough to get to Kaifeng. The train's departure time was drawing closer by the minute.

'Papa, it'll be okay. I'll just get a platform ticket and sneak on a train.'

Yong bought a platform ticket for 5 fen and entered the station, then got on a train that left at one in the morning. His father waited on the platform to bid him farewell. As the train began to move off, he ran after it calling out, 'Number Four, you pass that exam and come top!' He was wearing only a thin shirt because his jacket had been stolen, and shook from the cold. A station employee grabbed him by the arm and roughly pulled him away. Yong stood watching and weeping on the jolting train.

You'll see, Papa. This time I'll beat those bastards.

Next morning Yong arrived safely in Kaifeng and again met the pupils of Cao Xinlin at the examination hall. He concentrated hard and drew with all his might. An invigilator Professor Liu Pandong stood behind him the whole time watching him sketch.

That first night, Yong slept outdoors in the university grounds. Next day he was able to meet up with his friend Liao Hong, who'd entered Henan University the previous year. Liao Hong immediately gave him some food and a place to sleep. Their firm friendship dates from this time.

Yong again passed the second-round exam and took top place. His family was overjoyed. No-one else from Xinxian had passed, and Hu Damao and the Li brothers had failed yet again.

Not long after, however, a letter arrived from Henan University. The headmaster of the advanced middle school and the superintendent of the Culture Hall, jealous of Yong going to university while their own sons had failed the entrance exams, had written to Henan explaining the reasons for Yong's rejection the previous year and saying how badly behaved he was. Henan University couldn't simply reject a student who'd taken top place in the practical examination, and tried to pass Yong on to Jingdezhen Institute of Ceramic Art. But the two teachers who'd acted as invigilators, Liu Pandong and Qu Feng, spoke up on his behalf: 'The boy is still young – there's still plenty of scope for educating him. Not admitting a talent like this would be a great loss to our university.'

The university decided to accept Yong. But on the day of the entrance ceremony, the head of the Department of Art addressed the several dozen new students: 'There is one among you who paints quite well, but we have had a warning from his home town that he is badly behaved and delinquent. However, in consideration of the fact that he is still young, we have decided to admit this student. We will observe this student for one month and then decide whether or not to allow him to continue with his studies.'

The students whispered amongst themselves and turned to stare at Yong.

From that day onwards, there was always someone at Yong's back. The first person was Gao Wei, a model student who became the class leader. He was a most unpleasant person who never neglected to deliver his secret reports. The other students also only ever thought about seeking favour with the teachers, and almost none of them were serious about painting. This, coupled with the fact that from the very first day he'd been labelled a troublemaker, made Yong start to hate painting in the classroom. He decided that if people thought he was a delinquent, he might as well behave like one. He began to work by himself, falling into the habit of going to the train station every day to use the people waiting there as models.

One day, on the way back from sketching, he called in to the Beijing Restaurant near the station.

'Hey, do you draw? Are you an art student?' the head cook asked when he saw Yong carrying a drawing board.

'That's right.'

'I've got a young guy in here says he wants to study painting. I don't suppose you'd teach him?'

A young man who'd been frying noodles came out from the kitchen. Yong immediately accepted the offer to be his tutor.

The youth was a Hui called Wang Baoguo and was an excellent cook. Wang lived with his mother near the station, and Yong started staying with them after sketching late. He came to spend almost all of his time at Wang's house painting. He loathed the people around the university; he didn't want to meet them, nor did he want them to see his pictures. His dormitory room housed eight students, but Yong had made a private space for himself by enclosing his top bunk next to the window with scraps of plastic and wood to make a fortress.

Only when the model for life drawing came would Yong appear in the classroom, since there were no other opportunities to draw a nude female body. At the time, pornographic magazines and nude pictures were strictly regulated in China.

'Cao Yong's a delinquent like they said he was – a slacker who never even comes to class. He's too busy having a good time and out of control,' the teachers and students gossiped.

That first summer after Yong entered university, he'd take himself off to the outskirts of the city to sketch. It was here that he first glimpsed the Yellow River and was inspired to draw the boatmen.

One day, a boatmen with whom he'd become friendly gave him a ride as far as Jinglonggong on the opposite shore, where he disembarked at a village called Jinglongtun, situated on a shoal on the river side of the Yellow River dyke. The farmland here was good, fertile soil that had washed down the river, and when Yong saw it he became excited because at the time he was infatuated with the French artist Jean-François Millet, and this was exactly the kind of subject he'd been looking for. He grabbed his drawing board and feverishly began to sketch. The day slipped by in no time.

The sun had set and darkness was falling when Yong at last emerged from his trance to realize that there was no boat to return on. Nor had he any money. In front of him lay a watermelon field with a straw hut on one side for guarding the watermelons. A young man came out of the hut.

'Oy, what's up? Wotcha doin'?'

'I'm a university student in Kaifeng. I was sketching.'

'You came from Kaifeng? It's dark. You got somewhere to stay?'

'Would you let me stay in your hut?'

'You're alone? What about food?'

'It's already dark, so I can't do much, but I'll catch some sparrows to eat. Don't worry.' He showed the youth his catapult.

'Hey, come to my place. What's this about staying in the hut? Let's go.' The youth took Yong home. His name was Wang Dalin.

When they arrived at the mud-walled house with its thatched roof, Wang's mother, an old lady with a kind face, came out to meet them. She didn't look in the least put out by this uninvited visitor and welcomed Yong inside. Wang's father and siblings were away in another town for work and education.

'I haven't been out of this village for forty years, you know, ever since the enormous flood,' Wang's mother explained. 'It was a summer just like this one. We escaped with just what we could carry.'

Yong stayed on in the Wang house and sketched. The villagers gladly posed for him during breaks from their work in the fields. Jinglongtun was a charming village, a far more hospitable place than the university. Yong felt thoroughly at home there, and the time flew by.

One night, after he'd been living with the Wangs for a couple of weeks, there was a loud cry in the small hours: 'Flood!'

'Run to the dyke!' Yong leapt out of bed to find the floor already submerged.

'The river's flooding! Run!' Wang Dalin shouted.

Although there'd been no rain in the village itself that day, there must have been heavy downpours upstream. There was no warning – just this sudden assault. Wang and Yong loaded food and a few other important items onto their backs and left the house carrying Wang's mother. Rain pelted down as they joined the villagers all frantically headed for the dyke. Situated as it was on the dyke's river side, there was nothing between Jinglongtun and the river. The village was already becoming submerged as Yong and the Wangs ran for their lives.

They had to cross a bridge over a tributary of the river, but by now the two had merged to form a single stream in which the bridge was submerged and lost to sight. In the confusion Yong became separated from the others. Carrying the Wang family's belongings on his back, he searched for the bridge in the darkness, but since he didn't know the village very well, he didn't have the faintest idea where it might be. He was unlucky enough to lose his footing and was swallowed up by the raging torrent. He struggled in the water, managing at last to cling onto a telegraph pole that was also being swept away, but the pole kept slipping, so when a big box came floating alongside he grabbed that instead. Other villagers, donkeys, pigs and cows were also being swept along, so at least Yong wasn't alone. To his astonishment some despicable people were even taking the opportunity to scavenge from the flotsam that floated past.

Clutching the box tight, Yong was swept several dozen

kilometres downstream. As the new day dawned, the flood began to abate and he saw land ahead. In a daze, he tried to clamber up onto the ground, but after such long immersion, the right leg that had been badly broken when he was a child had become so chilled that he couldn't move it. Then several men appeared and helped to lift Yong out of the water.

'Are you all right? Where did you come from?'

'I'm a relative of Wang Dalin in Jinglongtun. Please tell Wang Dalin I'm here,' he pleaded, but the flood waters hadn't abated and there was nothing the men could do for the moment.

The land they were standing on was an apple orchard located on high ground that hadn't been engulfed by the flood and stood out in the middle of the river like an island. Villagers, rabbits, donkeys, pigs and cows had also swum ashore there. Yong stayed with everyone else in a hut, waiting for the water to recede. They ate apples to stave off hunger, but eating the unripe fruit every day turned the inside of his mouth so sour that it felt like his teeth would fall out. He was never able to eat apples again after that.

Even after the water subsided, Yong was still unable to move his leg. All the apples in the orchard had been consumed. On the fourth day, Wang Dalin at last heard where Yong was and came on his bicycle to fetch him. He put Yong on the bicycle and took him to the Jinglonggong People's Hospital.

Yong learned later that large artillery had been lined up on the Kaifeng side of the dyke during the flood. The population of Jinglonggong was much smaller than that of

Kaifeng, and if the flooding had worsened, the government apparently was planning to blast the guns at the Jinglonggong side of the dyke and destroy it so as to protect Kaifeng from damage. It hadn't come to that, but a great many people had died nonetheless.

During the Cultural Revolution foreign literature had been prohibited in China, but by the time Yong was at university, translations were finally becoming available again. He devoured literature and philosophy by such writers as Nietzsche, Sartre, Romain Rolland and Stendhal. He was greatly influenced by Somerset Maugham's *The Moon and Sixpence* and spent a great deal of time travelling around the Yao and Miao autonomous regions in order to paint these undeveloped areas.

Throughout his years at university, Yong continued with his independent-minded production of paintings, but eventually the time came when he had to think about his future. He was still not sure which path he should follow, though his interest in south-west China had been sated after his extensive roaming there. It was then that he remembered Bald Shen's war stories, his tales of wide horizons and vast wildernesses in north-western China, of the magnificent environment of Tibet and Xinjiang.

In 1983, during his last spring at university, Yong set off for Tibet. He hitched a ride on a freight train carrying coal, and arrived in Xining black all over from smoke and coal dust but in high spirits. The smell of lamb wafted through the cool, clean air, while Tibetans gathered in the station square sang and danced merrily. Smelly and dirty: this was

Yong's impression of the first Tibetans he ever saw; they gave off a rancid yak-butter smell, their hair was wild and long like that of savages, and the jackets they wore with the fur side turned in were shiny with grime and mud.

'Hey you! *Ni hao!*' A sturdy-looking Tibetan with long hair wrapped casually around his head called over to Yong. The locals were amazingly open and natural, unlike mountain people in the south.

It grew dark, and Yong decided to sleep on a bench in the train station, since his money didn't stretch to paying for accommodation. But near midnight a station worker came round to evict people sleeping there, and Yong was turned out into the bitterly cold wind. He was frozen and his stomach was empty to boot. Looking around, he noticed a number of Tibetans huddled together like stray dogs, asleep next to the station wall and looking surprisingly peaceful and comfortable. Yong went and sat at the edge of their huddle until finally, unable to endure the cold, he mustered the courage to creep into their midst. They were all pressed up against each other; there was no telling whose legs belonged to whom. Yong slipped his frozen legs in amongst the Tibetans': it was paradise. Even the stench of yak butter now seemed like a heavenly scent.

Next morning when the Tibetans awoke, they laughed sociably at this strange newcomer and didn't chase him away. Instead they lit a fire and set about making yak-butter tea, offering him some.

Yong had never drunk yak-butter tea before. He picked up the wooden bowl and gingerly took a sip. The sour smell shot up his nose and made him feel nauseous, but, being absolutely determined not to squander this goodwill, he drank it all down in one gulp. After drinking the tea he felt much warmer and more contented as the strength flowed through his body again.

The Tibetans had come on a pilgrimage from Chabcha in Hainan Tibetan Autonomous Prefecture. Yong was overjoyed to have met up with such agreeable people and went with them to see the Ta'er Monastery.

'Our home town is really beautiful. Great place.'

'Are there yaks where you live? And sheep?'

'You bet! Too right there are!'

So Yong set off towards their home town, deeper into the Tibetan interior.

Rolling grasslands, a clear horizon, limpid blue water such as he'd never seen before: Qinghai Lake was more beautiful than Yong had imagined it would be. He found the Heima River and approached some tents pitched there looking for somewhere to sleep. An old Tibetan man inside one of the tents just smiled, saying nothing, but, as if it was the most natural thing in the world, indicated that Yong should enter and gave him something to eat. The old man lived by the lake catching fish.

Tibetans live in tune with nature. When Yong drew the mountains, yaks or Tibetans, his charcoal pencil would beat in time with his heart. He'd never been one for singing, but when he was with the Tibetans he felt like joyously raising his voice in song. Tibet was a pure land, and free.

Yong got a ride on a PLA truck and headed even further west. The road from Qinghai was in a terrible state back then, added to which Yong had his first taste of the agony of altitude sickness. Nevertheless, he was glad to be heading up towards the sky. If you go to the sky's edge, you might fall off, but Yong didn't care – nothing else mattered but getting there.

When the truck stopped at Nakchu, it was close to the time when Yong had to return to university. By then he'd decided what he'd do after graduation. He was resolved to return to this land.

In China, you can't get a good job if you don't graduate from university. In addition, people aren't allowed to choose their own work units; the government assigns them. Although Yong had been painting as he wandered round China, he still had to make up attendance days and produce enough finished work to graduate.

When he arrived back from Tibet, he noticed a strange atmosphere around the university. In his absence, the class leader of the senior year, Qi Xiang, had circulated a petition demanding that Yong be expelled. Various charges — 'Always fighting. Reviles teachers. Carries concealed weapons' — were listed as justifications. Qi Xiang, one of the so-called 'good students', made all the other students in the Department of Art sign the petition. He'd also tried to ingratiate himself with the teachers and informed enthusiastically on those around him. Students spent nearly all their time on political activities instead of painting, and Gao Wei, who'd monitored Yong when he'd first entered the university, had even joined the Party. Now they were doing their best to find a victim with whom they could recreate the kind of struggle sessions that took place during the Cultural Revolution, raising their own status in the process. Yong, who had always gone his own way, was just the person to become their scapegoat.

If he was expelled now, it would all be over; he wouldn't be able to get a job, and four years of university would all have been for nothing. Yong was angry, but there was nothing he could do other than concentrate on completing his graduation pieces. As with every other procedure in China, it was taking a long time for a decision to be made regarding his expulsion.

One day, Yong consulted his teacher, Wang Wei, one of the few people who understood him.

'Take all of these pictures to the graduation exhibition room straight away. The teachers should see them,' Wang Wei advised him.

Professor Wang Zhaomin from the Guangzhou Academy of Fine Arts happened to be visiting Henan University at the time to deliver a lecture and saw Yong's paintings in the exhibition room.

'You have a student here doing some wonderful work. I'd very much like to meet him,' Wang said. When he found out about the attempt to have Yong expelled, he angrily exclaimed, 'To expel this student would be to discard a treasure of the university!' This appraisal brought the expulsion process to a halt. At the graduation exhibition, Yong had far more works on display, and of a far higher standard, than any other student. Yet in spite of his outstanding work, the university didn't give him a good evaluation. Politics were more important than artistic ability.

As graduation drew closer, Yong discovered that the university had assigned him a job at a primary school in

the coal-mining city of Pingdingshan. This seemed
ridiculous to him. With thoughts of Tibet still filling his
head, he wrote a letter to the State Council Ministry of
Education in Beijing conveying his desire to go there. By
chance the ministry happened to be trying to find model
young people willing to become 'Youth Assisting Tibet' at
this time. Yong received a positive response to his letter.
People in the lowland provinces regarded Tibet as a
barbarian hell; going there to work was a horrifying
prospect, a kind of exile in the remote land of savages. Life
in Tibet, where the air was thin and there was virtually no
system of health care or even basic infrastructure, meant a
great deal of hardship. But Yong had made up his mind.

When the university learned what he was about to do,
their attitude to Yong changed completely, and they began
trumpeting him as their 'model student'. There was
enormous publicity on the radio and in the newspapers
about Yong being a 'good young man' from Henan with a
fine ideology. He received many fan letters saying things
such as 'When I learned of your actions, I thought you
must be like Lei Feng. I was moved to tears at the idea of
you, a young man headed for Tibet to do your best for the
motherland.' Yong got goose pimples when he read them.

Lei Feng had been a PLA soldier who'd died in August
1962 in the line of duty and who'd been honoured as 'a
good soldier of Chairman Mao'. His spirit of sacrifice was
held up as an example for the populace, and there was a
nationwide campaign to 'Learn from Lei Feng'. Later,
when the Lei Feng effect had worn off, the government
began a 'Learn from Zhang Haidi' campaign. Zhang Haidi
was a disabled girl who was said to be imbued with good

ideals and to have performed worthy deeds without giving in to her disability.

About to set off for Tibet, and regarded as a model of sacrifice for the motherland, Yong was treated as a 'good boy' for the very first time in his life. Journalists gathered around him, taking photographs and planting microphones in front of him so that they could interview him.

'Are you going to Tibet because you were encouraged by the spirit of Comrade Zhang Haidi?' a journalist asked.

Yong had seen pictures of her, but all he could remember was that she was crippled. 'Comrade Zhang Haidi? Who's that? Ah, that chick with the bad legs!'

The journalists, who'd gathered to laud Yong as a model youth 'assisting the frontiers', switched off their tape recorders.

Yong went to Lhasa as one of the 'Youth Assisting Tibet' in August 1983. He chose work at Tibet University because he'd heard that university teachers had a lot of free time. At first he was diligent, but before the first month was up he'd become extremely bored, realizing that the students' heads were filled with nothing but girls and drinking. They hadn't come to the university because they loved art, but because they wanted to enter a good work unit. Most of them were also around thirty years old. It became too depressing to get out of bed in the morning.

'Oy! Wake up! It's time for class!' Every morning the senior art teacher would knock on the door of Yong's room in the teachers' dormitory block.

'Teacher, Teacher, class has started!' Occasionally the students themselves would come to wake him.

It became Yong's habit to throw on some clothes without even doing up the buttons before going reluctantly to class. 'Good morning, students. Today we will draw plaster casts,' he'd say, or something to that effect, and then he'd lie down on the models' dais and go back to sleep. Or he'd say, 'Good morning, students. Today we will sketch outside.' Then he'd send the students to the Barkhor and spend all day sipping *tiancha* tea in a teahouse.

'Wow, that's nice. You're good, you know.' His comments to the students were vague and half-hearted; he would lazily praise everyone. When it came to marking, he'd ask each student, 'Hey, what grade do you want?'

As might be imagined, the students therefore welcomed Yong with open arms – no other classes were as enjoyable as his.

As time went by, Yong started imagining how awful it would be to spend the rest of his life like this – what a waste! In the spring of 1984, unable to bear the tedium any longer, he finally abandoned his teaching and set out travelling, aiming for Chomolungma – Mt Everest.

Yong arrived at base camp just as an English and German team was about to begin its ascent of the mountain. Yong followed the Sherpas carrying the team's luggage. The team was well equipped with oxygen tanks, high-quality down jackets and tents, while Yong wore only a Chinese down jacket. The Sherpas let him sleep in their tents, and he kept climbing. As they went higher, however, sleep wouldn't come: he was tormented by altitude sickness and groaned with pain through the nights, believing that he'd die at any moment. In the mornings he'd awake with a thumping headache, his lips swollen as he gasped for breath. Despite everything, however, Yong was exhilarated at witnessing this snowy world.

The team members had apparently spent several months doing training climbs. If they'd been told to, the Sherpas probably could have ascended the peak with ease. To

Yong's eyes, the earnest-faced foreign climbers looked supremely comical. When they reached the summit, there would be cries of 'It's a miracle! What a record!' and their names would go down in history. But of the Sherpas who carried their luggage up and down Chomolungma as easily as if they'd been walking through a garden, not a single name would be remembered.

At around 7000 metres, one of the liquid-fuel cylinders exploded, injuring several of the climbers. Weather conditions were also bad, and there was an avalanche. The expedition decided to make an emergency descent, and Yong too followed the Sherpas down.

After a few days' walk from Chomolungma, Yong arrived at Tingri, an isolated village on the plain linking the Himalayas at an altitude of around 4000 metres. Tingri is also on the China–Nepal Highway connecting Lhasa and Nepal, and in summer nomads pitch tents there to graze their sheep and yaks.

Yong was walking through Tingri when by chance he met an acquaintance in Lhasa, a well-off Hui of around fifty from the Ningxia Hui Autonomous Region, called Lao Ma. Lao Ma, who'd been buying sheepskins from the nomads, was a trader with a goatee and cunning eyes. He went from place to place selling everyday items which he obtained in Gansu, Ningxia and Nepal, using his connections to run a private business. Without these connections he would've been prosecuted as part of the 'strike at economic criminals' campaign and had all his assets confiscated. There were many traders like Lao Ma in the western frontier regions. Yong had, in the past, been asked by him to paint a backdrop for a friend who worked as a photographer. Lao Ma and his friend were delighted with the result – a tank set against a battle scene – which Yong had designed to suit Tibetan taste.

'Hey, aren't you Cao Yong? What are you doing in a place like this?' Lao Ma seemed surprised to encounter Yong at the side of the road. Yong looked like some kind of monster with his enormous swollen lips, peeling face and over-large Sherpa climbing boots.

'Oh, just hanging around painting.'

'You really are a strange one. I'm going to Zhangmu from here. Do you want a lift?' Lao Ma asked jokingly, looking down at Yong from his truck.

'Yep, I sure would.' With his eyes alight, Yong boarded the truck in a flash.

Lao Ma smiled wryly. Yong could see how taken aback he was at this unexpected acceptance of his offer, as if he was thinking that now he'd have to provide food and a bed as well.

They travelled along the bumpy China–Nepal Highway, eventually reaching Nyalam at an altitude of around 3700 metres.

'Let's rest here tonight. Tomorrow is Zhangmu.'

Nyalam was a village on the slope of a steep valley in the middle of the Himalayas. Blocked from the warm breezes off the Indian Ocean, it was swept by bitterly cold winds.

Next day, the truck descended about 1400 metres in the space of 30 kilometres. Down, down, down the twisting mountain road they went. The change of scenery was dramatic; desolate plains and snow-heaped roads gave way to broad-leaf forests, and the air became hot and sweet. In just half an hour they'd left winter behind and burst into summer. Yong's body and soul tingled with life.

'This is Zhangmu. If you keep going down this road, you'll reach Kathmandu,' Lao Ma informed Yong as he stopped the truck in the middle of town.

Keep going down and reach Kathmandu! Mmm, you can almost smell the freedom from here. Goods from Nepal come into Lhasa too, like that Swiss-made portable stove, which sure is handy for cooking. My friend treats it like the family jewels. It worked great when I cooked those legs of mutton – no comparison with Chinese stoves. And there are those playing cards with nude women on them that the Tibetans sell in the Barkhor – they must've come from Europe through Nepal … and the photos of Nepalese temple carvings I saw with animals and women, horses and women, elephants and women, and lots of men and women all tangled up. Mmm, you can smell the lust wafting in from Nepal too.

The Kathmandu of Yong's imagination was a pleasure-filled paradise.

Zhangmu clung to the steep slopes at an altitude of 2300 metres. A trading base between China and Nepal, it was like some sort of primitive exchange, its roadside market overflowing with fruit, Chinese shoes, thermos flasks, quilts and other everyday necessities, and it was thronged with Sherpas, Nepalis and Tibetans. Yong was dazzled by the bananas, oranges and apples from Nepal.

Residents living within a 60-kilometre radius of the border didn't need visas. They came and went freely between countries, and when night began to fall, the Sherpas and Nepalis returned to Nepal.

I didn't know it was this easy to cross the border! Yong

loitered around the Friendship Bridge, thinking about Kathmandu on the other side of the mountain. On closer observation, however, he noticed that the people returning home at dusk were showing something at a checkpoint on the bridge.

There's a checkpoint. Shit! Yong went back into the town, shoulders drooping in disappointment. He was sitting on a bench in front of one of the small roadside shops when he saw Phuntsok, a Tibetan he knew from a teahouse in Lhasa who, like Lao Ma, must have come here to do business.

'Oh, it's Cao Yong, isn't it? What are you up to?'

'Just looking around.'

'Fancy running into you here. Come, let's have a drink.'

Inside the shop, several Sherpas and Tibetans were embarking on a drinking session. 'Hey, he's Han, isn't he? You don't often see Hans hanging around here.' They stared at Yong with interest. The only Han Chinese who ever came to these frontier regions wore uniforms – in other words, they were Party officials or soldiers. Yong accepted a drink and sat cross-legged on the ground.

Observing him closely, the other men fell about laughing. Yong's over-large climbing boots, which he'd exchanged for two packets of cigarettes when climbing Chomolungma, were falling to pieces. These men were all neatly dressed, well-off traders.

From the window of the shop nestled against the mountainside, Yong could see the peaks of Nepal in the distance.

'Hey, what is it? What're you looking at? Drink up.' Yong was startled back into the present when Phuntsok spoke.

'I want to go over there.'

'Over there? You mean Nepal?'

'That's right. I'm set on getting to Kathmandu.'

'Hah, this guy says he wants to go to Nepal!' Phuntsok burst out loudly, and the other men laughed again. They seemed to think it very strange that Yong would just be hanging around like a drifter, without business or any other purpose.

'It's easy.' This time Phuntsok spoke seriously.

'Can I get there?'

'Ah, there's some who'll take you for a small price.'

Yong searched his pockets. All he found was a sketchbook and around 50 yuan. He had no idea how much a wealthy person like Phuntsok would mean by 'a small price', but it was sure to be more than he could afford. He sighed with disappointment.

As darkness fell, Phuntsok passed out drunk on a bench and fell fast asleep. Everyone else had dispersed except for one young Sherpa who made preparations to leave, then stood up and beckoned to Yong.

'Let's go,' he seemed to be saying.

'Go where?'

The young man pointed out the window.

'Nepal?'

'Yes.'

Of course, he's a Sherpa. He's going back to Nepal! Yong scrabbled for some money in his pocket and thrust it at the Sherpa, who simply laughed and shook his head.

'We'd better hurry,' he urged.

Yong followed the Sherpa down to the valley floor, to a forest illuminated by the moon, where they crossed a fast-flowing stream by holding onto tree branches and rocks. The young man knew the path well and crossed the stream easily while at the same time helping Yong, whose feet kept slipping. Yong became grazed all over from falling many times, but he was so elated about crossing the border that he didn't care. It was completely dark by the time they arrived at the young man's home in a small Sherpa village. The stone house was silent and the family already asleep.

Is this really Nepal? There's no barbed wire, guard patrols or anything – it was a cinch to cross the border! Yong stayed at the Sherpa's home that night, still doubtful as to whether he really was in Nepal or not. But next morning when he looked around the village, he was excited to discover that there was no-one who looked like an official of the People's Republic of China. The brown-skinned residents were barefoot and looked poor, wearing only a cloth tied round their waists. The cars on the roads were also unfamiliar, with strange patterns and pictures painted on their worn-out bodies.

'If you find a lift here, you can get to Kathmandu.' The young Sherpa found Yong a truck. 'How much to Kathmandu?' Yong asked the driver eagerly, but his Chinese wasn't understood. He pulled out all the money he had and showed it to the driver. The old Sherpa laughed and extracted a single large note from the worn Chinese currency. Yong climbed onto the back of the truck, and they were off to Kathmandu at last. Along the way, Yong greedily drank in the scenery, his excitement mixed with a little fear. To think that just a few days ago he'd been in the middle of the Himalayas, and now here he was in a verdant forest breathing warm, sweet air! He'd quite forgotten about the Swiss stove and nudie playing cards, and felt dizzy with curiosity.

Yong was still walking on air when they reached Kathmandu. He alighted from the truck and wandered around the city open-mouthed. Kathmandu was a veritable feast for the eyes; he'd never seen anything like it. There were rows of shops filled with an abundance of goods, flowers and fruit in a multitude of colours, and Nepali women wrapped in richly coloured saris. Yong was thrilled by whatever sight met his eyes.

He also noticed images of Buddhas and temples all over the place. He stood rooted to the spot before one particular temple adorned with superbly carved wooden images, stunned by the realistic erotic poses. *This is filled with the scent of sex. Nepal … Kathmandu … What a wonderful place!* Yong stood there in front of the temple and laughed out loud. *The architecture here is so beautiful! This mountain country is a real pearl! That's right, the Himalayas are said to be a woman lying on her side. I've finally found her secret flower garden! Kathmandu! This temple is a jewel in a flower garden!* Yong walked the streets, his face wreathed in smiles, but when his stomach growled suddenly he was instantly dragged out of his reverie. He went to a food store and attempted to communicate through gestures. But when he pulled the crumpled Chinese notes from his pocket, the Nepali storekeeper shook his head. 'This money is no good,' he seemed to be saying. Yong's stomach continued to growl relentlessly as he tried every shop in sight, but everyone shook their heads when they saw the Chinese money.

Finally, around evening, the owner of a shabby restaurant took several notes from Yong's hand and handed him an aluminium plate heaped with queer-looking food. Yong took one bite and nearly gagged. The unfamiliar rice and hot, salty food was cold and tasted strange, but he had no choice. He wolfed it all down and somehow his stomach was satisfied.

This is strange ... does Chinese money stop being money when you leave China? This was a forlorn thought. It was growing dark, and Yong needed to find somewhere to sleep. He walked into a place that looked like a hotel, once again employing gestures to convey his needs. The owner looked at him suspiciously. 'Passporrut, passporrut,' he insisted, drawing a rectangle with his hands. Some women, maybe the owner's family, emerged to see what all the fuss was about. Yong pulled his money out, but the owner shook his head when he saw it. What on earth was he saying? He seemed to be speaking English, but the only English Yong knew was 'hello' and 'okay'. They were all pointing and shouting at Yong, and the expressions on their faces began to make him feel nervous.

Uh-oh. I haven't got a passport or any identification. I'll be in big trouble if I'm caught here illegally. I'll be thrown out of Kathmandu! Yong ran from the hotel. By now it was completely dark, and the bustling shops were all closed, but with his down jacket he could sleep in the open. He recalled a magnificent temple by the river and decided to go there. Struggling to remember the way, he eventually arrived at the river after a long walk. The elegant temple floated up out of the night. A dim light filtering from the building created a dreamlike atmosphere that drew Yong towards it, as if he was possessed. He stood there looking up at the temple for some time. On the opposite bank he noticed a series of small shrines and crossed a stone bridge to reach them. This side of the river also offered a full view of the temple. When he peeked inside the shrines, he discovered that there was enough space for one person to sleep – perfect! – but almost all of them were already occupied. Eventually he found an empty one and spread his down jacket inside for a bed. Having spent the whole day walking around, he fell asleep immediately.

Next morning he awoke with a start to something licking his face: a stray dog. It was becoming noisy outside, so Yong crawled out to investigate. Around the shrines were lots of monkeys, which he hadn't noticed the previous night, and he also observed some peculiar old men with long, untrimmed beards and hair and grubby cloths wrapped around their waists, who were basking in the sun while the monkeys checked their grime-covered bodies for fleas. These were the Babas, holy men who lived in the temples of Nepal. Yong often saw them together in the daytime, the monkeys stretched out beside them or climbing on their shoulders.

Yong had found his way to the Pashupatinath, the largest Hindu temple in Nepal dedicated to Shiva, the god of destruction. In front of it flows the Bagmati River, which further downstream becomes the holy River Ganges and flows to India. Yong saw women in saris and elderly people bathing. *Why are they bathing in water this dirty?* Next to them, women were washing rice, drawing water and scrubbing vegetables.

Mmm, something smells good … meat grilling. Yong's

empty stomach led him in the direction of the smell. On the opposite bank smoke rose from a stone platform onto which two men were stacking straw and sticks. *I wonder what they're cooking?* He crossed the bridge and drew closer. Two waxen legs stuck out from one edge of the straw. *It's a person! They're cremating bodies!*

The cremated bodies were thrown into the Bagmati. This in itself was no great surprise to Yong, since he was familiar with sky burials from Lhasa. Bathing, food preparation and funerals – every aspect of daily life was conducted in this one river.

Yong left the Pashupatinath and began to walk the streets again. He needed to fill his empty stomach, but most of the shops he tried refused his Chinese money, of which he hardly had any left anyway. Finally he was able to buy a cheap stack of *roti* – flat, round fried bread – which he stuffed into his pockets. Thus supplied with provisions, he spent the rest of the day roaming the city.

At nightfall he returned to the Pashupatinath – apart from the nuisance of fleas and mosquitoes, it was the perfect place to sleep – where he entered the same shrine as yesterday, spread out his jacket and lay down. In the quiet night he could hear the river flowing. Just as he was dozing off, Yong sensed a presence and raised his head drowsily to see a tall man peering in at him. Yong stiffened. The man entered the shrine, bent over Yong and prodded him with his foot. *What's with this guy? Is he telling me to push off?* Yong looked up at the man. *It's not the police. The bastard's got one of those cloths tied round his waist like the Babas and a weird cup hanging down.* In the dim light, Yong noticed that the man's beard was yellow. He was also speaking a language that sounded like English. *It's not a Nepali – this guy's a stranger here too. Who does he think he is, telling me to get out?!*

Yong stood up angrily and yelled at the man in Chinese, 'What's this crap! I slept here yesterday! Piss off!'

The man rattled on and on in English. Yong didn't listen; he simply grabbed his jacket and threw it down on the floor with all his might, then sat down on it with a thud to show the man that this was *his* spot. This sent up a cloud of dust, but even as he coughed the stranger didn't let up pouring out a stream of invective. Yong ignored him and lay down. After a while, the man gave up and lay down next to Yong with an exaggerated sigh.

Next morning when Yong awoke, he found the man's feet thrust under his down jacket. A good look at his face revealed him to be a thin, unhealthy-looking Westerner whose appearance was far worse for wear than Yong's own. His long, unkempt blond beard was filthy with rubbish and snot, his bony feet were bare, and he was wearing a grubby, torn T-shirt and a grimy white cloth tied around his thin waist.

What a filthy bastard! So foreigners can get this dirty too. Yong felt a twinge of sympathy, but his anger from the previous night had still not cooled, so when the man opened his eyes he felt no desire for conversation. Instead, he went and sat on the riverbank to nibble on his leftover *roti*. A monkey ran up and stole the *roti* from his hand while he was momentarily distracted.

'Aagh, I'll get you!'

The monkey nimbly made its escape to the top of the bank.

'You slick little bugger!'

The Babas nearby guffawed loudly.

Yong grinned in embarrassment. *How do they manage to eat, I wonder, sitting there every day?* Knowing neither Nepalese nor English, Yong tried to communicate with the Babas using gestures and facial expressions. The oldest Baba had a female monkey sitting on his shoulder that seemed extremely attached to him, zealously grooming his hair and beard, and picking out the fleas. He took a black, greasy, crud-like lump from his loincloth and crushed it with his grimy hands. Then he mixed it with some cut tobacco, rolled it in a scrap of newspaper, lit it and started to smoke. Several Babas gathered, and they passed it around. It was hashish. They pointed the cigarette end at Yong, offering him a hit. Yong didn't know how to smoke it properly and didn't feel anything special.

'The king presents this to the temple over there. It's a gift for us,' the oldest Baba said staring off into space.

One small Baba with a long black beard and long hair beckoned to some Western tourists over near the bridge. Yong followed him to see what he was up to. The Baba led the tourists to a secluded spot behind a small shrine and pointed to a stone on the ground big enough to wrap his arms around. The middle-aged men and women stared curiously at the Baba while he wound a white sash round the stone. Then he made one of the men hold the sash and indicated that he should try to lift the stone with it. The face of the well-built, solid man turned red as he strained to pick up the rock, but he could barely budge it. Next the Baba pulled a long, shrivelled penis out from his vermilion loincloth and rubbed a pinch of dirt on it. He bent forward, hooked the sash onto his penis, grabbed the end of his penis and stood up. Lo and behold, the stone was lifted easily off the ground! The puny-looking Baba lowered the stone and smiled with satisfaction as he thrust his hand at the Westerners. They laughed and handed him several notes. In just a short time the Baba had made several hundred rupees.

Yong found some cover and tried pulling on his own penis to see if he could do the same trick. *Mine certainly wouldn't be any good …*

Yong's money had all but run out, so he took off his jeans and attempted to sell them to one of the rickshaw pullers – by that point even a rickshaw puller seemed far richer than he was. But when they saw the torn, dirty jeans, the rickshaw pullers fell about laughing.

'What a dirty beggar he is, ha ha ha!' One of them picked up the jeans with pincer-like fingers and put his eye up against a hole in a clownish pose. The other pullers rolled over, doubled up with laughter. Yong blushed bright red and he snatched the jeans back.

Next he tried the hawkers selling their wares by the road. One old Nepali woman who was packing up to leave looked sorry for him and exchanged the jeans for seven ripe tomatoes and a few extra squashed ones.

Yong was down to a pair of long underpants, but that was nothing compared to his hunger. Famished, and with no strength to walk any further, he sat in the small shrine back at the Pashupatinath, pulled out his sketchbook, chewed on his short pencil and began to sketch the beautiful temple towering in front of him. While he sketched, he forgot about his stomach.

'Hi, hello!' This sudden voice behind him belonged to the Westerner with whom he'd ended up sharing his sleeping place. Every night they slept cheek by jowl, yet since that first quarrel they hadn't exchanged a word. In the middle of the shrine was a Shiva lingam that marked the boundary between them. Today the Westerner had returned earlier than usual. Yong smiled at him, his temper having cooled down at last.

The Westerner mimed smoking a cigarette. Yong shook his head.

'My name is Robby … you?' The man smiled and spoke slowly in English.

'Cao Yong. I am Cao Yong,' Yong replied, feeling a hint of gladness at this overture.

Robby leaned over and peeked at Yong's sketchbook, saying something to the effect of 'What are you doing?' or 'Cool! Fantastic!' Thumbs up accompanied by a smile must mean the same thing the world over.

Fascinated, Robby turned the pages of the sketchbook. 'Did you draw all of these?' he seemed to be asking, pointing at Yong.

'Yes, I drew them,' Yong replied with a nod.

Robby let out a deep breath and shrugged. Yong couldn't understand his English, and of course Robby didn't comprehend Yong's Chinese. They spoke to each other, but most of their words kept missing the mark. The only certain thing was that they were becoming friends. When it grew dark, Yong offered to share his jacket with Robby. That night the two of them slept nestled against each other for the first time.

'Caoyong, Caoyong.'

Yong was sitting on the riverbank in the morning light, stomach hollow and feeling light-headed, when he heard Robby's voice. Robby brought him the dented aluminium cup that always hung from his waist and offered it to Yong: it was half-filled with milk.

'Drink it,' he urged.

Yong drained the cup dry. He felt the strength flow back into his body as he digested the much-missed protein. Robby bent over to look at him, then laughed and retrieved the cup. Robby appeared to have been living at the Pashupatinath for quite a while. Although he looked almost like one of the Babas, in fact they were cleaner and healthier.

Yong had decided to part with the down jacket that day – it was all he had left to sell. Although it was worn out and torn, and the stuffing was coming out of the sleeves, he thought he could probably exchange it for a little food. Feeling slightly better for having drunk the milk, he walked to the stalls to try his luck, but everyone he appealed to shook their heads and laughed mockingly when they saw the dirty jacket.

Yong went back to the restaurant where he'd bought food on his first day in Kathmandu. The owner looked shocked at his appearance. He took the jacket and put it to one side, then, without a word, took several deep-fried cakes off a shelf and placed them in Yong's hands. Yong was wearing only his long underwear, which he'd cut short with a knife borrowed from the Babas because it was so hot. Following their example, he'd tied the rest of his possessions around his waist with scraps of his underwear cut into thin strips: he was a pitiful sight.

While gnawing on the cakes, Yong couldn't suppress a feeling of uneasiness when he thought about how light he was travelling now, with nearly all his belongings gone. *What am I going to do?*

When he returned to the Pashupatinath, he saw that Penis Baba must have just finished performing his great feat again for the tourists, for he was counting a bundle of notes behind a shrine where no-one could see him, and he hastily stuffed the money into his loincloth when he noticed Yong.

'You are really something,' Yong told him in admiration. 'Do you reckon I could do it with mine?' he asked, gesticulating to indicate the trick with the stone.

'Show it to me.'

Yong motioned the Baba over, pulled down his underwear and showed him his penis. The Baba took it in his grubby hands and looked it over, front and back, before sighing in disgust and tossing it back.

'I spent a long time training mine,' he seemed to boast, thrusting his chin out with pride. He pulled his own penis out from the vermilion loincloth to show Yong. It was indeed very big and long.

'So mine is no good. Shit!' Yong went back to the shrine, where he slept for a while and then began sketching the temple again.

Robby returned at dusk. Entering the shrine, he smiled at Yong. 'Hey, what happened to your jacket?' he was evidently asking.

'This is what.' Yong showed him the crumbs of half-eaten cakes, and Robby laughed.

'Don't you have any money?'

'It's all gone.' Yong turned out his pocket to show him.

'You idiot! You've got this, haven't you?' Robby cried out and snatched up the sketchbook. 'Look at these! Pictures! These are money, you know! These will fill your stomach!' Robby spoke animatedly, gesturing impatiently to show a full stomach.

'A sketchbook will fill my stomach?'

As soon as morning came, Robby woke Yong and they went into the city together. Robby took Yong down a street of cheap guest houses in the centre where a group of Westerners was hanging around outside.

'Okay, give me that sketchbook,' Robby gestured to Yong. He promptly called out something to the Westerners and began to show them the sketchbook.

'Amazing!' The group of people examined the drawings closely, all speaking at once, occasionally shifting their gaze to Yong.

'This is bullshit, right? Did this dirty-looking Sherpa here really draw them?'

'He really did. I see him sketching every day,' Robby explained eagerly. At first the group seemed to give him a lukewarm reception, but then they began to listen more attentively.

'Okay, let's go,' Robby prompted Yong, and they went inside the guest house. Next to the window there was a rough chair and table where one young Westerner sat writing. Robby caught his attention and asked him something. The young man turned over the pages of Yong's sketchbook, said, 'Okay' and disappeared up the creaky stairs. Robby looked pleased and smiled at Yong. Soon the man came racing back down with several sheets of white paper in his hand. He handed them to Robby along with some pencils. Robby clapped him on the shoulder.

'Look here, we've got paper!' he said to Yong.

Robby seems to be telling me to draw some pictures. Yong picked up the high-quality white paper, but his fingers left grubby marks on it; horrified, he rushed into the courtyard to wash his hands under the tap. Robby looked hard at his own hands and followed Yong's example. Their eyes met and they laughed. The others in the guest house laughed loudly at the sight of Robby and Yong going to great pains to shake their hands dry. One of the girls lent them a handkerchief. Hands clean at last, Yong solemnly took the drawing paper.

'Look, there're pencils too.' Robby showed him the pencils in several different colours as if to say, 'Draw pictures on this paper, then you'll be able to fill your stomach.'

I have to find something to use as a drawing board. Yong looked around and saw a broken pane of glass propped up by the window. He wiped the dust off the glass and placed the paper on it. Just the thing. Robby laughed and patted his shoulder.

Right then, I'll start drawing. I still don't know what'll happen after that, but I do know one thing – it'll lead me to my next meal!

They stood before the temple that had caught Yong's eye on his first day in Kathmandu, the one he'd wanted to sketch ever since. It rose magnificently in front of them.

'That's it. That's what I'll draw.' Yong placed the paper on the glass and sat down. He was thrilled to be using the beautiful foreign coloured pencils. At once he focused his concentration and effortlessly drew lines on the fine-quality paper.

'Oh, great! It's beautiful!' Robby sat alongside him clasping his knees, watching as Yong sketched, exclaiming excitedly every so often. A crowd soon gathered to watch this odd pair, wondering what they were doing. Some tourists also wandered over, and Nepali policemen as well. A wall of people formed in front of Yong, but Robby jumped up and briskly moved them on.

'Excuse me, don't stand there. You're getting in the artist's way.' It was the first time Yong had seen Robby this animated.

Yong sweated under the hot sun as he poured all his energy into drawing. Robby went and filled his aluminium cup with water and handed it to Yong. The day's food depended on it, so he was literally drawing for his life. By sunset, three sheets of paper had been transformed into three pictures.

'Okay, let's rest.' Robby patted Yong's shoulder and smiled at him. 'Caoyong, you go to the Pashupatinath and wait there for me.' *Pashupatinath* was the only word they both understood. Robby took the three pictures and disappeared in the direction of Thamel, where the luxury hotels were located.

When Yong returned to the small shrine and lay down, he felt fiercely hungry. On top of having drunk only water and barely eaten, he'd been drawing all day and now he felt dizzy. *If I draw then I can fill my stomach, surely that's what Robby said. Did I misunderstand? Why did Robby take the pictures?* It was completely dark now. Yong couldn't sleep for the growling in his stomach. *It's late and he still hasn't come back. What's Robby doing? Where the hell did he take my pictures?* Worried and impatient, Yong couldn't stand it anymore, so he got up, walked over to the bridge and stared down the street that led into the city. The row of small shops and restaurants across the Bagmati were all closed. Looking at the quiet street, Yong suddenly felt anxious. *Won't I be getting anything tonight after all?*

He sat down on the riverbank, hunched over with disappointment. Mosquitoes buzzed around his body as he stared at the candlelight from the temple reflected on the water. From the row of stone cremation platforms, wisps of smoke were rising from the ashes of bodies burnt earlier that day. Behind the platforms was a stone-pillared building where the elderly and sick lay waiting to die. Stray dogs wandered around the area. Sounds of their howling, faint groans from the sick and the clearing of throats echoed through the darkness.

Over a week had passed since Yong had arrived in Kathmandu. He thought of his mother back home. *How poor we were, and we kids wolfed down food like stray dogs from the single plate that Mama filled. We didn't have any sense, so when there wasn't much food left, we'd each spit on it to try to get it for ourselves. Sometimes we'd fight, and the plate would fall to the floor and break. Mama never ate anything – just a bowl of rice. She always looked at us and turned away so we wouldn't see her tears. I wonder how she is?*

Yong heaved a long sigh. These last few days he'd been

troubled by diarrhoea; this, in combination with the fatigue of sketching, had sapped his strength entirely. *But today the diarrhoea settled down a bit at last. There's nothing left to come out, I suppose.* He staggered to his feet, about to go back to his sleeping place, when he caught sight of a solitary figure walking quickly towards him. *It's Robby ... he's come back!* In a flash Yong's spirits lifted, and he raced across the stone bridge.

'Caoyong! Caoyong!' Robby hugged Yong tight. 'I sold the pictures. We've got some money!' Robby took Yong under a streetlight and, hands trembling with excitement, pulled some notes out of a cloth bag hung around his neck. 'Caoyong, we did it!' Robby put the foreign notes, one by one, into Yong's hands.

Are these US dollars?! Yong gaped at the notes he was seeing for the first time.

'I'm starving. I bet you're hungry too.' Robby grinned, then looked around. There wasn't a single shop still open. 'Okay, okay, wait one second,' he said, and went and banged loudly on the iron door of one of the closed shops. Silence was the only reply. Yong joined Robby, and together they banged on the doors of each shop in turn. There was no reply from any of the restaurants, but a sleepy Nepali youth finally emerged from one of the shops. He sold them a packet of biscuits and a tin of canned beef, and the pair sat down on a log beneath a streetlight to eat. They forced the tin open with a knife and crammed their mouths with biscuits. Tears of joy ran down their faces. It was the most delicious food Yong had eaten since coming to Kathmandu, and he devoured his share in no time. But still his stomach rumbled.

'Let's knock again and buy more,' he motioned to Robby.

'Caoyong, we can't. Tomorrow we have to buy paper and paints with the rest of the money.' Robby looked Yong in the face and spoke seriously.

'I sold two pictures. There's still one left. Tomorrow we'll sell it.'

'All this money for two pictures?!' Yong looked at Robby in disbelief. But at least there was food in his stomach, and that night he slept well.

When Yong awoke the next morning, there was no sign of Robby. Crawling outside, Yong spotted Robby on the riverbank holding a fragment of broken mirror in one hand as he concentrated on shaving off his beard with the other.

'Hi! Good morning.' Wiping his face with a dirty cloth as he climbed up the bank, Robby looked quite different. In fact, with his hair smoothed down and the beard shaved off, he could've been mistaken for another much younger person. Yong was delighted by the transformation.

'Let's go and buy paper and paints,' Robby suggested enthusiastically.

Yong nodded eagerly in reply. *I get it. We have to have enough money to buy materials. If not, then we just eat up the lot. Today we do the same as yesterday. And if we keep at it, then we might make heaps of money.*

'Okay, then, let's go into town. The first thing, though, is to eat.'

Carrying the glass pane between them, they went into the city. Robby bought a cup of milk and gave it to Yong with a biscuit.

'I'll go and get the paper and paints. You wait here.'

Yong sat down on the steps of the temple he'd drawn the previous day and waited for Robby to return. While he was waiting, several tourists from Hong Kong entered the temple grounds. '*Ni hao*!' Yong flashed them a grin. They stopped in surprise on hearing him speak Chinese.

'Do you have a dictionary? An English–Chinese dictionary?' Yong was holding the drawing left over from the previous day. He was full of confidence. *Yesterday I got all that American money for the other sketches, so it should be easy to exchange this one for a dictionary.*

'An English–Chinese dictionary? I do have one. But … what do you want it for?'

'I just need it. Hey, you wouldn't exchange it for this, would you?' He held out the drawing to show them.

'That's this temple! It's lovely. Who drew this?'

'I did.' Yong laughed and pointed at himself.

'You're kidding!' They looked Yong up and down disdainfully. Reflected in their eyes was a small, filthy, young Chinese man who looked like a beggar with his torn, dirty underwear, strange objects fastened to his waist by dirty strings and oversized climbing boots that flapped open.

Yong felt a bit put out by their reaction. 'This is my sketchbook. Take a look.'

They turned the pages and finally seemed convinced. 'You really are an artist. Incredible! Do you live in Tibet?'

'Er … how about it, will you exchange the dictionary for the picture?'

'All right. You're sure it's an English–Chinese dictionary you want?'

'Yes, I need one.'

The young man who made the exchange was delighted with the picture.

'Have you only got one? I want one too. I'll buy one,' another member of the group offered.

'I've only got one at the moment. If you want another, come back here again tomorrow.' *Now I can talk to Robby using this dictionary. Our business starts today!*

Robby returned a short while later with a stack of drawing paper under his arm and handed it to Yong. He also had paints and pencils. Robby was pointing to the paints and trying to explain something when he noticed Yong's English–Chinese dictionary and flung his arms around Yong's shoulders, laughing delightedly. Robby flipped through the pages.

'Water. Colour. Paints.'

Aha! The colour of water. Yong was elated at learning the English word for the first time.

'Can. You. Paint.'

Um, Robby is asking me if I can paint watercolours. Yong hastily turned the pages of the dictionary, searching for the words to answer: 'Of course!' He immediately began to paint the temple. Robby had told him that a watercolour picture would fetch a much higher price; thanks to the dictionary, the scope of their conversations was expanding tremendously. When three new paintings were ready, Robby again told Yong to wait while he went to sell them. He returned much more quickly than he had the previous night, having exchanged the paintings for US dollars and Nepalese rupees. Robby then took Yong into a pharmacy, explained something to the shop assistant and bought a box of medicine with some of the money.

'Caoyong. Your stomach's bad, isn't it? This is medicine.' It seemed Robby was aware that Yong had diarrhoea. Yong was touched by his thoughtfulness.

They went into a restaurant that, until then, they'd only glanced at as they'd passed by. It was a smart place where foreign travellers gathered, but when Yong stiffened nervously, Robby put his arm around his shoulders and ushered him in.

The owner stared at them incredulously, then walked over. 'May I help you?'

Robby was a well-known character in the area – the strange American who'd been living in Kathmandu for ages – but when the restaurant owner shifted his gaze to the equally dirty Yong standing beside him, his eyes showed contempt. Robby, however, proudly introduced Yong to him, showing him Yong's sketchbook and flashing the wad of notes. The owner's attitude immediately became deferential, and he respectfully showed them to a table at the back.

'Caoyong, let's eat beefsteak!' Robby said as he looked at the menu.

'Beef?'

Robby flicked through the dictionary. 'Here it is.'

'Beef. Cow meat.' *Beef means cow meat ... beef ... beef.* Little by little, Yong was learning English.

Their business flourished. They sold watercolours for around 30 US dollars each, sometimes selling five or six a day and making over 200 dollars. They wasted no time in buying themselves some new clothes. Robby became the consummate businessman and held his head high in his new outfit. The Babas at the Pashupatinath were baffled by the pair's transformation.

'Oy, what've you two been up to?' One evening, Penis Baba and some others came over to them and stared closely at the smart new jeans and shirt that Yong was wearing.

'Is it this?' Penis Baba asked with a suspicious look on his face, miming lifting up the rock with his penis to show what he meant. It seemed he was afraid they might be trespassing on his professional territory.

'No, he's a great artist,' Robby explained. He showed the Babas the sketchbook, and Penis Baba looked at Yong with amazement.

'It's true. I've often seen him drawing,' the Baba next to him said.

'Okay. You no problem!' Penis Baba smiled and embraced Yong.

The two young men sat down in the little shrine, and Robby spread out their takings to show Yong. By the light of a candle set on the lingam, they found that they had more than 500 dollars.

'Caoyong, this is your share.' Robby handed 300 dollars to Yong.

'No, Robby, we go halves. Half,' Yong repeated, and Robby accepted with an 'okay'. His eyes were moist.

'Caoyong, we can really make a go of this. Let's open a gallery. We can make it your combined gallery and studio!'

'Gallery?'

'Yes! Caoyong! We can be rich! We can have houses anywhere! We can buy a big car and go around the world. Hey, wouldn't it be fantastic to keep going west and reach

Africa?' Excitedly, the pair dreamt up big plans that now seemed to have every chance of being realized.

The next day they rented lodgings in Thamel, the luxury-hotel area where rich tourists stayed. They'd amuse themselves in the mornings, and in the afternoons Yong would paint while Robby went around the hotels selling paintings. Sometimes he'd bring back a group of Westerners to their room, which was becoming like a gallery with pictures hanging on the walls.

'Did he really paint all these?' In disbelief, people would stay to watch the puny young Asian man at his work. On these occasions his paintings always fetched high prices.

One day, Robby came back to their lodgings carrying a large wooden box of oil paints that he'd ordered from a Nepali trader who often went to India. 'Caoyong, look what I got! It's your speciality – oil paints!'

'Robby, you're incredible!' Yong squeezed some of the foreign-made oil paint onto his finger and gazed at it entranced.

Robby also had a tradesman make up an easel and canvases and frames for the pictures as quickly as possible, while he busily set about making alterations to the 'studio'. When the easel was placed in the centre, the room was transformed; when they hung several framed paintings on the walls, the atmosphere changed completely. The place became a high-class gallery.

'Robby, I feel like I've just become a great artist.' Yong sat proudly in front of his easel.

*

A few days later, Yong and Robby were awakened early in the morning by a loud knocking on the door. Robby threw on some clothes and sandals, and turned the key in the lock. Abruptly the door was pushed open and three policemen burst into the room.

'You! You don't have a passport, do you?!' the policemen barked out in English, looking at Yong. Robby stood between the two of them as if to protect him, and answered something back.

'This man is an illegal immigrant. He will be deported.'

Robby looked at Yong in surprise but then quickly pulled some dollars from his pocket and put a hundred into each policeman's hand. The policemen glanced at the money and cocked their chins arrogantly at Yong: 'We won't arrest him today, but get out of here fast! Next time there'll be no mercy!'

Yong cast back in his mind. Recently he'd spoken with some Chinese he'd met on the street who'd come to Nepal to work, glad of the chance to use his native language after such a long time. *They might have figured out I don't have a passport. Is this all because of them?* His face paled at the memory.

When the policemen disappeared, Robby rapidly began packing their things. 'Caoyong, let's get out of here!'

Yong had been standing there stunned, but he came to and set about gathering everything together. They moved to different lodgings, but Yong stopped going out whenever he felt like it for fear the police might return.

'Caoyong, it's all right. We can save our money and get out of here.' Robby was smoking marijuana and muttering as if he was delirious. Yong began to realize how serious their situation was. Robby was spending more and more time in a grass-induced haze.

Once again there was an early-morning knock on the door. It was one of the same policemen as before.

'The boss knows about you! Why are you still here? Didn't he say there'd be no mercy next time?!'

Robby tried to argue.

'If you don't want to be arrested, pay me!' He intended to make a bit on the side. Robby pulled two hundred-dollar notes from his pocket, but the policeman shook his head and didn't move. When two more were handed over, he left with a satisfied grin. Yong sat down on his bed, his shoulders drooping.

'Caoyong, hey, cheer up.' Robby gave him a hug.

But a few days later, the young policeman was back, demanding another bribe. Yong's eyes filled with tears at the sight of Robby cajoling the guy – if they were going to be continually squeezed like this, everything would be for nothing. *All the money we earn will go down the drain.* When Yong started packing his things in earnest, Robby didn't say a word.

'Robby, I'm going back to China. This is my address.' Yong handed Robby a piece of paper. 'I'll write. Will you go back to America? Give me your address there.'

Robby shrugged his shoulders and laughed wryly. Silently, he picked up the dictionary, then looked at Yong. 'There's nowhere in the world I call home. My parents divorced when I was small. My father took me, but he died when I was five. My mother had a new family and more children. I was raised in my uncle's house. My uncle loved only his own children and hated me, so I ran away when I was thirteen. Since then I've gone from one job to another. I've been wandering the whole time. I haven't got a home to go back to.'

Robby stood up and went out to the veranda. Yong was about to go over to him when he noticed that Robby, hunched over his cigarette, was crying.

Later Robby left without saying anything more. When he returned that night, falling-down drunk and raving incoherently, he fell into Yong's arms. Yong removed Robby's shoes and clothes and put him to bed, where he soon began to snore. Yong stared at his thin back for a long time.

Next morning, Yong stood beside Robby's bed, holding his luggage and looking at his friend's sleeping face. From his pocket he pulled the money that he and Robby had earned, then extracted all the hundred-dollar notes from the wad and gently slipped them under Robby's pillow. Robby didn't stir. Yong locked the door behind him and left.

Yong hitched a lift in a truck headed for the Himalayas, and the Nepal–China border drew closer. *The border! Such a cruel line dissecting those giant ranges, up there in those beautiful snowy mountains. All our dreams, all our hopes … destroyed by the border!* Yong's eyes were glued to the magnificent peaks before him as tears streamed down his face.

When he returned to Lhasa in the autumn, not only did Tibet University refuse to give Yong work, they withheld the monthly salary of 180 yuan from this delinquent teacher who was always wandering off. Yong considered selling his paintings to foreigners as he had done in

Kathmandu. But China wasn't open to foreigners then; it was not only difficult but also dangerous to have contact with the few outsiders there.

Yong had a girlfriend from his university days, and at some point she visited him in Lhasa and they married. But she couldn't get used to the city and soon became ill, so he was now not only poverty-stricken but trying to support a sick wife.

Painting isn't my only talent. But I can't paint if I can't even make a living. Okay, then, I'll go into business – old ladies and illiterates make money from business, don't they? I should be smarter than them! Right, I'll make some money, and then I can paint again. Racking his brains for a way to make money, he recalled the peacock feathers he'd seen in Zhangmu and Nepal. *That's it! Peacock feathers were selling for 2 yuan each at the White Peacock Art World and big department stores in Beijing when I went to see that European exhibition. I could sell peacock feathers from Lhasa down there. I wouldn't have to invest much, and the return would be good.* The only problem was, he had no capital. But then he remembered his meeting with the trader Phuntsok in Zhangmu. Phuntsok was in the business of supplying the Barkhor with peacock feathers. He knew that Yong had sold pictures in Nepal and trusted him. So, promising to split the profits fifty-fifty, Yong borrowed tens of thousands of peacock feathers and headed for Beijing with them stuffed into hemp bags.

There was a long tradition of trading in Tibet. Each year when the barley harvest was brought in, one man from each household would set out to trade. The traders would form caravans of mules, yaks and camels, and travel south to

India, north to Mongolia and east to China. They took musk, sheepskins, salt, gold dust, furs and Chinese caterpillar fungus to exchange for cigarettes, silver ingots, horses, bricks of compressed tea, tools, Russian silk, Japanese matches and American perfume. Under Chinese rule this trade was strictly controlled, but many traders continued with their business, using their contacts to get around the law. The Party naturally regarded such trade as smuggling, and anyone caught under the policy of 'strike at economic criminals' was severely punished. Those who turned their hand to commerce were almost all Tibetans and Hui.

In Beijing, Yong went around various shops and hawked the peacock feathers at prices ranging from 5 jiao to 1 yuan. Most peacock feathers in Beijing came from Yunnan, because the Tibetan route was still unknown. They sold like hotcakes in privately run shops, general stores, university kiosks and department stores. Yong made thousands upon thousands of yuan, and returned to Lhasa in high spirits.

Phuntsok was delighted but unfortunately passed the good news on to other Tibetans, who also started taking stocks of peacock feathers to Beijing, selling them for around 2 jiao per feather. The market was soon flooded.

Yong's next enterprise was to take Indian bracelets and perfumes to Chengdu, but he only managed to break even. However, by chance he also had with him a sample of *raxa* cloth from India that he showed to buyers. It was actually fake, but when the clothing factory in Chengdu saw it, they agreed to buy more for 22 yuan per metre.

Yong sent five or six bags of the cloth to the factory on a

trial basis and received a good response. Immediately he started transporting *raxa* to Chengdu and bringing Sanjiao cigarettes back to Lhasa on the return journey. He was now transporting goods on a large scale, so in addition to Phuntsok, he involved another Tibetan called Thoden. Yong used their capital in return for acting as their negotiator, since they couldn't speak Chinese. They obtained *raxa* in Zhangmu in exchange for Chinese-made shoes, thermos flasks and pencils. The *raxa* they bought for a few yuan per metre sold for at least a dozen yuan per metre. On the return journey from Chengdu they hid cigarettes by covering them with biscuits. Cigarettes were a government monopoly, hence strictly regulated, and it was prohibited for individuals to trade in them, so sometimes the smuggling ring had to pay bribes to avoid being caught and having the cigarettes seized. Everything was transported along the Sichuan–Tibet Highway.

Despite making a lot of money, Yong felt a gaping void in his life. Whenever he met his artist friends, his heart felt ripped in two. Sometimes he tried to draw, but with his head full of business worries, he couldn't concentrate. Even though he was now able to obtain paints, an easel and everything else he needed, he simply stared at them, feeling totally ashamed of himself.

He went home to show his parents how prosperous he'd become. His father was furious when he learned what Yong was up to: 'What are you doing with those dirty smugglers? You fool!' Even then, Yong's father still worshipped Mao Zedong.

'In Tibet you have to do this kind of thing; otherwise you can't survive!'

'That's enough! You take your work seriously and set a good example as a model teacher!' Yong's visit ended in a huge quarrel with his father.

Yong struggled with his dilemma. But it wasn't easy to break away from his business partners.

Then he found himself under investigation. In 1986, the government of the TAR established the Office to Identify and Strike at Economic Criminals; numerous campaigns were spasmodically launched in China, and the 'strike at economic criminals' campaign was one of them. Somebody had informed on Yong, and the new office lost no time in opening an investigation into his crimes, since he bought guns, rode around on a motorbike and drove a Beijing jeep.

That spring, Yong bought a horse in Shigatse and fled to Ali. His idea was to make reproductions of the frescoes there while hiding out. Although that was the background to his visit, he of course became totally captivated by the place. When he returned to Lhasa, the storm from the 'strike at economic criminals' campaign had blown over. Yong completely washed his hands of business. 'Ten-thousand-yuan households' were much talked about in China at the time, but Yong, who'd become one overnight, had already discovered what wealth meant. About the greatest pleasure he'd been able to have when he'd been in business had been to go with prostitutes.

With the money he'd made from smuggling, Yong was able to concentrate on his art at long last. He became a new man and began painting in a state of intoxication day after day. Possessed as he was by inspiration, the pictures simply poured out of him.

He began to sell his work in Lhasa. This wasn't easy, but the Australian manager of the Holiday Inn there, who was interested in art, gave him a contract and took the initiative to arrange for him to exhibit and sell his work in one of the hotel rooms.

Yong also showed several paintings in an exhibition at the Potala Palace Exhibition Hall. One of these works depicted a lama with several flies on his head. A German visitor stood in front of the picture and tried to brush the flies away with his hand. He subsequently bought the work for 4500 US dollars, an enormous sum in Tibet, where the monthly salary was less than 200 yuan.

After that, other artists in Lhasa became jealous. Whenever there were opportunities to exhibit, they'd shut Yong out, even refusing to let him enter his pen drawings in a competition for small-format illustrated storybooks. He was also excluded from contributing to a government-published collection of works by Tibetan artists.

The Chinese art world is full of trashy pictures like dog shit that only get shown because of the artists' connections. That lot are useless – they do nothing but act like government slaves or pander to fashion. My spirit won't let me be part of all that. Untouched by the other artists' jealousy, Yong secured Western collectors by means of his own resources, thus increasing his support base even more. And he began to plan his one-man exhibition in Beijing.

Sanya at night, silent as the grave. The clicking of geckos echoes through the seaside hotel where I lie inside my mosquito net. A cool wind blows sporadically through the latticed window of our bamboo hut.

Suddenly, something heavy envelops my body. I can't move. Oh, it's so heavy! I can't breathe. In the darkness I feel like a limp doll wrapped in seaweed: damp, clammy, cold. Two eyes shine. A chill runs down my spine. I try with all my might to move. I scream.

The light bulb sways and flickers.

'Aya, what's up? Are you okay?' Yong's worried face appears. He's sitting on my bed, and I notice that the mosquito net has fallen to the floor.

'You gave me a shock. I heard a scream, and when I got up there was this white thing rolling and thrashing about on the floor. I was scared … thought it was a ghost. So in a panic I screwed the light bulb back in and saw that it was you! You got caught up in the mosquito net. Don't you remember?'

My entire body is soaked in sweat. 'I'm the one who saw a ghost.'

Abruptly a voice calls from outside, 'What's happening!?' All the residents of the bamboo huts are awake. I must've let out a terrible scream.

'Sorry. No problem. Big mouse.' Yong goes outside and good-humouredly explains the situation. Everyone seems satisfied.

'That scream was so loud the whole hotel heard it,' he says.

'There really was a ghost. Maybe it was the spirit of someone who died along this coast.'

'It's that hash we smoked last night. You were hallucinating.'

24 May. A month has passed since we came to Sanya. Yong is constantly glued to the radio, listening to news of the student movement in Beijing: the pro-democracy demonstrations are building in strength. I've given up thinking about what we're going to do, or what will happen in the future, because whatever we decide never goes to plan.

We walk down to the beach in the evening, but tonight the ocean has a different look about it. A strong wind whips the South China Sea, turning the normally quiet deep-blue waters turbulent and leaden. The enormous, bird-like coconut palms rustle loudly in unison, while high up in the sky small black birds dance on the wind. Heavy, dark clouds advance from beyond the horizon and begin to fill the ash-blue sky. A typhoon is coming!

The storm arrives in the middle of the night, blowing off the roof of our hut and destroying the bamboo frame as if it were little more than matchsticks. We snatch up our belongings and follow one of the staff through the deluge to take refuge inside the steel-reinforced concrete hotel building. The power's been cut, and everywhere is pitch black. Flashes of blue-white lightning illuminate the room continuously.

'It's time to leave Sanya,' Yong says, lighting a candle. 'Let's send a telegram to Lhasa and find out what's happening there.'

When I throw off my soaking-wet clothes, I notice that my breasts feel awfully swollen. Come to think of it, I haven't had a period for a while either. Could it be? I feel the blood drain from my face.

27 May. We leave Sanya. Yong's brother in Lhasa has sent us a telegram saying that martial law still hasn't been lifted. We disembark in the desolate town of Hai'an and take a bus bound for Zhanjiang, where there's a railway. The battered old bus is jam-packed and we can't sit down. When we stop for a toilet break, my shoes get caked in mud. Then the wearying, bone-shaking journey continues.

When we finally reach Zhanjiang, the railway station is unusually deserted for China. We buy hard-seat tickets and catch a train to Liuzhou. This city lies on the way to our destination of Dali in Yunnan Province, a place the travellers in Sanya praised unanimously.

The train is also rather empty. I stare out at the evening, conscious of my tight painful breasts. I've tried to be careful about birth control, but apparently I've failed. It's odd, but even as I feel upset about being pregnant, my body feels strangely content.

'Do you want to have it?' Yong asks.

'I don't need a child. I want my body back to normal as quickly as possible.'

'Well, we aren't in a position to even help ourselves at the moment. If we had a baby now, it would only end in unhappiness.'

I think of the paintings confiscated in Beijing and sense that they're like children to Yong, dearer to him than any flesh-and-blood child could ever be.

30 May. The banks of the river that runs through Liuzhou are lined with willows. We take a room in a hotel not far from the station to rest after the non-stop journey from Sanya.

Next morning, we ask for directions to the People's Hospital. Yong assures me that it has the best reputation in Liuzhou. On arriving there by rickshaw, he pleads with the doctor to take particular care of me because I'm Japanese. As expected, a test confirms that I'm pregnant. I've been making out that it isn't such a big deal to have an abortion, but now that it comes to actually doing it – here in a Chinese hospital – I start to panic.

'Will you give me an anaesthetic?' My voice sounds feeble even to me.

'Anaesthetic? No, it's a simple procedure. You're not far gone, less than a month,' the woman doctor answers coolly.

I feel like fainting. Having an abortion is a run-of-the-mill occurrence in this country of birth restrictions.

'Don't worry. Everyone does it.'

If I don't have an abortion here, then I'll have to return to Japan. Otherwise, I'll be running around China with a big pregnant belly.

'That woman doctor is the oldest and most experienced specialist in the Obstetrics Department. It'll be okay,' Yong assures me.

The doctor, in her fifties, has a composed, dependable-looking face.

I look around the waiting room and see a girl who's just had a termination sitting on the long bench, her mother's arms around her. She's younger than I am and not even crying, just sitting there silently. In China there's no sense of sin or guilt about having an abortion; there's no need for grief. Japanese and Chinese bodies are the same. If Chinese women can do it, I should be able to as well. This thought helps my resolve to go through with the operation. I sit on the bench and wait to be called.

Yong squeezes my hand.

Prompted by the doctor, I enter a large room with a dozen or so operating tables for abortions arranged in rows along two sides, so that several women can lie waiting at the same time with their legs spread open. Today, though, there's no-one else here. I lie down, open my legs and try to keep the lid on a growing feeling that I'm on the verge of losing control.

Presently the doctor comes along and, with a practised hand, inserts the forceps into my vagina. I scream from the pain and terrible humiliation. Seemingly unaware of my agony, she pokes around and plucks out the bud from my womb. Teeth clenched, I lift my head and see a blood-drenched lump of flesh pincered between the forceps. She throws it with a plop into an aluminium container.

'It's over. You can go now.'

I'm forced to leave the operating room straightaway. I

walk over to the door on shaky legs and lean against it to open it, whereupon Yong's face greets me; he's been glued to the other side, waiting. He carries me to the recovery room. He's saying something, but nothing makes any sense; I'm sobbing uncontrollably and oblivious to everything around me. Eventually, I calm down, and we take a rickshaw back to our hotel.

'I've really been through the wringer this time.' I fall onto the bed and start crying again.

'Why doesn't anything go right for us? I wish I could take your place.' Yong strokes my hair to console me. But there's nothing he can do. If only this nightmare would be over.

'At any rate, you have to eat something nutritious.' Yong goes out to the market and buys a live fish. He takes it to a restaurant near the hotel and has it steamed and lightly flavoured with ginger, leeks and salt.

On the second day, I'm able to get up and go for a walk. I notice that the weight Yong had put on while we were in Sanya is starting to fall away.

'Yong, let's go to Dali tomorrow.' In Dali there's something that can help me to forget my pain. From the travellers in Sanya we heard about the wild hemp that grows there.

'Can you travel already? Sure, I'll go and buy the tickets.'

Liuzhou has an atmosphere all its own; a mournful air hangs over the rows of willow trees along the riverbank.

'I suppose it's called Liuzhou because of all these trees,' I say, referring to the character *liu*, which means 'willow'.

'Now you mention it, there's a Chinese saying that goes

"Born in Suzhou, live in Hangzhou, eat in Guangzhou, die in Liuzhou",' Yong recalls. 'Liuzhou's coffins are famous.'

Maybe it isn't a coincidence that I had an abortion here. As we walk along the riverbank, I think of the tiny foetus plucked from my womb, about the size of a gecko, and pick a wild flower. That night, we hold a funeral for our little gecko in our hotel room.

2. DALI

3 June. 'What a beautiful place! This is really something!'
Yong exclaims at the sight of stone gates emerging dreamlike out of the morning mist.

We're immersed in a rustic scene of traditional houses
with tiled roofs and low eaves; an old man squatting by the
roadside is using a burning bundle of straw to singe the
bristles off a dead pig's skin.

Having spent a bumpy night on a bus from Kunming,
we've arrived in the tranquil old fortified town of Dali.
High up on a mountain plateau, Dali faces long, narrow
Lake Erhai. Some call the area the Switzerland of Asia. The
bus passes through the arched gate and comes to a halt.

'Hello, change money,' some Bai women call out in
English. Beautifully dressed in ethnic costumes, they
approach us despite the early hour to try and change
money or sell us local craft items.

We take a sunny room on the second floor of the Dali
Number Two Guest House. Showing Yong's work ID
enables us to stay at the Chinese citizens' price of 7 yuan
per night.

'How long are we going to be able to travel like this? I'm worried about our money running out.'

We pull out all we have and count it.

'There's the money left over from your exhibition-preparation fund, from the sales of the pictures that weren't confiscated … Put that together with my money and it comes close to 6000 US dollars. If we're careful, the two of us should be able to live on that for a year,' I say.

'It'll be all right. If we get stuck, I'll paint some pictures to sell.' Yong sounds full of confidence. Well, that's a relief, because if we use up all our money and discover we can't leave China, then he might very well have to do that.

Bai peasants move about the streets while elderly people sip tea and play chess at teashops inside stone arches. The literal term for 'marble' in both Japanese and Chinese is 'Dali stone', and I can see why; large quantities of local marble lie outside shops, and there are also many finished pieces – ornaments and so forth – for sale. Closer observation reveals that this marble is used everywhere: for small shelves in shops, the entrances to teashops and even tables. Unlike other Chinese cities, Dali appears to be brimming over with cultural activity: the beautifully embroidered costumes of the Bai people; indigo cloth with batik patterns; bright yellow cigarettes from Yunnan; glass and bamboo pipes; traditional wooden houses; even churches.

'Hui food!' Yong spies a Muslim restaurant and immediately goes inside. Large pots of tripe soup and the beef that's central to this cuisine are bubbling away gently. The meat is simmering in soy sauce and herbs, and doesn't look at all heavy or greasy; after tasting some, I can imagine eating a vast quantity of it. Yong polishes off several bowls of the soup, which glistens with globules of floating fat.

Back in our room, Yong listens to international broadcasts on his radio. 'Apparently the students have built a Goddess of Democracy statue in Tiananmen Square. Some have even been throwing eggs filled with paint at Mao Zedong's portrait there! It's that lot from the Central Academy of Art.'

Yong's eyes had shone with excitement as the demonstrations were building up; over time, however, his expression has gradually turned more and more sombre. The situation isn't as optimistic as it seemed at first.

'Hunger strikes are no use. Democracy – or anything like it – will never be achieved unless the students commandeer the machine guns and start firing at the government without asking questions first!'

In Beijing the heavy tread of troops enforcing martial law can already be heard.

4 June. Morning. I return from the communal shower to find Yong listening to the radio, his head in his hands.

'What's happened?'

He gives a start. 'The government has massacred the students.' His voice is trembling; his face is distorted with anger and grief. 'The fools! Stupid idiots! They should've known their hunger strike would come to nothing.' Yong continues listening to the radio, biting his lip so hard that it starts to bleed.

Tiananmen Square has been transformed into a killing field. Students and others, aged fifteen to seventy, are reported to have been slaughtered. The numbers may be in the hundreds, even the thousands. Our friends from Beijing are very likely amongst them.

'Ever since I was born, China has never been at peace – not once!' Yong is flushed and trembling.

'In the end it was the government who fired the machine guns without asking questions first, wasn't it?' I sigh in despair.

On the radio we hear prayers of condolence from Taiwan, cries of sorrow mourning the students' deaths. These fearless students and citizens had continued their protests under martial law, distributing leaflets, dashing off wall posters, finally erecting the Goddess of Democracy statue. At dawn today, tear-gas and bullets had suddenly been fired over their heads; the air had been filled with bursts from automatic guns, while tanks and armoured trucks had appeared in Tiananmen Square. The indiscriminate firing had continued almost until noon. The government had announced that there'd been no deaths, but more than three hundred were said to have died. The day had become 'Bloody Sunday'.

Individual lives carry very little weight in China, and since the beginning of history there have been many such cruel incidents, as if they're nothing out of the ordinary. The fact that this time events are being reported on around the world as they happen perhaps augurs well for change.

Yong continues to listen to the international broadcasts. We've come to Dali for rest and quiet after the abortion, but there's no chance of that now. Why is there never any peace in China!

'Both of our birthdays are in June,' I venture. 'Mine's on the sixth and yours on the ninth. Let's celebrate.'

'Birthdays ... I just came one step closer to death' is all Yong can say.

I decide to go out into the town by myself to look around the shops. Yunnan is famous throughout China for its cigarettes, with luxury brands such as Ashima, Yunyan and Hongtashan being indispensable gift items. Ordinary cigarettes cost 1 yuan a packet, but those manufactured in Yunnan can fetch up to 10 yuan a packet. Here at the site of production, however, they're cheap at 3 yuan 5 jiao. You can also find wild marijuana growing all over the city in cracks in the pavement. It's treated like any other weed; the Bai are always snacking from bags of marijuana seeds.

When we go into the city for dinner, Yong suggests that we take a walk. Leaving Dali behind, we see a peaceful scene of oxen plodding slowly through paddy fields spread beneath a golden sky, a trail of reddening clouds hanging in the distance. We're amazed to discover a profusion of marijuana growing along the path between the rice paddies. We've never seen so much before! Apparently it's left uncut because it's a perfect fertilizer for the crops. Sniffing the pungent odour brings back memories of ecstatic times, and we happily pick young shoots from the chest-high plants to fill our cloth bag. When we put our hands into the bag, it feels mysteriously hot.

Marijuana is a truly powerful plant.

Next day, the leaves have completely dried out in the highland air, and we roll them up in papers to smoke. You can climb up to the hotel roof from our windows, so we go up there and light our joints. I gaze up at the azure sky and see particles of light like snow come pouring down. I feel utterly free, as if I might fly off into the distant sky at any moment.

Back in the room, Yong turns on Voice of America again.

'I can understand why opium became so popular in China,' I speculate. 'There's no other way of escaping from the quagmire in this country except through drugs.'

Yong suddenly leaps to his feet and yells, 'Damn it! When will China ever have peace and quiet!' He grabs the radio and throws it against the wall with all his might.

It makes a splintering sound.

'It's broken now.'

'Yep, I think it's broken.' Yong makes a wry face, perhaps regretting this fit of temper.

But I'm totally blissed out. Whatever might be happening several thousand kilometres from here has nothing to do with me. We'd be better off enjoying the day while we can; it's so peaceful here in Dali.

We visit the weekly Bai bazaar, catching an early-morning bus to a place called Shaping. The market, like a barter exchange, has rows and rows of goods to delight the eye: chickens and ducklings, varicoloured fruits and vegetables, baskets of straw sandals, sugar cane. Bai arrive in droves carrying their wares in bamboo baskets on their backs. The market becomes increasingly crowded. Elderly people sit beneath broad, shady trees enjoying the cool breeze. At the food stalls, Bai men eat with great relish from plates heaped with some kind of finely chopped raw meat.

'What's that meat they're eating?' Yong asks one of the elderly men.

'Pork. You dip it in soy sauce with vinegar and chillies. Taste it.' The old man offers Yong a plateful, but he recoils from the raw meat swarming with flies.

'I didn't know they ate raw pork here. In Tibet I ate raw lamb and yak, but I'm scared of parasitic worms in pork.'

When we return to Dali, many small stalls have appeared at the roadside. One vendor sells candy sculptures of dragons and phoenixes. Spinning tops and sweets … there's a nostalgic feel about it all, reminiscent of the festivals we used to have in Japan. An old man sells books laid out on a piece of cloth he has spread at the roadside. Yong buys one and walks off, but the old man comes running after him.

'I'm sorry, I didn't give you enough change,' he apologizes.

'I don't believe it. Is this China?' Yong looks astonished. 'I've had people come after me yelling because I didn't give them enough, but this is the first time in my life that anyone's done something like give me money back because they took too much!'

Maybe it's because of Dali's isolated position – in a mountain basin at an altitude of 2000 metres – that the people don't lie or try to swindle outsiders like they do in other Chinese cities. The old people are absorbed in playing chess from morning to night, while the Bai women are busy selling their handicrafts to tourists. There are beautiful teahouses where you can enjoy delicious green tea, and the locals are so welcoming.

We walk out of the city to beautiful Lake Erhai, where

children are swimming and playing. In the distance, massive thunderclouds are billowing up in the clear blue sky.

'Look! There's a temple.'

A grove of large trees grows alongside a ruined temple; illuminated by the rays of the evening sun, it reminds me of the eerie landscapes by the German Romantic painter Caspar David Friedrich. The temple's stone gates are still standing and its external appearance is unchanged, but it's a hollow shell. There are no Buddhist images here, for they were all destroyed in the Cultural Revolution.

'This temple is beautiful. One day I'd like to build a house about this size in the woods and live off my painting.'

'I hope that day will come.'

'It will. I'm certain of it. One day I'll find some land I like and build a house there!' Yong declares passionately.

Since the radio broke, Yong has, not surprisingly, been anxious to know what was happening in Beijing, and as we walk through the town he pauses to watch the news on a television in a small shop. CCTV, the national television station, is transmitting what it calls 'the truth' about the counter-revolutionary violence. It's a far cry from the information coming from Voice of America and the BBC.

'Martial-law troops did not kill a single person in Tiananmen Square,' CCTV states emphatically. It calls Fang Lizhi, who's taken refuge in the American Embassy, a traitor. The announcers repeatedly condemn the 'insurgents' for damage they've inflicted on the PLA and praise the PLA's outstanding behaviour in difficult circumstances. Leaders of the student movement such as Wang Dan, Wu'er Kaixi and Chai Ling have fled, and participants are on the wanted list.

Despite the turmoil in Beijing, daily life continues almost uninterrupted in Dali. There are many shops catering for foreign tourists, and at some that sell Bai clothing and batik cloth, you can select material and have garments made up for you.

'The cloth here is good. Let's get some clothes made,' Yong decides and immediately sets about sketching some practical travelling outfits. Something tells me that this is another one of his talents, since he informs me that he also designed the crimson-coloured clothes he was wearing when I first met him in Xinjiang.

'I hate the clothes sold in China. I feel embarrassed wearing the same things as everyone else. That's why I make my own.'

Dali also has many restaurants catering to foreigners, and we often relax at a Tibetan café managed by a man from Shanghai. The extensive menu includes treats such as beefsteak with scrambled eggs, toasted sandwiches and apple pie. I'm delighted since I'm tired of Chinese and Hui food. At this café we always run into a bald young Frenchman whom the waitress has nicknamed 'Beansprout' because he only ever eats stir-fried beansprouts. Beansprout is a photographer. He takes black-and-white pictures with an old-style single-lens-reflex camera and develops them in his hotel room. One day he tells us about 'spacecake'.

'You can buy it at the Coca-Cola house. Just a little way down the alley over there.'

Spacecake is marijuana hotcake. Dried, crumbled

marijuana is baked into enormous aromatic hotcakes –
larger than a human face – which sell for 7 yuan each. We
eat some of this spacecake, then return to our hotel room
to follow up with our own joints. Now we're walking on
air! Through our window the evening sky unfolds; in a
gorgeous contrast, blue sky peeks through gaps in the
reddening clouds that shine golden at their edges. The
world looks beautiful and profoundly transformed.

Smoking marijuana dries the throat and stimulates the
appetite. Yong goes out and returns with a paper bag
containing some yoghurt and toasted sandwiches from the
Tibetan café. We've just started to eat when there's a sharp
knock on the door. Our breath catches and we look at each
other. I hastily wrap up the marijuana drying on the floor,
open the windows wide to chase away the smoke, then sit
on the bed munching on a sandwich as if nothing is amiss.
Yong opens the door apprehensively.

Seven or eight policemen barge into the room. They give
Yong a steely look and order him to show them his
identification.

Yong calmly takes out his personal and work IDs.

'When did you come to Dali?'

'4 June.'

'And before that?'

'I had business in Guangdong.'

'Is that right? Let's go, everyone.'

And they disappear – just like that. The smell of
marijuana permeating the room apparently didn't interest
them in the least. For some time after they leave, Yong,
who'd sobered up instantly, keeps an eye on the way they
went.

'They're searching for students who fled after Tiananmen.'

The winds from Beijing have finally reached here; apparently all hotels in Dali where Chinese citizens stay are being thoroughly searched. For policemen in pursuit of the 'insurgents' who started the student movement, offences like smoking marijuana are neither here nor there.

3. BACK TO TIBET

19 June. We leave Dali. Before we go, Yong stocks up on Yunnan cigarettes to use as bribes when he applies for his passport.

As expected, the search for students continues, and there are a number of checkpoints on the journey to Kunming. We see several students being dragged off the bus.

In Kunming the next morning we buy tickets to Luoyang from a scalper. We're going to see Yong's sister, Cao Qing, who should've received the documents sent by my parents to enable Yong to leave China.

23 June. We arrive in Luoyang. Cao Qing and her family are happy to see us despite our having arrived unannounced. Even though she's very busy with her baby son, she buys a carp and some lamb to cook us a special welcome meal. She hands us a letter from Japan. In order to reassure my parents, I'd written them an upbeat letter enclosing a carefully chosen photograph from Sanya to show how much fun I've supposedly been having. They'd been quite shocked by all that'd happened to me, but at

least if they thought I was well, it would have put their minds at ease. When I open the envelope containing the documents and read my mother's anxious letter, I nearly break down in tears at the thought of having caused her to worry.

China has been in constant tumult this year. Beijing is a whirlpool of confusion, and martial law is unlikely to be lifted there for some time. Foreigners are scrambling to leave China, package tours are being cancelled, and the whole world is raising its voice in condemnation of 'Bloody Sunday', while, in contrast, the people we meet on buses and trains keep their mouths tightly shut. Yet the Tiananmen Square affair – one of the major political incidents of the century – could be taken as our salvation: Yong's case is probably so insignificant that it has been pushed to one side.

'Look at this!' He's reading a three-day-old newspaper. '"Tibet is open, and parties of foreign tourists have begun to visit Lhasa."'

We've only just arrived in Luoyang, but he hastily begins preparing to leave again.

'Cao Qing, do you think you could you ask someone to get us hard-sleeper tickets to Xining in a hurry?'

Cao Qing helps us to procure tickets, and the next day we set off west once again.

Five days later we're in Golmud, standing stunned in front of the station.

'Shit! What the hell are we going to do now?' Yong explodes.

We've just heard that only foreign tour groups are being

allowed into Lhasa; individual travellers are still not permitted to enter. The newspaper article he read was in fact misinformation released by the government to calm the domestic situation in the wake of Tiananmen. Chinese news is always a mixture of lies and nonsense, which the uneducated peasants, who comprise 80 per cent of the population, probably swallow whole.

'Now we've come this far, we can't wait anymore. Just running away, going round in circles like this, isn't going to achieve anything. Let's go to Lhasa.'

'But I don't have a travel permit, do I?'

Yong tries to think of a way to get into Lhasa. There are bound to be many checkpoints on the Qinghai–Tibet Highway, but if I pretend to be ill with altitude sickness and only speak in monosyllables, maybe no-one will notice that I'm a foreigner. The fact that I don't have a travel permit issued by the Public Security Bureau is a problem, though.

We take a room in a small hotel directly across from the station, and Yong spends the whole day mulling over what to do.

29 June. Morning. Yong gets out of bed and says, 'Aya, let's go to the Public Security Bureau and get you a permit.'

'The Public Security Bureau?!'

My immediate reaction is one of misgiving, but then I think of Tiananmen Square and the fact that the affair of the exhibition must be on hold as a result. Without delay we get ourselves over to Golmud Public Security, housed in a small reinforced-concrete building only a short walk from the bus terminal. We pass through the gate, ask one of the employees where the travel-permit counter is, then proceed through the building to the office in the back. My heart thumps violently.

Just outside the office, Yong signals for me to wait by the door and enters alone, a nonchalant look on his face. 'A permit for Lhasa, please,' he says to the middle-aged official sitting behind the desk. He produces his employment and identification papers, upon which the official promptly pulls out a form and begins making up the document.

'Where are you from, then?' he asks casually.

'Henan. I'm one of the "Youth Assisting Tibet". I came to work at Tibet University after I graduated. Oh, and I have a favour to ask. I plan to take my fiancée with me to Lhasa, but the thing is, she completely forgot to get herself a letter of introduction … And, well, I'm sorry to trouble you, but would you mind putting an entry for her in my travel permit, please?'

The official shoots a quick glance at me standing by the door.

'Aha, what's her name?'

'It's He … er, He Cai,' Yong says, nearly giving my real name in Chinese but changing it just in time.

'Okay, this should be all right.' The official finishes writing out the permit and hands it over.

'Thank you, Sir.'

We take the permit and calmly leave the building, keeping our mouths tightly shut, but, once there's a safe distance between us and Public Security, we look at each other and whoop loudly.

'He didn't have any doubts at all! Look, he's written your name in here too, Aya!'

There in the travel permit, next to Yong's name, is written 'He Cai', the Chinese name he made up as a bluff.

'When we get to Lhasa, I'll show Public Security that newspaper article and say I was convinced that martial law had been lifted. Then I'll get a passport somehow.'

We feast on lamb in a Muslim restaurant, preparing ourselves to plunge back into Tibet.

30 June. At noon we catch a bus bound for Lhasa. The only other passengers are Chinese and Tibetan. I gaze out at the scenery and take care to keep my voice down. Early summer in Tibet is pleasant and refreshing; blank-faced yaks sprawl on the grass beneath a limitless blue sky, and the land is green with thick vegetation. I have no symptoms at all of the awful altitude sickness I experienced four months ago.

It was a major decision for Yong to take me back into Lhasa under martial law. If the worst happens and we're discovered en route, he will well and truly be headed for prison. Even if the affair of his Beijing exhibition doesn't come to light, just the business with the travel permit would be enough to put him in gaol. Once again I'm overcome by the feeling that we're walking on thin ice.

The first checkpoint is at Budongquan. A young PLA soldier boards the bus and checks the identification and travel permits of all of the passengers in turn. We nonchalantly show our permit and get through the inspection without incident.

'I didn't realize checks were still this strict even after four months. Martial law has gone on for ages this time. Tourism companies won't be getting any business, I bet,' Yong sighs.

In March, when we'd escaped from Tibet, there'd been a rumour going around that the Dalai Lama was going to send military planes to attack the PLA. With the United States and other countries imposing sanctions on China after Tiananmen Square, the Tibetan independence movement found new inspiration. Hence the prolonging of martial law.

In the evening we arrive at Amdo. We eat a meal at a restaurant and rest in our lodgings. I have no nausea at all and sleep well.

1 July. Early morning. The bus crosses a mountain and passes through grassland. Just before Lhasa there's a roadside checkpoint.

'This is the last one,' Yong whispers.

So far, the checkpoints have all been manned by young PLA soldiers, but the official at this one wears a different uniform: he's a senior Public Security policeman. Yong shows him our travel permit, and he stares at it wordlessly. The silence seems to go on forever.

'Where's your ID? Show it to me!' the policeman suddenly demands of me.

I break out in a cold sweat and wait for Yong to come to the rescue.

'I'm very sorry, but my wife has lost her ID ... Here's mine.' He hurriedly thrusts his own identification and work ID at the policeman.

'I'm not asking you! Let her answer!' the official barks.

'Excuse us, but my wife has altitude sickness. She's not well.'

The policeman gives me a long, hard stare as I lean against the window feigning illness.

'My head hurts, altitude sickness …' I murmur in Chinese with my eyes closed. The policeman stands there for a while longer, then looks once more at our travel permit and turns on his heel, moving on to the next passenger. I make a show of my condition getting worse.

'Are you all right? Is the headache bad?' Yong asks me, playing along.

When the inspection is over, the policeman has one last look at us before getting off the bus. We wipe the sweat off our faces.

'That policeman was sharp. He thought there was something fishy about you as soon as he saw you.' Yong smiles weakly but looks scared all the same.

At dusk we arrive in Lhasa and go straight to Tibet University. Walking through the grounds to find Yong's friends, we pass by the teachers' dormitories. But for some reason Yong's old room – the one I saw in March – is nowhere to be seen.

'Wasn't your old room around here somewhere?'

The ground all round has been transformed into a pile of rubble. There's no sign of the room. Yong stands there in disbelief, a look of bitter grief on his face. 'Let's go,' he urges and walks off, as if tearing himself away. 'It's a message from Tibet warning me to get out of here fast.'

We can't find anybody we know, not Husheng and his wife, not Li Qinpu, not Pei Danfeng. It's the summer holiday and the place is deserted. We've nowhere to stay and naturally can't go to a hotel. On top of that, since we're afraid of getting Yong's brother, Cao Gang, into trouble, we're reluctant to go to his house. We'd been depending on being able to stay in Yong's old room.

'Cao Yong!' Turning around, I see a man about the same age as Yong.

'Well, if it isn't Shi Ming'er! What a surprise! How're you doing? It's been ages.'

Yong's spirits lift upon seeing this friend, a music teacher at Tibet University, and we go back with him to his room straight away. The room is filled with empty bottles rolling around on the floor. According to Yong, Shi Ming'er grabs for a bottle first thing every morning and his hands shake if he runs out of drink, but he has an easygoing, sunny disposition. Yong explains our situation, although obviously he can't tell a heavy drinker like Shi Ming'er the whole truth.

'Hmm, I see.' Shi Ming'er's face becomes serious as he makes tea. 'You've had a rough time. Stay in my room tonight. I don't mind crashing at my girlfriend's place.'

'Sorry about this, Shi Ming'er. Thank you. My place is just a heap of rubble now. I'll see what I can do tomorrow about getting another room. It looks like we're in for a long battle.'

2 July. Morning. We go to a restaurant not far from the university that serves Sichuan-style dumplings. Yong's a regular there.

'The dumplings here are famous,' he says. 'In just two or three years this shop has really grown. It even has branches now.'

Inside are several large round tables with round seats; on the shiny surface of each table are bottles of vinegar and soy sauce.

'Four bowls of boiled dumplings!' Yong orders loudly. Warm steam billows out of the kitchen. We've eaten nothing to speak of since the previous evening and are famished. A while later, four bowls full to the brim with boiled dumplings are plonked on the table in front of us. Yong goes to get a plate of chilli powder from the kitchen, and we add chilli, vinegar and soy sauce to the dumplings. We cram them into our mouths and instantly feel our energy reviving.

'*Kochi kochi kochi.*' Shaking their dirty bowls, a crowd of Tibetan children and old women has gathered to beg. I don't know what '*kochi*' means, but I hear it whenever Tibetans beg for something. Stray dogs also wait patiently under the table for scraps to drop. We sit in the midst of all this, silently eating our dumplings.

On the way back to the university, we see Yong's dog, Ahuang, sitting outside a butcher shop. She wags her tail at her master.

'Ahuang!' Yong calls out to her loudly, but Ahuang stays put.

'Ahuang!' When Yong races over to her, she quietly gets to her feet at last. Does she perhaps sense that Yong will soon disappear again? She follows him, her eyes cool and expressionless.

Yong goes to negotiate a room and succeeds in being assigned one immediately. For the time being, our home will be a room in one of the teachers' dormitories close to Husheng's place. In fact, it turns out that Husheng is in town. Apparently Xiao Mei has gone home to Beijing on a visit, but he has stayed behind.

Our room is about 5 square metres in total, part of a row built from concrete and dried mud bricks. Floating over from a small cowshed out in the back comes the sound of cattle lowing and the smell of manure. A concrete partition about two-thirds the width of the room divides it into two sections, with a dilapidated old steel-pipe bed in the back corner. We decide to use the front room as a kitchen and the back one for sleeping.

Outside in front, communal water pipes stick up out of the ground. Our neighbour to the right is a Han Chinese man, and to our left is a Tibetan family. The first thing we need to do is to give the room a thorough clean, so Yong fills several buckets and sluices them over the floor with a practised hand, then sweeps it roughly with a broom to get rid of the water. Such rough-and-ready cleaning methods are perfectly adequate in the dry climate of Tibet; all dirt and dust are swept away, and the floor dries quickly.

Just when we've managed to get a reasonable amount of cleaning done, Cao Gang and his wife arrive by car, having heard that we're here. They bring with them bedding, pots, a bicycle and other necessities, including a pressure cooker. For the moment we have everything we need.

In the evening, Yong buys food from the free-enterprise market and we prepare dinner in Husheng's room. All Chinese men are good cooks, it seems. Shi Ming'er makes a salad of finely sliced cucumber, Yong prepares stir-fried pork with garlic shoots, Husheng cooks stir-fried tomato and eggs, and in the blink of an eye the table is buried under a mountain of food. Each of these men has a determined pride in his cooking, and the spread they've produced is delicious. With our stomachs full for the first time in a long while, we can relax. Serious conversation begins, and Husheng quickly turns up the volume of the television. When people voice their true thoughts and feelings in China, they make sure there's no-one lurking outside and turn up the radio or TV to prevent their words being overheard and reported. You never hear anyone criticize the government in public.

Since Tiananmen Square, Yong has become even more cautious. Now that I speak Chinese, he worries that I'll say something careless. Whenever we're on trains or buses and I come out with statements like 'the Chinese government is really awful' or 'the Chinese government is frightening', he hastily cautions me, saying 'Keep your voice down.' Nor can I give too much detail in my letters to Japan for fear of the censors.

'Shi Benming came here, you know,' Husheng says, drinking his tea.

'Really?! Where is he now?'

'Well, I don't know. He stayed at my place for two nights a week ago.'

Shi Benming, the artist in whose house we'd stayed in Beijing and who'd helped Yong in various ways with his exhibition, is in Lhasa! At the end of February, he'd been shaken to discover that Public Security was investigating everyone who'd signed Chen Jun's petition calling for the release of political prisoners. 'If anything should happen, escape to Tibet. I'll introduce you to friends in Lhasa,' Yong had said to Shi Benming the day before we'd left Beijing.

'If Shi Benming fled as far as Lhasa, it means that Beijing Public Security must've been in hot pursuit.'

'Hmm, apparently almost all the others who signed the petition were arrested.'

'Chen Jun was deported.'

'Cao Yong, if you'd stayed in Beijing, you would've been done for.'

Yong and his friends discuss these and other sombre topics late into the night.

3 July. We go into town to buy some essential supplies: soy sauce, salt, light bulbs, white cloth, blue netting for making screens, insecticide, fly swats and so on. When we return home, we stick the cloth on the walls so that when we lean against them the colour doesn't come off on our clothes, and we put netting across the back window where flies from the cowshed can get in. Fixing the room up takes half the day. Around dusk, a figure suddenly appears at the entrance.

'Shi Benming!' Yong is overjoyed by this unexpected reunion. He asks about the situation in Beijing.

'Right after you two left, Public Security began arresting people who'd signed the petition. Some had their homes turned upside down. I left in a panic ...'

An unspeakable apprehension seizes me as I stroke Ahuang, who lies sprawled out on the floor.

5 July. Morning. Yong returns from seeing some of his contacts, his face ashen. 'Someone's informed on us!'

'Informed? What do you mean?'

'Apparently Public Security knows I brought a foreigner into the city.'

'We made it through all the checkpoints! How could they know?'

'I don't know. But maybe I should go and see them before they turn up here.'

Yong sets off for the Public Security Bureau with grim determination. How did they find out about me? His friends at Tibet University are hardly likely to have informed, and, apart from them, no-one else knows I'm here.

It's dark when he returns. 'Public Security want to charge me.' Glumly, he recounts his interrogation:

'Do you know what a crime you've committed? The Japanese girl will be deported immediately, and you will be detained.'

'We came because I read that martial law had been lifted. I never dreamed it was still in force.'

'There were checkpoints on the Qinghai–Tibet Highway, weren't there?! Exactly how did you get here?'

Yong couldn't let them know about the travel permit. 'We came by truck,' he answered off the top of his head.

'So who does this truck belong to, then? The one you came here on.' They began a tenacious cross-examination.

'Er … I don't remember the name. I think it was a Dong Feng truck from Gansu. Yes, I'm sure of it.' Yong maintained his balancing act, inventing the story as he went along and showing them the famous newspaper article. 'Look, it says here that Lhasa is open to travellers again.'

'Cut the crap! Martial law is still in force. We'll decide what action is to be taken in a couple of days. Until then, the Japanese woman will be kept under surveillance. You are to wait for our decision, and she is not to go anywhere!'

'Detained? Surveillance?'

'It's all right. I know a few of the Lhasa police.' But even as he speaks, Yong's face is tense.

The surveillance begins that night. Torches are shone into our windows, and several Tibet University security guards prowl around outside, relentlessly peeping in during the night.

'This is awful!' I say angrily. Yong says nothing in reply, but his look tells me that if this is all we have to put up with, then we are doing well.

7 July. Monday. The appointed day arrives. Yong rises early and leaves for the Public Security Bureau. He returns before

noon, bringing with him my favourite potatoes and cucumbers, as well as eggs and Chinese cabbage. His face is as white as a sheet. 'It's no good. They said that for me to leave China, I need to have permission from both Tibet University and the Chinese government of the TAR. I've heard that they've been restricting people leaving the country since Tiananmen. It's looking bad. I don't think I'll be able to get a passport.'

'What about deportation and detention?'

'A friend helped to wangle it so you'll just be kept under surveillance.'

'But at least you won't be going to prison – that's good, isn't it? And I'm not being deported. Isn't there any hope for a passport?' I don't really have a full understanding of the situation. Yong looks upset but doesn't explain further.

We go to Husheng's place, where the three of us share a simple meal of stir-fried cucumber and egg, with a salad of cucumber and Chinese cabbage.

Husheng teaches and researches Tibetan history and is also a very good writer. Having turned his living room into a coffee shop and billiard parlour in order to supplement his meagre salary, he was reprimanded by the university for running a business and forced to close down his amusement parlour. In his garden there's still a large billiard table he obtained from somewhere. The next plan he and his wife came up with was to use the washing machine in their garden to offer a laundry service for students. In Lhasa there are hardly any washing machines at all, and students have no means of washing their clothes other than by hand, so the business was a great success. So far the university hasn't found out about this venture. Husheng is shrewd in everything he does, though it seems there's one person he can't fool, and that's his wife, Xiao Mei.

Husheng listens attentively while Yong tells him about the passport situation.

'The first thing you need to do is get permission from the university. I'll write the letter for you.'

'Much appreciated. I was thinking that your writing skills were my only hope.' Since Yong isn't in the habit of reading newspapers or going to the university political-study sessions, administrative jargon is like Greek to him.

'You need to use reasonable language that will also touch the university president's heart,' Husheng tells him.

Yong and Husheng sit at the desk together and begin to compose a letter. Husheng racks his brains to think of the appropriate turns of phrase. Finally they finish.

'We've done it! Aya, we're ready to go! Husheng, I really appreciate this.' Yong's voice rouses me just as I'm dozing off on the sofa.

8 July. At nine in the morning exactly, Yong jumps out of bed and rides off on his bicycle, saying, 'I'm off to give the university president our letter.' An hour later he returns, announcing, 'They said they'll let me know in three days', before flopping back down on the bed and falling asleep again. I look at him lying there snoring and sigh over these incomprehensible Chinese procedures.

9 July. Yong is busy now from morning to night, running around frantically seeking a way to get a passport. I'm still under surveillance, prohibited from leaving the university grounds, and with someone always loitering nearby. Many

people in China specialize in surveillance, which they carry out with great enthusiasm and skill. Along with informing, this is a useful route to promotion. If you weren't paying attention, you'd never notice them.

I resolve to enjoy my life regardless. I amuse myself by sketching or painting, which has the effect of a tranquilizer. This surprises Yong, who asks me if I regard painting as fun; he always has some goal he wants to achieve with a painting and is relentless in its pursuit, whereas I paint to soothe my spirit.

Our only source for water is the communal supply, which is right outside our room. I can't wash myself all over, but in the Tibetan climate it doesn't matter. As the supply is cut off at night, every day I fill two large iron buckets. We wash plates and pans at the tap, and birds and dogs clean up any scraps of food. A 50-metre walk from our room is a Chinese-style toilet for 'chatting while doing your business'. The building is a simple construction of mud bricks and concrete, with a line of ten or so narrow rectangular holes and chest-high partitions between them. There are always dogs lying around inside, waiting to scavenge for faeces and urine. Yong hates this toilet.

'It makes me feel sick standing there with warm air coming up from where other people have just done their business. I never use it.'

'But where else can you go?'

'See that long grass over there? Sit in there, do what you have to do and watch the sunset at the same time. It's the best feeling.' Yong encourages me to relieve myself outside, but I hesitate.

'That surveillance man might be watching.'

The Tibetan climate and atmosphere are mysterious. There's no sense of perspective; the distinct outlines of distant mountains seem to gouge into the sky. Organic matter doesn't decay easily under the strong sunlight in the thin, dry air. Substances just drop like sediment to the ocean floor and emit no signs of life. Even dog and human excrement lying on the ground doesn't bother me here. I have the feeling that I'm not on earth, that I've arrived on another planet.

Nothing goes to waste; everything that comes out of the body is utilized. Excrement is fed to pigs and dogs, while human corpses fill the stomachs of vultures, dogs and crows. Anything edible circulates amongst all living things. The Tibetans raise yaks and make butter with their milk, eat their meat, then make durable tents and clothes from their skins that last for years. Yak dung is dried and used for fuel. Yak butter is preserved and applied to the face and body as a skin-protection cream, or used for lamps, or drunk mixed with tea, or eaten mixed with *tsampa*. One yak can fulfil almost all the requirements of human life. The only crop that can be grown here is *qingke* barley, and a feast consists of yak, lamb and *tsampa*. Nowadays pork, vegetables, chickens, rice and wheat are brought up for sale from the Chinese interior, but these are expensive.

The only garbage in the rubbish tips is fruit peel and vegetable scraps. In fact, the Chinese word for 'rubbish bin' means 'fruit-peel bin'. In contrast, Japanese rubbish bins contain huge amounts of waste plastic and polystyrene. In Tibet, people use to the utmost what they receive from nature and lead a life in harmony with the ecosystem. I can understand why people are attracted to this land.

Tibetans sit in the sun sipping their yak-butter tea from morning until night. Dogs sleep in the daytime without moving, scattered around the ground like stones. There's barely any movement at all. 'Tibetans are the laziest people in the world. It takes two of them, sometimes even three, to hold a shovel and dig a hole in the ground, and they sing while they do it, shovelling in time with the song.' I remember Yong telling me that Tibetans wear the same clothes for years on end and as far as possible avoid washing them, because frequent laundering soon causes them to wear out in the strong sun. Dogs too are rarely bathed, and the long-haired ones look like sheep covered with muddy wool.

Since coming to Tibet I've not had a proper bath; I've been wearing a wide-brimmed felt hat and hemp clothes, and I've come to blend in with the local environment. Recently I've realized that I can wash my hair perfectly well with just three bowls of water. When I stroke my hair, which has begun to feel stiff like that of the Tibetans and their dogs, I marvel at how people can survive so well with so little.

In front of Husheng's rooms is an open space with a large tree where many stray dogs gather to frisk about. One day, when Yong's been gone since early morning yet again, I'm sitting beneath the trees. The shade is surprisingly cool because of the dry air. While playing with Husheng's dog, Huazi, I suddenly notice a black dog I haven't seen before. I imitate a dog sticking out its front legs and nose, inviting the black dog to come and play, and it comes bounding over as if this is what it's been waiting for. It pounces on me and pretends to chew my hand. It has long legs and short black fur with white on its stomach and paws, its ears are floppy. Only the area around its nose is covered with long fur. Its appearance reminds me of a jovial English gentleman.

'That's one of Ahuang's pups,' Husheng informs me when he comes outside.

'It's Ahuang's?! There's no resemblance at all. What about the others?'

'There's one called Heizi, with bad legs. Look, that's him. These two are the only ones of Ahuang's that are left.' A thin, black dog comes over from the side of Husheng's place, twitching as it goes.

'What about this one, doesn't it have a name?'

'That one's dirty. Always sleeping in the toilets,' Husheng says in disgust.

I see what he means. Closer observation reveals that this is one filthy dog: her bottom teems with squirming maggots, presumably from eating human excrement after she was left to starve, and they plop to the ground when she walks. Yet she has an exceedingly lively and cheerful disposition. Whenever I call her, even from a distance, she comes racing over in a flash with a happy expression. I name her Furugomi. Furugomi becomes very attached to me, probably because no-one has ever petted her dirty body before.

Ahuang's puppies were born last autumn when Yong was in the midst of preparing to leave Lhasa, and have now grown up. Ahuang has always been protective of Heizi, giving him food first whenever she found it. And if other dogs try to steal it from him, she scolds them with a good bite.

When evening comes, I let the dogs into our room because it rains most nights during the summer, and even dogs need a dry place to sleep. We start off with three, but the number rapidly swells to eleven; all the stray dogs in Tibet University must have heard about this place where they can sleep on rainy nights. There are Tamanegi, Nyoden, Amida, Kurofun, Pusa, Lao Jiu, Lao Xi and even Huazi, Husheng's dog. Huazi has a pointy face like a fox and long, soft brown-and-white speckled fur. He's a handsome thing despite the reddish-black swelling that hangs off one side of his jaw. I get the impression that Huazi is Furugomi's boyfriend. When day breaks, the dogs go racing outside again.

I've developed a routine of walking along the river every day with the dogs. First comes Ahuang, followed by the others. The eleven dogs file after me in a grand parade in order of size. People stop and stare at us in disbelief.

I love these dogs – free spirits who've never been tied up. They eat rubbish and excrement to survive, often die of parasites or infectious diseases, and sometimes are shot by the security guards to prevent outbreaks of disease, but they live their lives in free-wheeling abandon. I'm sure they're far happier than dogs in Japan who spend their whole lives stressed, under-exercised and chained up.

On nights when it doesn't rain, Yong and I stroll with the dogs through the university grounds. On moonlit nights – so light that every wrinkle on the palm of my hand is visible – I wish that I could walk like this forever.

*

Since I can't leave the university, Husheng sometimes asks me in for coffee or tea. He has cocoa and instant coffee left over from the days when he ran the coffee shop.

'Husheng, why is it so difficult for Yong to get a passport?'

'It's because he's the biggest thug in Hebalin.'

'Hebalin?'

'That's what this area is called. See the Lhasa River? Well, the university neighbourhood is called Hebalin. The area around the Potala is called Xue. Actually, Yong even got the better of a guy called Huang Xiaolin in Xue, so you could say he's the biggest thug in the whole of Lhasa.'

'Who's Huang Xiaolin?'

'The boss of Xue. People are the same as dogs – they form gangs around anyone who's sharp and make him their leader. There are rumours about Huang Xiaolin. A tough macho guy, a head taller than Cao Yong. He's also got lots of Tibetan followers. When there's a fight brewing, Huang Xiaolin just has to say the word and several hundred brothers turn up. They're all really brave; they'll put their lives on the line in a fight.'

'Did Yong really beat someone like that?'

'Everyone knows Cao Yong ranks alongside him as the toughest guy in Lhasa. Cao Yong's a crack shot, and good in a fight. He also had lots of weapons hidden in his room: grenades, shotguns, rifles, gunpowder, bombs, tear gas, blinders and stuff. It's what you have to do here. The officials are all a bad lot. It makes no difference whether you're Tibetan, Han or anything else; ethnicity's got nothing to do with it. Almost all the police here are gangsters too. You can't rely on people like that for help. We have to protect ourselves – there's no other way.'

'I heard about Yong being beaten up by the police when he first came to Lhasa in 1983. And about the legend of his fight with the Hui in the Barkhor.'

'Well, I suppose it's all right to tell you about this, then. Three years ago, when Cao Yong went to Ali on his own, it was amazing what he managed to do. I was really impressed ... travelling out to that inaccessible place. At that time, everyone had forgotten about Guge, and after the Cultural Revolution it'd just been left to rot. Cao Yong was hugely excited by the fact that such incredible remains still existed. When he came back to Lhasa, he was in a panic that they needed to be restored in a hurry.

'So as soon as he got back he went to see the person in charge of the Cultural Heritage Administration Committee at Norbulingka, a guy called Cai Xianmin, and discussed the site with him. Cai spoke about this to an artist called Pei, who was working in the Lhasa Exhibition Hall. You see, Cai and Pei both graduated from the Sichuan Fine Arts Academy, and at the time Huang Xiaolin was studying painting under Pei. Everyone's eyes lit up when they heard about Ali. Cai decided to survey and restore the site under the auspices of the Cultural Heritage Administration Committee.

'He found a big truck and got together a dozen or so publishers, that lot from the Culture Union, Lhasa artists – and they all set out for Ali in high spirits. Amongst them were Li and Yu Xiaodong, a couple of teachers from the Tibet University Art Department. What I'm about to tell you is what I heard from Yu Xiaodong.

'Cao Yong was included in the survey team since he knew the geography and general situation in Ali. But even though he'd busted a gut travelling there and given them the information he'd collected, he was only taken along to act as a guide.

'Soon after the survey team departed, Huang took over as leader. That's how it is in the wilds of Tibet; the tough, strong one becomes boss. Huang is Han, but he can speak Tibetan. Not to mention that he's also big. He used to carry around this old Japanese army bayonet rifle more than a metre long and was full of big talk. Cai is the tame type, and he was soon under Huang's thumb.

'One day, they were sitting in the back of the truck when Huang started provoking Cao Yong by hitting him on the shoulder with his bayonet. The five or six Tibetan painters were followers of Huang, and Cai just shrank into a corner. Cao Yong said nothing, but when he pointed out that they were going the wrong way, Huang turned a deaf ear. If Cao Yong said west, they'd go east. Yong got more and more angry.

'Now, the survey team wanted to see Chomolungma, so they called in at Rongbuk Monastery, at the base of the mountain. Everyone had dried provisions to eat, but the lamas at Rongbuk knew Cao Yong and kindly gave him a leg of lamb. He hadn't eaten meat for days. Cao Yong, Li and Yu Xiaodong started boiling the meat in a beat-up old pot next to the lamas' living quarters. It stank and was slightly off, but once it was cooking, it smelt good.

'Several people smelled the lamb cooking and came over to ask for a bit, even offering to pay for it. Then Huang came over to see what was going on and flicked up the lid

of the pan with his bayonet. The lid clattered to the
ground. Cao Yong looked daggers at Huang. "Mmm,
smells good," Huang said, stirring the pot with his
bayonet. Then he speared a piece of meat and put it in his
mouth.

'Cao Yong was furious and yelled at him, "Oy, Huang
Xiaolin! If you want to eat, you have to pay! This lamb
cost 16 yuan. If you eat any, you'll have to pay me 5 yuan!"
Ignoring Yong, Huang brought his bowl over and began to
eat.

'Cao Yong decided to shove Huang's head in the pot. He
jumped up, yelling "Get fucked!", but the others stopped
him. Everyone was afraid that if Cao Yong and Huang
Xiaolin had it out, one of them would get killed. Huang
always punched really hard, and on the journey to
Chomolungma he'd already thumped several members of
the team. I reckon that Huang was planning on having Cao
Yong become one of his men, seeing as he knew the local
geography. Anyway, somehow Cao Yong managed to get
through this incident as well.

'After leaving Rongbuk, the team stayed at a guest house
in a small town. But there was only one room in this guest
house, with two beds in it. Cao Yong put his bags on one
of the beds. Of course he and Cai should've been the ones
to sleep there. But Huang came and grabbed Yong's things,
threw them to the ground, then plonked himself down on
the bed. Again Cao Yong wanted to have it out with
Huang once and for all, but again the others stopped him.

'When they arrived at Gaize, Cao Yong shot a dozen or
so rabbits and some ducks with a rifle – enough to feed
everyone. Later the group met up with a Sichuan

engineering team on the road and exchanged some rabbits for rice. So now they had meat and rice, and were able to prepare a good meal for the first time in a while. Everyone started cooking straightaway. Everyone, that is, except Huang, who just hung about watching, doing nothing to help. Then, to top it off, when the food was ready, he went right up to take some.

'"Fuck you! Son of a bitch!" Yong was livid, and Cai and Li desperately tried to hold him back.

'"Cao Yong, drop it. Stop! Don't go starting anything!"

'But Yong's back was up and he was out of control.

'"Huang Xiaolin! There's nothing here for you. Don't you dare eat any of that meat. You still haven't paid me for the lamb, so you have no right to eat anything more. Everyone else cut wood and did some of the cooking, but what did you do? Nothing! Did you?! I want you to pay for today's meal, and for the lamb last time. And until you do, I'm not letting you have anything to eat!"

'"Pah! If these other jerks can eat, why can't I?" Huang retorted, not to be beaten.

'"People I invite are allowed to eat. When did I invite you?"

'"Right then, so that's how it is. I'm going to have a good feed today, and then show you what for," Huang threatened.

'Yong walked over to the truck in a silent rage. Yu Xiaodong knew what he was thinking.

'"Cao Yong, stop it. You can't do that!"

'"Yes, I can. I'm going to shoot that bastard." Yong was reaching into the truck to get his rifle.

'"No, you can't! What'll happen if you kill him? Think

about it!" Yu Xiaodong implored Yong. "The border's a long way away. It'd take a few days to get there from here. And the truck's always breaking down, so if anyone came after you, you'd never get away."

'After this frantic speech, Cao Yong stopped to think a bit. "Okay, I'll kill him when we get to Zanda. It's close to the border with Kashmir, and there's hardly anyone around – there's no law and order there. That's where I'll do it." Cao Yong at last suppressed his anger and put down his rifle. Yu Xiaodong, Cai and Li quickly gave him a big plate of meat and rice. When Yong looked at the three of them all in a panic, he calmed down completely.

'The sun set and the moon was bright. Cao Yong decided to sleep outside. He and Yu Xiaodong spread their sleeping bags out in the truck. Gaize was a tiny place with only a few houses, and it was deadly quiet. The two of them were in their sleeping bags when Huang, who was supposed to be asleep in the guest house, came over to the truck with two of his Tibetan followers. Cao Yong had decided to sleep in the truck because he couldn't stand to be near the guy, but now here he was!

'"Oh, it's you two – are you sleeping here?" Huang asked.

'Cao Yong couldn't believe it: this guy should be dead, but instead here he was still throwing his weight around.

'Huang was the arrogant type. Without so much as a by your leave, he jumped up on the truck and began shoving Yong's things out of the way.

'"Huang Xiaolin!" Cao Yong yelled, then jumped up and punched him in the face at long last. Huang fell with a thud. Just the one blow seemed to leave him reeling. Cao

Yong picked up a torch the size of two fists and hit the fallen Huang hard on the head, over and over.

'Huang was crying out, "Spare me! Spare me!" until at last he lay there not moving. The torch was bent and twisted. A puddle of blood formed under Huang's head. Cao Yong was amazed it was all over so quickly. How could the boss of Xue fall so easily?

'But you can't be sorry for him or anything like that. Huang Xiaolin was an anarchist – a guy with the balls to smash the system with his own hands. In other words, it was a case of take what you give.

'Cai, Li and the others had woken up and come outside. They carried Huang to the small clinic in Gaize. He was covered in blood, and the skin was peeling off his head. Cao Yong went to see if he was dead or alive. The doctor had just started cleaning his head.

'"Ow, it hurts! It really hurts. Ow!" Cao Yong stood watching at the window and heard Huang moaning. He was satisfied because Huang was still alive.

'Next morning, Huang's face was all swollen; he had seventeen stitches in his head and bandages wrapped all around it. When Cai asked if he was coming along with the others, Huang nodded meekly and got into the truck. From then on, Cao Yong was king of the Ali survey team. At any guest houses after that, if there was only one bed, it was Cao Yong's – no arguments. In other words, this fight settled everyone's place.

'But Huang had guts, and even though he'd been beaten, he wasn't one to be mean-spirited about it. So Cao Yong began to regret what he'd done. He started thinking, "This guy's just like me. There are heaps more people I should've beaten up before I hit him. I shouldn't have done it." After that Cao Yong kept trying to get close to Huang so he could make it up, but Huang kept avoiding him. Of course if Cao Yong hadn't beaten up Huang Xiaolin, he probably would've been bullied relentlessly.'

'That was quite a tale.' While listening to Husheng, my palms had started sweating and my eyes were pricking with tears.

'That's who Cao Yong is, and that's why he's on the Tibet University blacklist. His file is stuffed with bad reports, and it's going to be a really hard fight for him to get a passport,' sighs Husheng. 'He's just as likely to do something reckless, like punch the Party secretary and university president, as do anything else.'

'So is that why these application procedures are so difficult?'

'No, in truth, the biggest problem is that the whole of Lhasa knows Cao Yong brought a foreigner into Lhasa under martial law. There was something in the Lhasa *Youth Daily* about the two of you.'

'The *Youth Daily*?'

'Yeah, it's a Lhasa newspaper. Lao Peng wrote it – unfortunately. And then somebody informed on Cao Yong.' The article was apparently a kind of gossip piece with the headline 'Lhasa's Prodigal Son, Cao Yong, Finally Falls in Love with a Japanese Girl'.

'The Lhasa Public Security Bureau has lodged a complaint against Tibet University, saying, "What's this about one of your work-unit members, etc." The university president has to write an apology.'

'An apology?'

'Yeah, to apologize for Cao Yong bringing a foreigner in under martial law.'

'I didn't know this had all blown up so badly!'

From the moment Chinese citizens are born, they're watched – when they eat and when they fart – and reported on, and all the details are recorded in their files. Everyone is afraid of having bad records because their files decide people's futures, for better or worse. No-one is allowed to see their own file – files are controlled by work-unit departments – but it's possible to get them rewritten with a bribe. With a bit of luck, a person can go from being a bad citizen to a good one overnight.

Surveillance and informing are also excellent paths to 'becoming an official and getting rich', as the saying goes. In Tibet University, there are a number of people in high positions who got there by means of their informing activities. Someone once informed on a friend of Yong's for having a naughty party. The friend was hauled in by Public Security, who forced him to strip naked and dance while wearing a cloth sack filled with salt. Since Yong is a notorious thug, no-one has dared inform on him until now. Even though people felt resentful, he was beyond their reach. Informants would suck up to him, at times passing on confidential information. Nobody lifted a finger against him because they knew that unless it was certain that he could be brought down completely, he would take his revenge later.

That evening, I race outside at the sound of the dogs barking and hear a bicycle approaching. Yong has returned, exhausted. Recently, this has become the daily pattern. He comes inside and his eyes immediately blur with tears.

'Does it look like you'll be able to get your passport?'

'It's very difficult.'

'Isn't there even a tiny bit of hope?'

'In China, whenever you try to apply for something, the person in charge always says, "Research, research". The word for "research" has the same sound as that for "cigarettes and alcohol". In other words – bring a gift! After that they'll think about it!'

'Is it so difficult to get the letters you need?'

'I need a mountain of them: "1: Tibet University Art Department; 2: head of the Organization Department; 3: decision from the university president's Work Unit Committee; 4: Personnel Bureau in the Education Department; 5: head of the Education Department; 6: head of the Foreign Affairs Section in the Public Security Bureau; 7: head of the Public Security Department; 8: Foreign Affairs Office of the TAR; 9: Standing Committee of the Tibetan People's Congress; 10: three Party Committee secretaries; 11: Marriage Application Section in the Bureau of Civil Affairs; 12: examination by the Centre for Hygiene and Epidemic Prevention; 13: TAR Notarization Bureau." That's thirteen letters of consent! I have to use my connections carefully and ingratiate myself, all the while going along with their under-the-table demands as well! Every day I'm seeing people who might help me, but ...' Yong coughs violently, and his eyes dim with tears.

Known as the tough guy of Hebalin, Yong is having to bow and scrape to everyone. Some who had previously regarded him with hostility are encouraged by this change and see it as the perfect chance to squash him. He goes to and fro between people likely to support him, but even they apparently don't want to be involved with the person who scandalously brought a foreigner into Lhasa under martial law.

Meanwhile he's grown thin, the flesh completely melted from his body. His travels back and forth between the Chinese interior and the Tibetan plateau have also brought on bronchitis. He has a terrible cough and vomits every morning to boot. He's in a pitiful state. 'I met Chang Yan on the street, and the bastard looked the other way. Son of a bitch! It-looks like I'll be seeing my friends' true colours more and more now,' he exclaims bitterly. Chang Yan is a friend from the same province as Yong.

The dogs have been capering around the room, but now I draw them close. 'Don't worry. Look, we've got eleven comrades.'

'Brother Cao! Long time no see! I heard the rumours.' A thin brown-skinned youth has come to visit.

'Xiaoming!' Yong's face lights up. He puts his arm around the youth's shoulders and ushers him inside.

'*Ni hao*, Aya. I'm the one who brought Yong your letters.'

'*Ni hao*, Xiaoming. Yong has talked about you often.'

Xiaoming and Yong have a cast-iron friendship; if something ever happened to Xiaoming, Yong would put his life on the line for him. They're like brothers, 'iron brothers'.

I'd sent my letters from Japan to Xiaoming's address because the university administration read and destroyed letters sent to Yong from outside China. Destroying his letters was one of the university president's punishments for Yong the delinquent teacher, and as a result he'd lost many opportunities and friends, one of whom had been the German friend who'd promised to help him leave the country after his Beijing exhibition. When my letters arrived, Xiaoming would immediately cycle the 3 kilometres to the university to deliver them to Yong.

'Brother Cao, I hear you've had a tough time. I suppose you're planning to leave the country?'

'It's fucking awful! What are they doing to me? Damn it!'

'The whole of Lhasa knows the story. I guess you're having trouble getting a passport?'

'I can't wait anymore. I think I'll escape over the Himalayas to Nepal,' Yong announces out of the blue. 'There are lots of Tibetans who've escaped to Nepal, and Han Chinese as well, so I should be able to find someone I know there. I know how to get a passport too, by getting hold of the family records of a dead person in Nepal. About 200 dollars will fix it. Aya, you go back to Japan and wait for me. I'll think of a way to get to Japan from Nepal. Xiaoming, could you arrange a ride for me as far as Zhangmu?'

'Brother Cao! The border's heavily guarded now because of the protests. It's too dangerous!' Xiaoming tries to talk Yong out of his plan. 'Apparently people were even killed at the border during the riots in Lhasa. It's really unsafe. You've still got plenty of ways you can try to get a passport. I'll see what I can do to help and ask if my older brother's friends can do anything. Come on, cheer up!' Xiaoming leaves. A true iron brother.

After he's gone, Yong lies sprawled out on the bed, his arm over his face. 'Something's wrong with me. I never used to be scared of anything. I never even valued my life. I've been scared of dying since I met you, Aya. Before, I wasn't afraid of anything when I crossed the Nepalese border. Now I'm afraid to take risks. I don't want to get into fights anymore, or do anything illegal either.'

'I've stayed with you all this time so you could get a passport and leave the country legally. If you can do that, one day you'll be able to come back to China again, and to Tibet too.'

'All right. Tomorrow I'll go and see someone else I know in the government.'

'You think they might be able to help?'

'I often used to play with his child. He's a good person, so there's a chance he might help me out.'

Next morning, Yong goes out early. Close to noon, Xiaoming drops by again.

'Is Brother Cao here? I wanted to let him know that I found someone who might be able to help.'

I offer him some *tiancha* – the sweet black tea simmered with milk powder that Tibetans often drink. We sit on chairs, basking in the sun and waiting for Yong to return.

'Whenever letters came from you, Brother Cao would be wild with happiness. Even though he'd hadn't been interested in being with a woman since his divorce.'

'Yong's wife ... what was she like?'

'It was a long time ago, but about a year after Brother Cao arrived in Lhasa, this girl from his university days arrived. She'd promised to marry him.'

'Why did it end in divorce?'

'There was an incident – a really painful one for Brother Cao. When he got married, he'd been living on his own for so long that he was accustomed to using up all his money as soon as he got it. He'd had an advance on his teaching salary and didn't even have any proper bedding in his room. He slept rolled up in a dirty wad of cotton stuffing on top of some straw he'd spread on the floor. He didn't have any furniture or anything – just one bent bucket and a single silk quilt cover his mother had sent as a wedding gift. That was all.

'The girl couldn't get used to Tibet and soon got sick. She just stayed in bed with a high fever. Brother Cao was in a panic and flat broke, so he decided to sell the quilt cover to get some money. Taking the cover, he went with another art teacher, Yu Xiaodong, to the Barkhor. They stood there for half a day, holding it between them. But Tibetans don't use things like Han quilt covers, so they couldn't sell it. Brother Cao hid his head in shame behind the quilt. There he was, he was thinking, over twenty and not worth anything. He decided that from then on he'd do whatever it took to make money. Around evening, they sold the cover to a Hui egg-seller for 4 yuan. With that money, Brother Cao bought a bag of rice, three eggs and a few mandarins.

'After that, Brother Cao changed completely and started smuggling with the Tibetans. He got goods from Nepal and India, and sent them to the Chinese interior, and he also painted lots of signboards and wall signs all over Lhasa. He managed to do really well for himself. He was riding around in a Beijing jeep and owned a Suzuki motorbike too. He became one of the rich young men in Lhasa and even wore a suit.

'But after a year, he and the girl began living apart. Because she'd graduated from the Foreign Languages Department at Henan University and could speak English, Brother Cao pulled some strings for her to start working in the Foreign Affairs Office. Once her life had settled down though, her attitude started to change. At first Brother Cao lived with her in the housing she was assigned by the Foreign Affairs Office, but after a while he shifted back to a university room.

'In her rooms she had everything you could ask for – a television, refrigerator, washing machine and tape recorder. Brother Cao asked her for a divorce many times, but she kept refusing. You wouldn't be able to buy a television on her salary, even if you didn't eat for two years and saved every penny. Whenever they met, they'd only ever argue.

'One day, Brother Cao was getting ready to go out on his motorbike when he suddenly had this strange feeling and rode over to her place. Her rooms were on the ground floor of the two-storey Foreign Affairs Office building. He arrived and knocked on the door, but it was locked. Her colleagues and neighbours said she must have gone with a foreign tour group to Shigatse. But Brother Cao still felt like something was wrong and kept knocking. Then he went round the back, where he could see through a barred kitchen window. The inside door was shut, which he thought was odd. And it was quiet inside, not a sound. Deadly silent. He grabbed the iron rail hard and bent it – later, no-one could believe he'd got the strength! Look, the window in this room's got thick iron bars too. He bent one of these. Just as he was about to go into the kitchen, the bedroom door opened suddenly. The girl stuck her head around the door and yelled, "I don't want to see you! I'm sleeping! I don't want to see you." It looked like she wasn't wearing any clothes.

'Brother Cao climbed inside and yelled back at her, "I'm tired of this – either we live together or we separate. One or the other! If not, I'll find some way to get you sent back to the interior!" He thought there was something odd about her. She was flustered and jittery. "Let's go back to the university and talk. People in my work unit can hear us here," she said. "Why?" he asked. "We can talk here, can't we? Let's settle things now ... if we're going to separate or ... what we'll do." She refused to discuss things any further.

'Brother Cao got really mad then and picked up a fruit knife from the table. "I can't stand this anymore. I won't put up with it. Why don't you kill me! I'd rather be dead than have to keep on like this!" he shouted.

'Then the girl started screaming hysterically. Brother Cao had already been in the room for half an hour by this point, but it wasn't until he heard her scream that he noticed something. The space under her bed was dark. He stormed into the bedroom and yelled at the shape under the bed, "Come out!"

'She went nuts, screaming, "Help, somebody! Someone's going to get killed!" Then Brother Cao heard a man's voice under the bed, begging for his life to be spared. He grabbed the naked man, a fellow called Jiang. Jiang was in the same work unit as the girl and had often visited Brother Cao's room. They'd even gone hunting together, and once Brother Cao had saved his life when Jiang had fallen through the ice on a lake. The girl held Brother Cao back from beating Jiang up.

'People had heard the screaming and were gathering outside. They knocked loudly on the door. Brother Cao ignored them and punched Jiang anyway. "I'll kill him ... where's that knife?" He picked up the fruit knife again and went to stab Jiang in the throat, but he missed because the girl had her arms around him and only cut his shoulder. The girl herself was hit and had injuries to her forehead and arm, and her face was covered in blood. Jiang was badly beaten up as well. Both of them ran for their lives.

'So then Brother Cao was alone in the place, and he went crazy, smashing up all her stuff in a rage. The television, camera, necklaces, electrical goods – everything. After that he rode back to the university in a hurry to get a knife from his room and went off to kill them. They weren't at the People's Hospital. Next he went to Jiang's place. They weren't there either. He searched the house but couldn't find them. Jiang's father had forced them to leave immediately and escape to the lowland provinces.

'Jiang's father was a Tibetan, and his mother was a Han. His father was head of the Tibetan People's Congress and was called a traitor by Tibetans because he was one of the signatories to the peace treaty between Tibet and the People's Republic of China. Both Jiang and the girl fled, she to Gansu and he to Wuhan.

'She's back living in Lhasa now, though. Her present husband loves gambling and even mortgaged the Hitachi television that Brother Cao smashed up. Hitachi TVs are really something, you know. Brother Cao sliced off the corners of that one in a rage, but it still worked perfectly.

'But Brother Cao was hurt real bad, and then went broke as well. People in Lhasa, all our pals, everyone felt sympathy for him. Even his friends in the police were on his side. From then on, he began to hate women. And it was then that he went to Ali. Even though he'd go out with lots of women, he couldn't feel the kind of love that'd make him want to live with someone again.

'Yong has numerous scars from knife and bullet wounds, but the scars on his heart seem much deeper than any of those. He didn't paint when he was with his wife. He was too busy making money from smuggling, for one thing. But after that incident, he never got involved in business again, and now he always asks, "What good did money do me?"'

'Thank you, Xiaoming. I'm glad you told me all this. I understand Yong even better now.'

Xiaoming smiles.

'I met with that government fellow. He's different from the rest. He might come through for me,' Yong says that night in Husheng's room. He sounds exhausted.

Anyone who's willing to help us is doing it either for money or because they expect something out of having a connection with Japan. Acquaintances who occasionally visit us try to take advantage of our vulnerability by asking us to change money into foreign currency or to help them with applications to study in Japan.

'Procedures, procedures! Why should I have to grovel to so many people to get a passport? In return I only get squeezed for bribes and stuff!' Yong rages. The day he can escape from this country seems to be receding further into the distance, like a dream.

14 July. I have a bad cold, my cystitis has returned and my back hurts so much that I can't walk. Yong wants to take me to the People's Hospital, but the university security guards stop us, saying, 'It's out of the question, she is prohibited from going out.'

'Mean bastards. They're not human.' Yong is seething, but there's nothing we can do. He himself has a terrible cough and his bronchitis is getting worse. If he doesn't get an injection of antibiotics, it could turn into pneumonia. In spite of his condition, he carries me on his back to the university clinic. The doctor there is well disposed towards Yong – in fact there are quite a few people in the university who show him goodwill – and after an examination, she gives me an antibiotic injection and a prescription. Yong also receives an injection of penicillin for his bronchitis. A day later, I'm able to stand up and walk again.

Two weeks have passed since the surveillance began. On 21 July, Yong goes to the Public Security Bureau to ask permission for me to go out. A friend there tells him to pay a fine for the time being, explaining, 'It's hard to talk to the bosses about getting permission.' So Yong pays a fine of 300 yuan in FECs, and I'm given an extension on my expired visa and permitted to go out. I can go anywhere. Hurray!

Yong has done everything he possibly can towards getting a passport. All we can do now is wait.

We waste no time going out on bicycles with Ahuang and Furugomi. We pedal along the road that runs beside the Lhasa River to Gumolingka, a park on a shoal in the river commonly known as *Xiaotou'er lingka* – 'Pilferer's Park'. *Tar-choks* – prayer flags printed with Buddhist scriptures – in shades of red, yellow, white, blue and green flutter from a suspension bridge linking the shoal to the riverbank. Across the bridge is a small teahouse where we order a thermos of milky tea and some glass cups, then settle ourselves in the shade of a tree. It's a perfect spot with a crystal-clear view of the Potala. Tibetans nearby are engrossed in playing cards and have probably been knocking back *qingke* wine since early in the day.

'The *Xiaotou'er lingka* is quite the red-light district. There are prostitutes here.'

'In the middle of these woods? Here, on this island?'

'Yeah, nomad women who come to Lhasa on pilgrimages. They're waiting in the woods. It costs about 2 yuan.'

'Here ... in the grass?'

'Yeah, see that plastic greenhouse back there? You find a woman you like and go to that greenhouse.'

'You mean ... you do it inside the greenhouse?'

'That's right.'

'You seem to know a lot about it. Have you been with them often?'

'Er ... me? Nah.'

22 July. We ride our bicycles in the direction of Sera Gompa to see a place called Dog Castle. The moment I heard about this Dog Castle, I knew I wanted to see it.

A few years ago, Yong tells me, the Chinese government proposed a major cull of stray dogs to contain over-breeding and the spread of rabies. The Tibetans, however, were fiercely opposed to this slaughter and nearly started rioting. A meeting of the Chinese–Tibetan Administration Work-Unit Committee was held; the top brass spent as much as half a year racking their brains over what to do. The upshot of this long deliberation was a brilliant proposal by one quick-witted man: 'We'll build a dogs' castle! Separate the dogs by sex and they'll be extinct in one generation!' This idea was well received and applauded as the best solution. And so Dog Castle was built on a mountain on the outskirts of Lhasa, to the tune of half a million yuan. The choice of location was also pure genius, with Sera Gompa behind and a nunnery on the mountain top.

Several hundred dogs were shut up in two large concrete buildings, and the government appointed a caretaker whose only job was to feed them. Inside the concrete buildings – several dozen metres long and enclosed by sturdy iron bars – the dogs embarked upon a life of aristocratic bliss, basking in the sun and enjoying meals brought to them by their own cook. Newspapers throughout Tibet unanimously reported that 'Dog Castle, a bridge to ethnic unity, is finally complete. The Chinese government treats every single Tibetan dog with care!'

Over time, however, the male dogs were driven to distraction by the nearby barking of large numbers of bitches on heat. With a strength born of necessity, they eventually managed to make a hole in the concrete wall and invaded the females' cage, pouring in like a flood. The bitches became pregnant and gave birth all at the same time, so in the end, Dog Castle became a giant breeding facility.

There's no sign of the dogs in the long concrete buildings, though we do see several decrepit old beasts, too feeble to move, sprawled motionless in a corner. Some Tibetans sit in another corner drinking tea. Looking closer, we see the remains of campfires dotted about, lit by pilgrims who've stayed here. Dog Castle is gradually evolving into a rest house-cum-lodging-cum-shop for pilgrims. The location is perfect for those visiting Sera Gompa, and the castle's value as a guest house is growing. The giant buildings on the rocky peak will no doubt go down in history as a grand monument to ethnic unity.

On the way back from Dog Castle, we stop off at the Barkhor. In the square fronting the Jokhang Temple, clouds of smoke from burning incense billow up out of large stone urns; pilgrims from outlying regions prostrate themselves and offer prayers; elderly people spin their *mani* prayer wheels; Tibetan women clad in *chupas* with turquoise and other precious stones fastened into their countless long plaits mill about; young men do heroic prostrations in return for money; and old people sit at the side of the road absorbed in reading sutras.

Some Tibetan women in native dress approach us to try and sell their folk crafts.

'We'd better say we're Japanese here.'

Tibetans are directing their bitterness at the deaths of friends and family members during the independence movement against all Han Chinese, but they show unconditional friendliness to foreigners who support the movement.

I enjoy wandering around examining the folk arts and crafts on display. From them I get a sense of the distinctive culture out here in the west: nonchalant displays of bowls made of human skulls and trumpets fashioned from thigh bones; lines of sheep's and yaks' skulls with scriptures etched into the brows; silver bracelets made in the shape of skeletons; necklaces carved from bone; and flintstones. I purchase a necklace carved out of sheep's horns and a bone bracelet.

An old beggar sitting at the side of the road bangs stones against some mud-covered bones. He carefully picks up the fragments of bone and sucks out the contents.

'That's a real treat. I love that stuff. I can't understand people who just eat meat and don't eat the marrow,' Yong says, as if this is the most natural thing in the world.

On the way home, he catches sight of a slightly-built old Tibetan man and stops him, calling out, 'Tseren!'

'Teacher Cao!' The old man's face breaks into a joyful smile, and he stretches his arms out as far as they will reach to embrace Yong. 'What's happened to you! Teacher Cao, you've changed a lot ... you're thinner! Who's this? Your wife?'

'*Ni hao*, pleased to meet you.' I smile and greet him.

'Oh ... oh ... your wife's Chinese is strange. Is she from Hong Kong?'

'Nah, she's Japanese.'

Looking pleased, the old man chortles, revealing chipped black-red teeth as he claps Yong on the back. With his dirty dark-blue trousers and threadbare woollen sweater hanging off his small frame, he looks like any other impoverished Tibetan.

'That was Tseren the sky-burial master,' Yong tells me after we take our leave.

Immediately I turn around to look back, but the old man's small shape is already lost amongst the crowds.

In 1983, Yong had been in Lhasa less than a month when curiosity led him to see a sky burial, the early-morning funeral rite in which the bodies of the dead are fed to vultures. In the Tibetan order of things, cremation is reserved for those well born or of high rank; burial in the ground is for victims of infectious diseases; suicides and newborns receive water burials; everyone else receives sky burials. The men who carry out this last rite are called sky-burial masters.

The biggest sky-burial site in Lhasa is an enormous, oblong boulder on a rocky slope near Sera Gompa. It protrudes from the ground at a gentle angle, with rocks placed underneath to support it. The boulder's surface – bigger than two four-ton trucks combined – is pitted with many holes large enough to fit a human head comfortably. Essentially a chopping block, this rock is where the dead are prepared to be fed to the vultures.

On the day Yong went there, one sky-burial master stood on the rock in the early-morning light. Yong and his fellow new-arrivals in Tibet took up a position where they could watch the rock yet be far enough away to be out of reach of stones the sky-burial master might throw at them. Tibetan law prohibits foreigners from watching sky burial, and the masters are very accurate at hitting intruders with their slingshots; they've injured a number of Chinese and other foreigners, as well as smashed their cameras. If someone tries to drive up close in a car, the masters will attack the vehicle with swords and stones and totally wreck it.

Looking down, Yong and his friends noticed a frail old man pulling a cart up the road below them. In the cart was something wrapped in white cloth. It appeared that the old man's wife had died, and he was single-handedly hauling her body all the way out to the sky-burial site. Ordinarily, family members don't attend such burials – friends and acquaintances do that for them – but it seemed that there was no-one to do it for this old man.

The sky-burial master climbed down off the rock and ran over to him, indicating that he should bring the body up to the rock. The old man struggled to pull the heavy cart along the narrow track that wove its way up the steep slope, but it wouldn't budge any further. Unable to stand by and watch, the master tried to help, but the cart was too heavy even for the two of them.

'Hey! You over there,' the master shouted to Yong and his friends. 'You want to see a sky burial, don't you? Well, if you do, get over here and help us!'

The friends looked at each other in alarm. 'Cao Yong, you go,' said one.

'Yeah, you go over,' they all agreed, looking at Yong.

Yong, only about twenty at the time, was the most daring and spirited of the group. He was also keenly aware of the two girls with them. Clearly, he couldn't run away from this, so he mustered up the courage to walk over to the cart.

With his help, the cart proceeded easily up the rocky mountain road. Once they reached the top, however, the sky-burial master suddenly started barking instructions at Yong as if he were an assistant.

'All right, put the body on the rock. Grab the feet,' he ordered while unwrapping the white cloth covering the old woman. Yong's friends had followed and now stood about 20 metres away watching him.

Yong forced a smile and did as he was told. The old woman lay naked in the cart, curled up like a foetus. The sky-burial master grasped her arm. Yong took the legs. Together they tugged at the corpse until the stiff resistance of death suddenly dissipated and the body straightened. Yong broke into a cold sweat. He saw the woman's eyes staring up at him from under the partially closed lids in her dark-skinned face, and his arms holding her ice-cold legs shook like jelly. They carried her to the top of the rock, where a terrible stench assailed him. Finally the old woman lay on the chopping block.

Noticing that meal preparations were underway, a flurry of vultures descended from the sky. *Thud!* They swooped down on wings as wide as a person's outstretched arms, hitting the ground like cannon balls, and edged haughtily over to the sky-burial master.

'Hey, quick, pass me that knife over there.'

Yong cursed his misfortune as he handed over the long blood-slicked knife. The sky-burial master promptly set about preparing the body, tying a cord around the neck that was then secured to an anchor rock nearby. He turned the corpse face down, made an incision extending from the Achilles tendon up to the buttocks, then began to peel the flesh away from the bones.

Next, the master flung the chunks of flesh to the greedy vultures, who rose up with a whoosh and scrambled to devour it. He extracted the organs for the vultures too, and they fought over the long strings of intestines. Each time this happened, the master had to step in and mediate, severing the intestine in the middle. Yong was fighting to keep down the contents of his own stomach. More and more vultures swooped down from the sky, and in the blink of an eye the rock was hidden under fifty or more birds. The old woman's body rapidly disappeared into their stomachs.

The sky-burial master then rolled her severed head into one of the holes on the rock's surface and, with the flesh cleanly peeled away to reveal the white skull beneath, smashed it to pieces with a stone. Bits of brain flew up and scattered as the head became shards of shattered bone and scraps of flesh. He placed the fragments of flesh and bone left over by the birds into the hole, ground them thoroughly before mixing in some *tsampa*, then kneaded it all into dumplings which he threw to the vultures.

The old woman's corpse had vanished before their eyes; the vultures flew away with bulging stomachs. With the job completed, the sky-burial master turned to look at a chalk-faced Yong, and a laugh rose up in his throat.

'Okay, that's done. Hey, what's your name? I'm Tseren, head of sky burials.'

'Er, I'm ... Cao Yong.'

And that was how Yong met Tseren, a slightly built Tibetan man of barely fifty.

At the end of their day's work the sky-burial masters would sit on the edge of the rock and drink *qingke* to ease their tiredness. As usual, though, Tseren first washed his hands in urine.

'Why do you wash your hands in piss when there's a stream just over there?'

'Don't you know that piss can be used for sterilizing? Wash your hands!' the sky burial master ordered.

When Yong returned to his friends, the girls wouldn't come near him because he'd touched a corpse. He also found himself vomiting, unable to eat any kind of meat, and plagued by nightmares for the next few weeks.

After about a month, though, Yong recovered and started to think about going to another sky burial. In his travels until then, human corpses had been the thing that had frightened him the most, but if he was going to travel all around Tibet as he had resolved to do, he needed to strengthen his nerve. Around that time, he happened to see Tseren again on the Barkhor.

'Hey there! How's things?' Tseren remembered Yong well. And Yong, glad to see Tseren again, invited him to a teashop.

'Ordinary guys only pay attention to me when they want to see the sky burial. They ignore me later. You're different. Come and see me again, eh?' Tseren's eyes were moist with tears as he put his arm around Yong's shoulder.

The second time Yong went to the sky-burial rock, he was able to face the ritual calmly. After that he often went along to help out, learning composedly to cut up a corpse and throw the flesh to the vultures, who also soon got to know him. At times a hundred or more vultures would come flying down from the mountain peaks in the hinterland where they lived. Vultures who came regularly were given names like Gasang and Choden, and to the sky-burial masters they were like family or friends. In a way the sky burial was like a small Japanese company, with Tseren as the president, the other masters as the executives and the vultures as the workers. Every morning, the masters reported to the rock for work and lit a fire that sent a signal to the vultures, who'd come flying down as if to report for duty. Rankings among the vultures – their managerial positions, if you like – were determined according to relative strength.

At the time, Yong was working on a long series of pen-and-ink pictures for an illustrated storybook called *Female Buddha* that was to be published by Tianjin Press. It was work that demanded enormous patience; he had to draw more than a hundred pictures, each with many minute, finely detailed human faces the size of a little fingernail, using a fine-hair pen. He'd work on the pictures all night long and then cycle out to the sky-burial rock for a change of mood. It was still dark at that time of morning, and the sky burial was the only place where people might be about.

Since it was the masters' custom to wait for corpses at the rock, Yong usually encountered Tseren on these mornings. There was a spare-parts and car-repair shop a few hundred metres away; from there Yong could tell if Tseren was around by the smoke from his fire.

Climbing up to the rock one morning, Yong found Tseren already there, stoking his fire.

'Well now, it's Teacher Cao!' Tseren had taken to addressing Yong with this respectful title ever since he'd discovered that Yong taught at the university. 'Some Hong Kong people came here yesterday. They were really nasty pieces of work. I lost my temper and grabbed their camera.' Yong was astonished when he picked up the camera lying next to Tseren's cooking stove. It was a very good one indeed – a single-lens reflex, the kind a professional would use. He'd seen such a camera in a magazine before, but to have the real thing in his hands, smashed up like this, was too much.

'You idiot, Tseren! To get a fantastic camera like this and then go and break it! You really are a blockhead! Even if you smashed those Hong Kong jerks' heads in, there's no need to break the camera. Fuck!'

'Teacher Cao, I couldn't help it. I mean … I just got so burned up. Anyway, I didn't know you like this kind of stuff. If I did, I wouldn't have wrecked it so much.'

Awkward and embarrassed, Tseren moved away to join the other masters. 'Teacher Cao, Teacher Cao! A girl! A pretty girl! Come and look!' he called out excitedly to the still fuming Yong. Turning reluctantly, Yong saw that Tseren had raised something up off the chopping block and was holding it in his arms for Yong to see. The naked white body of a beautiful girl rose up like a vision out of the early-morning mist. Yong abruptly dropped the camera and hurried over.

'Is she dead?' he asked.

'Teacher Cao, she's pretty, isn't she?' Tseren chuckled bawdily, humouring Yong.

Young girls' corpses were rarely brought to the rock. For

the most part, the bodies belonged to elderly people who'd
died of old age or sickness. A sense of life was still
palpable in the girl's body lying on the rock – as if a heart
was still beating under those soft, round breasts. She was
probably about eighteen and her face was exquisite. Her
face and lower arms had been tanned dark brown by the
sun, but the skin was milky-white where it had been
covered by a fur *chupa*. That morning, she'd fallen from a
wagon, hit her head and died instantly. Her body was
unscathed, a small wound on the back of her head the only
sign of injury. Her thin pubic hair fluttered in the breeze.

Yong touched her arm and the coldness shot through
him. She really was dead.

Overcome, Yong and the sky-burial masters gazed awhile
in silence at the young woman's body. All sighed deeply.
Despite having attended many sky burials by then, it was
the first time that Yong was able to look at a corpse
without feeling the slightest bit sick. The masters set about
their work with unusual cheerfulness, and, as always, Yong
put the cord around the neck and secured it to the anchor
rock.

Such unimagined, beautiful white flesh! But then Yong
touched the girl's arm again, and the cold, hard feel of it
caused his perverse desire to wither. *It's a real shame. Why
did you have to die?*

Tseren lingeringly ran his sword through the girl's skin;
little by little, blood began to seep from the incision. Then
he opened up her thigh and his voice became excited. 'This
sweet young thing is a virgin!'

He spread out the excised genitals to show the others. A
smiling Tseren was telling him something, but Yong was

oblivious, sighing as he gazed at the beautiful girl becoming chunks of meat that disappeared into the vultures' stomachs. Blood and meat juice flowed, and the odour wafted over to Yong, jolting him back to reality. *Shit, why couldn't we have met when you were still alive? This is a hell of a day! First the camera's broken and now a beautiful young girl is dead.*

Tseren didn't shatter the head as usual; instead, he took his time in making a clean incision, starting near one ear, and cut the skull out in a shape that resembled a porcelain bowl. When their work was done, the sky masters sat on the rock to rest. Tseren then took a large container of *qingke* wine and poured some into the bowl he'd made from the girl's skull. The masters passed it around and each one drank from it.

'Teacher Cao, drink from a bowl made from a virgin's skull; it'll make you strong.' Tseren held out the bowl to Yong. Bits of human flesh were still lodged between the rings on Tseren's hands despite their being freshly washed in urine. Yong took a deep breath and received the skull bowl from those hands. Branching blue veins traced the inside of the pure white skull, as if they were still pumping warm fresh blood. The raw smell shot up Yong's nose. *If I drink this, maybe we'll be together in a way*, he thought and, closing his eyes, drained the skull dry in a single gulp.

Tibetans call the sky-burial masters 'black bones' and shun them completely. Not a single person will go near them, and of course there was no reason why a Han Chinese should have anything to do with them either. Sky-burial masters walk along the road and people make detours to avoid them. They're invited into homes when there's a death in the family, but any cups or plates they touch are immediately thrown away. Yet Tibetans pay handsomely with gifts and money to ensure that sky burials are conducted with care, believing that if a body isn't completely pulverized – every scrap devoured by vultures, not a trace left behind – then the spirit of the dead person can't ascend to Heaven.

Thus Tseren was a man very much alone. Despised because of his profession, he led an isolated life with only his family and the other masters for company. He passed his days drinking away almost all the money he earned from his work.

Around that time a new sensation appeared in Lhasa: Japanese-made tape recorders. Anyone who owned one became the envy of everyone else, but the only people who could afford them were wealthy businessmen, Communist Party officials, the Tibetan aristocracy and the merchants on Barkhor Street. And even they only used theirs on special occasions.

Tseren made the enormous decision to spend a large sum of money on one of these much-talked-about tape recorders. He took to carrying it while he wandered the streets with the volume turned up to ear-splitting levels. But Tseren only listened absent-mindedly to the music; his eyes darted hither and thither observing the reactions of people who, astounded, stopped in their tracks and stared at him incredulously. He was like a child who walked the streets at night singing loudly.

'Teacher Cao!' Tseren called out when he caught sight of Yong one day after he'd bought the tape recorder. Yong couldn't hear anything in the midst of such cacophony; it was only from the movement of Tseren's lips that he understood what the sky-burial master was saying.

'Tseren! What the hell are you doing? Ha ha ha!' Yong walked alongside Tseren and laughed comfortably.

'Eh …?' Tseren faltered. He was lost for words, overjoyed that Yong would actually walk next to him. He stretched one arm around Yong's shoulders – even though Yong was a head taller – leaving his other arm around the huge tape recorder on his shoulder.

'Out of the way!' Tibetans cried out in surprise and fear, avoiding the pair. Tseren walked along with Yong – the only person ever to walk side by side with him in public – and when they met people he knew from sky burials, he eagerly introduced Yong to them.

'Hey, look here. This is my very best friend – Teacher Cao!' The people he called out to mostly panicked and ran away.

'Right, Tseren, let's go, then.' Yong hoisted the tape recorder onto his own shoulder as well and they swaggered down the Barkhor, carrying it between them. Tseren let out great peals of laughter.

Yong was the first ordinary person ever to become Tseren's friend, and whenever they met, they had tea or went drinking together.

'I've made my first Chinese friend. You're my best friend,' Tseren declared, taking Yong's hand in a gesture of friendship.

One morning Yong, who was prospering at the time from his smuggling activities, drove by the sky-burial rock in his jeep just as Tseren was finishing work.

'Teacher Cao. How about it? Do you want to come to my home today?' Tseren asked as he shouldered a bag stuffed with leftover *tsampa*.

Yong invited him into the jeep and they set off for Tseren's home.

'Hey, Teacher Cao. Stop the car for a bit, will you?' Tseren shouted whenever they saw someone he knew. He'd hardly ever ridden in a car before and wanted everyone to see.

They arrived at Tseren's house, not far from the Barkhor. His family were mostly still asleep, but Tseren yelled out loudly anyway, '*Cao Laoshi laile! Cao Laoshi laile!*' announcing Yong's arrival in Chinese. At the sound of his voice, a cloth hanging across the entrance parted and Tseren's wife appeared. The smell of sleeping people and smoke from the yak-dung fire assailed Yong's nose. Small children wrapped in dirty scraps of cloth were still asleep beside the entrance, but they all soon awoke and jumped up when they noticed the guest – including Tseren's thirteen-year-old son whom Yong had met before at the sky-burial rock. Everyone was excited by this rare appearance.

'*Cao Laoshi laile! Cao Laoshi laile!*' they tried to imitate their father, but to Yong's ears, instead of '*Cao Laoshi*', meaning 'Teacher Cao', the words came out sounding like 'Cao the shit man'. Since they didn't attend school, the children hadn't learned to speak Chinese.

'Hey, what's this? Do I turn into shit if I come to Tseren's house?' Yong laughed and took the children in his arms.

Belongings were scattered throughout the long, narrow

building composed of three rooms in a row, each roughly 10 metres square. Six or seven children surrounded Yong and made him sit in the middle of the room. An old man and Tseren's wife welcomed him.

'This is one of my two fathers,' Tseren said, introducing the old man.

'Two fathers? Did your mother remarry?'

'No, my mother married two brothers who are both my fathers. One died.'

Polygamous marriages of one wife and two or more husbands, or one husband and two or more wives, are not uncommon among Tibetans. It's quite usual for brothers or sisters to marry the same person in order to prevent the dispersion of family property and assets.

Near the window a girl wrapped in a PLA greatcoat was leaning against the wall. She picked up a baby that had begun to cry and was comforting it.

'Your daughter's a real beauty, isn't she? Is she married?'

'No, she just had a baby.'

The girl opened her shirt, bared a large, round breast and began to feed the infant. Her breasts were white and full, but with brown marks here and there – perhaps where the baby had touched them with dirty hands. Tseren didn't offer any more details as to why his daughter had a baby but no husband. This daughter was beautiful, her looks equal to those of any Tibetan girl. Tseren's sons would work at the sky burial, but the chances of his daughters being able to marry were almost nonexistent.

Tseren handed his wife the *tsampa* he'd brought home. The masters would bring home clothes and possessions that had belonged to the corpses, plus any leftover *tsampa*.

Yong was offered some with yak-butter tea while he played with the children.

When Yong eventually made a move to leave, Tseren announced, 'Teacher Cao, I have something I very much want to give you. Please wait.' From a corner, he pulled out an ornamental box of the sort Tibetans use to keep their valuables in, and drew out something carefully wrapped in cloth. 'These are my family treasures,' he said. That box was the sole object in the house to exude an air of value. With great care, Tseren delicately pinched the cloth between his fingertips and gently opened it up. Inside was a time-worn knife and a round black object about the size of a thumb tip. 'This is the knife my dead father used. And this here – this is something I saved.' Yong stared at Tseren's mysterious treasure.

'It's very precious. You only find them in maybe one person in a few thousand. It's incredibly effective for warding off evil spirits. To find one this big is amazingly rare, you know.' The black object was a gallstone, taken from a human gall bladder. Sky-burial masters have the ability to discern the cause of death at a glance when they cut up people who've died of illness. This gallstone represented the achievement of half a lifetime's work as a sky-burial master and was Tseren's greatest pride.

'I want to give these to you. Take them, please.' Tseren's face flushed.

'No way. I can't take something so valuable.' Yong tried to refuse, but Tseren would not listen and begged him again to take the things.

'I know. I can't take the knife – it's a keepsake from your father – but let me take the gallstone.'

Tseren smiled with satisfaction.

When Yong went to leave, he discovered that all the tyres of his jeep – parked next to Tseren's house – had been punctured. This was typical of the kind of harassment that Tseren and people associated with him were subjected to.

Sometimes it happened that an acquaintance of Yong's would be brought out for sky burial. One day, the corpse of a traffic-accident victim turned out to be the father of Yong's friend Losang. Yong had known the man well, but his head had been run over by a truck and the face was almost unrecognizable. In total disbelief, Yong found a familiar mark on the arm. *Losang's father! This body is his. A man I drank with, who laughed and talked heartily. He's ended up like this!*

Tseren began to chop up the robust flesh. Sometimes the vultures would stage a slowdown. With only about thirty birds, there were going to be leftovers from a body this big. Yong, not wanting to prepare the body of Losang's father with his own hands, kept watch from the side. Tseren knew that this was a friend of Yong's, so he didn't handle the body roughly; instead, he worked up a sweat taking an unusually long time. They decided to crush and burn the bones left by the vultures.

Yong set about the job of burning the corpse's possessions as usual: in Tibet it's customary to burn a dead person's belongings. He lit the fire next to the rock and, one by one, threw into the flames all of the belongings that had been stuffed into a cloth bag. There were several photographs in the bag. These too he was throwing onto the fire when suddenly he felt as if he'd been struck – it was his own image he held in his hands. *Ah, that's right.*

We took a photo together during the Yoghurt Festival a few months ago. In the picture Losang, Losang's father and Yong had their arms around each other and were laughing. *Today Losang's father became chunks of meat eaten up by vultures. Now there's not a trace of him left.*

The sky burial had begun early in the morning and finished when the sun had already risen high in the sky. Tseren and Yong sat on the edge of the rock to rest. Tseren looked with concern at Yong, who was lost in thought.

'Teacher Cao, what's wrong?'

Yong stayed silent, then at last raised his head. 'Tseren, if I die in Lhasa, make sure you give me a sky burial, will you?'

'Of course I will, Teacher Cao. I'll feed the vultures so carefully that not a scrap of flesh or bone will be left. You have my word.' Tseren's eyes shone.

Yong and I set out by bicycle for the sky-burial rock. We ride along the road to Sera Gompa surrounded by a desolate landscape peppered with rocky peaks. A little farther along the road between the yellow-ochre crags, the sky-burial rock becomes visible. Nobody is there now.

'That's the rock over there.' Yong stops and points. I can see the large boulder where the ritual is conducted.

'I haven't been here for years, but it sure has changed. A new temple's been built.'

As we walk towards the rock, I notice human hair, teeth and nails littering the gravel that crunches underfoot. These are scraps left over by the vultures from this morning's sky burial. The sun is already low in the sky; apart from our footsteps, there isn't a sound. We climb up the slope and the sky-burial rock comes into view.

'That's the anchor rock over there.' Yong looks in the direction of a rock large enough to wrap one's arms around, and his eyes light up with nostalgia. Freshly dried blood glistens and a few scraps of flesh are scattered about. Yong gauges the size of the bloodstain and says, 'Only one person was done this morning.'

We sit on a nearby rock, light cigarettes and gaze at the scenery. Behind us is the gentle outline of a ridge on the peak where the vultures live. The sky-burial rock, which has absorbed the blood of tens of thousands of people, shines darkly in broad daylight. Presently, a dozen or so Tibetans appear near the rock.

'Who are they?'

'They're pilgrims who've come to Lhasa from Qinghai Province.'

Men and women, young and old, the pilgrims stand in a line below the sky-burial rock. One by one, they clamber up onto it, lie down like corpses with their heads placed directly beneath the anchor rock, look up at the sky and join their hands in prayer.

'What's this ceremony?'

'They're praying for the day they receive the sky burial and can ascend to Heaven.'

16 August. Yong has been gone since early morning, seeing about his passport. I take the dogs out for their walk, although you couldn't call it 'taking the dogs for a walk' so much as simply calling out to Ahuang and Furugomi and setting off. The others usually just follow behind. Nowadays people seem quite used to seeing us filing down to the river in a long procession.

These dogs are like family to us. Recently, Yong dared to ask the university president if he could receive a salary. 'I have a wife and eleven children,' he pleaded, and succeeded in receiving 400 yuan. Such are the possibilities if you stand the socialist state system on its head.

Down by the river, the sun beats more intensely the higher it rises. Watching the dogs chew on sheepskin and bones, I mull over the idea of living in Lhasa forever with them if Yong can't get a passport. Maybe it wouldn't be so bad.

All the students have gone home for the summer holiday, so it's very quiet. I'm accustomed to life here now and have grown to like the harsh climate. I'm also fond of our room;

although simple and sparsely furnished, it feels snug and homely. We have an enormous bed – larger than king-sized – fashioned out of a blackboard we stealthily removed from a classroom in the dead of night, and we sleep on it surrounded by the dogs.

The dogs and I are larking about as usual when we hear a bicycle, and they run barking in the direction of the sound. Yong has returned. He pedals towards me, going as fast as he can, with an unusually joyful expression on his face.

'Aya! I got it! I got it!' he yells, beaming. But I'm slow on the uptake and just stand there, uncomprehending. Still mounted on the bike, Yong pulls a brown booklet from his pocket.

It really is a passport! Issued by the Public Security Bureau.

'Everyone gave their consent! I needed thirteen bloody letters to get out of here, and finally it's been authorized!' Yong gasps.

'You did it! At last we can leave!' But then I remember the dogs and can't feel unqualified joy. What will become of them? I'm much happier here than I was in Japan – I don't want to return to my old life: deep down, that's what I feel. Even with the surveillance and worries about the passport, I've tasted a freedom here that I've never known before.

'Let's buy some meat at the market and give the dogs a good feed,' Yong says, as if reading my thoughts. 'Aya, look at that!' Yong stares upwards. Amongst the fleecy clouds scudding across the sky shines an enormous, mysterious rainbow-coloured ellipse.

'It's magnificent! Magical.'

We gaze up at it in wonder for some time.

At the free-enterprise market below the Potala, we purchase 4 kilos of lungs, tendons and other less saleable animal parts, then walk down to the river with the dogs. There in the grass we cut the meat up into large chunks. The dogs are beside themselves over this unexpected feast – such as they've never had before in their lives, I expect – and wolf it down ecstatically.

'When will we leave?' I ask Yong, who stares wordlessly at the dogs as they devour their treat.

'Tomorrow. Let's get plane tickets to Chengdu,' he answers with a frown.

That night we invite all eleven dogs into the bed to make the most of the little time we have left together. The unaccustomed meat, however, has affected their stomachs, with the result that they restlessly release gas half the night, while the puppies have diarrhoea. We can only laugh wryly at the terrible stink as we drift off to sleep.

17 August. At the national-airline office near the Potala we buy tickets for the earliest flight available to Chengdu, leaving in two days. From there we plan to take a train to Guangzhou – much less exhausting than catching a bus to Golmud. Guangzhou has the advantage of being far from Beijing and close to Hong Kong. We plan to get a visa at the Japanese Consulate there and then head directly for Japan. It feels like so much time has passed since I came to China, I can hardly believe I'll be going back to Japan.

After we get the plane tickets, I stand gazing up at the Potala.

'Do you want to climb up?' Yong asks.

'Of course.'

We walk to the bottom of the stone stairs leading up to the Potala but find it closed off with a wooden barrier. Yong asks a Tibetan man nearby why.

'Apparently it's closed for repairs.'

So we turn our bicycles around and ride out to take a farewell look at Sera Gompa instead. The building is a complicated maze built along the dun-coloured mountains, inhabited by many dogs as well as lamas. On the nearby peaks are several large, vivid images of Buddhas painted on large stones. The chanting inside the building comes to an end, and the ancient doors open to reveal the spectacular sight of a large group of lamas flicking their robes smartly as they leave. The elderly lamas' faces are evocative of tree trunks, as if they've been absorbed into their natural surroundings, and their expressions are serene, both stern and beautiful at the same time.

The sound of lively voices drifting on the air is audible when we enter the monastery. In a garden thick with trees, a question-and-answer session for the young lamas is in progress. A dozen or so groups of around six young lamas each – all clad in crimson robes – squat on the ground surrounding one lama who stands. *Thwack!* The lama in the middle claps his hands and asks a question, and the squatting lamas must reply instantly. The young men are in high spirits, and their study session grows more and more lively.

We climb up to the roof of the monastery. A strapping young lama stands framed against the evening sky holding a kitten in the palm of his hand. '*Tashi delek,*' he greets us with a smile.

'*Tashi delek*, we are Japanese tourists.'

'Welcome. Come. I show you something,' he says in English and beckons us inside. He leads us to a large room, open from the ground floor upwards, that was visible through a window. It's dark, but in the shafts of sunlight that filter through the wooden latticework, I gradually make out the contents of what appears to be a storeroom. There's a pile of objects on the floor – scriptures, altar fittings, Buddha images, building fragments – obviously from when the monastery was ransacked during the Cultural Revolution.

'The PLA really are terrible,' I try out in Tibetan.

'Yes, very bad. Tell people in foreign countries, please,' the young lama replies in halting English.

We sit on the roof, on a rock once used for sky burials, and gaze out over all of Lhasa lying beneath a calm evening sky. People are making their way home, on carts and pulling donkeys. The lamas too have finished chanting their scriptures and answering the day's questions, and a hush has fallen over Sera Gompa.

'I love Tibet so much. I don't know when I'll be able to come back. Six years I've been here, but I still haven't climbed up to the Potala. When I came, I vowed I'd only go there when the time came for me to leave Tibet forever,' Yong bursts out after a long silence. 'Today I took a chance. If we'd gone into the Potala today, then maybe I'd never be able to come back to Tibet again …'

'It's all right, then, because we couldn't go. I'm sure you'll come back.'

'I'm sure there's no other place in the world to beat Tibet.' Yong is overcome with emotion. 'When I saw

Chomolungma and felt how small and insignificant my own existence was, I was scared. But soon after, I realized something ... I realized that though flesh may be small, spirit can equal these mountains.

'If the wealthiest man in the world were to heap all his riches in front of these peaks, they'd be no match for the greatness of the mountains. My body may be insignificant, but my spirit can expand infinitely. And if I can do that, then it isn't impossible that I could transcend the mountains.

'The wilderness of Ali is uninhabited land. I lived there alone for months – only the wilderness, the sky and me. That's how it feels to be one with the universe. I don't believe in God or Buddha, but I feel something that resembles belief. Not belief in a false, made-up god but in a true god. Just time, space, nature, me ... I had to prove my own existence. And when you're out in nature and you demonstrate your own existence, can you predict what a person will feel? Jesus Christ, Sakyamuni ... I realized they were just ordinary men ... their actions totally natural. But people talk of those ordinary actions as greatness. A time will come when I will have to tear open and reveal my own soul – I'll have no choice. But I won't spare any effort to do it.'

Yong is a completely different person when he speaks about his time in Ali. Or perhaps this is when his true self appears. His spirit sparkles like the innocence in a child's eye but is also unsparing – and beautiful – like the vast wilderness and mountains of Tibet. For a moment, the dry wind blows and the intense sun pours down like a burning flame scorching my heart. At times like this, the giant monsters inhabiting Yong's mind also stir, and for this reason, too, he must leave Tibet.

'I hate farewells,' says Yong, and he doesn't tell his friends or even his brother the date of our departure. Only two people are there to see off the thug of Hebalin: Tudaji and Husheng stay up with us on our last night. Tudaji, whose command of English is so good that he could be mistaken for an Englishman, used to interpret for Yong when he met with Westerners.

'I'll be saying goodbye to Lhasa for a while. Husheng, would you look after the dogs for me?'

At six in the morning we give the dogs the last of the meat we bought to stop them following us when we depart. Ahuang seems to sense that Yong is leaving again, but pragmatically she turns away to eat. Furugomi follows us, though.

Even in summer, the Lhasa dawn is piercingly cold. The sky is pitch black and clouded over, with not a single star visible. Yong has a friend who works in a travel agency and he's going to the airport to meet clients, so we have a lift from the gates of Tibet University. Furugomi cocks her head and looks at me as if to ask why we're leaving. Innocent that she is, how will she survive in the Lhasa dog world? My tears spill over. 'Husheng, please, the dogs! We'll meet again sometime. We'll write!'

'Leave everything to me. Keep well!'

The van sets off for Gongkar Airport amidst farewells from Tudaji, Husheng and Furugomi.

'What are we doing asking Husheng to look after the dogs? I mean, when even people are having a hard time getting by.' Yong falls silent. From now on the dogs will have to do whatever they can to get by.

The van proceeds along the riverside road towards the airport. Still the morning sun fails to emerge, and cold rain begins to fall.

'The plane won't be leaving on time in this weather.'

Our flight is scheduled for 9.30 a.m. In China, however, people usually get moving early – well before time – so as to allow leeway in case something goes wrong. We arrive at the airport before eight.

'Ah, just as I thought, the plane's not on time. It's still not even on the runway,' the travel-agent friend says.

'This is the airport?'

'That's right. Lhasa Gongkar Airport.'

Gongkar Airport is smaller than the Golmud train station; just one square steel-reinforced concrete building in the middle of a vast, isolated area. At the rear of the building is the wide runway. The dim outlines of people are visible moving around in the rain outside.

'They still don't know what time the plane'll leave. Let's sleep for a bit in the van.' Tired, we drop off for a while. Some time later the warm, dazzling rays of the sun awaken us.

'Two planes are supposed to be coming in from Chengdu close to evening. If you're lucky, you'll be able to get on one of them,' Yong's friend puts his head through the window to inform us. Apparently in China, and especially between Lhasa and Chengdu, it's normal to wait a day, two days, sometimes even weeks for a plane. You have to let yourself go with the flow and be prepared to settle in for a while. We go to one of several small mud-brick restaurants and fill our stomachs with a simple egg soup and stir-fry.

When the two planes from Chengdu arrive in the afternoon, Yong's friend greets his clients and returns to Lhasa. It looks like we might have a chance of leaving before the day is over.

The Chinese-speaking French guide of a tour group that has also been waiting wearily since early morning strikes up a conversation with Yong. 'This is a damned nuisance, isn't it? I wonder if we'll be able to fly today.'

'Yep, we'll probably be on our way by seven or eight this evening.'

'You need real stamina to travel in China, what with planes being more than ten hours late and all!' The guide is getting fretful.

'He studied Chinese for three years in France apparently, but you speak better than he does,' Yong whispers to me softly.

We sit and wait ... and wait and wait. When I think about it, all I seem to do in China is wait. Not long now, though, and it will be farewell to Tibet and China. Today we fly to Chengdu, then the day after tomorrow we can go to the Japanese Consulate in Guangzhou, get Yong's visa and leave China. Once we're in Japan, we won't have tiresome waits like this or the Public Security Bureau to worry about. I suspect that Yong will feel rather cramped after the magnificent natural environment and freedom of Tibet, but China will improve in future. He'll be able to go to the United States and probably other countries as well. He's thin and gaunt now from this long journey, but his expression is cheerful and animated. The day of his release from this giant prison is finally drawing near.

At 7.30 p.m. boarding begins. We complete the inspection, check in our luggage, then board a bus. After a three-minute ride we alight on the runway and line up with the foreign tour group, Tibetans and other Chinese waiting for the entrance steps to be lowered.

'Look, that's something I painted a long time ago. To make money.' Yong points out a large signboard on the other side of the runway. 'I had to steer a ladder truck and paint at the same time – all in the middle of the night. It was so cold I nearly froze.'

The giant signboard depicts the Potala and a plane flying up towards it, and is inscribed with the words 'Welcome to Tibet'. Its colours are already fading.

'What a vulgar design! Surely it wasn't your idea?'

'I should say not! I thought up something much more artistic, but the person in charge wanted a plane and the Potala. So I had to do it.'

Just at that moment, I notice a uniformed man striding towards us. Next thing, a Public Security policeman is standing there. He's middle-aged, with a look of hatred in his eyes and alcohol on his breath.

'… permit.' He glares at me, mumbling something in a creepy, strangled voice. Yong tries to explain, but the policeman takes no notice and shouts at me again, 'Permit!' He wants to see my travel permit.

'We've already paid a fine to Lhasa Public Security for her being here during martial law without a travel permit. Lhasa Public Security also extended her visa. Please look at the date,' Yong explains politely while I hastily open my passport.

'Shut up! It's an offence not to have a permit! You two cannot board this plane! Wait here!' The policeman becomes increasingly belligerent.

'The Chinese authorities in Lhasa, and the Public Security Bureau, authorized a passport and gave me permission to go to Japan to marry this woman. The governor of the TAR and the Chinese government have all given their consent. You can confirm that with a telephone call,' Yong explains desperately. He shows the policeman the passport he received three days ago.

'Be quiet! I'm telling you to wait! Do as I say, or I'll charge the two of you. You'll never get on a plane again! You ... you're off to prison!'

The policeman pulls out a handgun and points it at Yong's head. The man is drunk, his eyes hazy and unfocused, his legs unsteady. It all happens so fast that Yong is lost for words.

'These passports are confiscated!' The policeman thrusts both passports into his pocket. Yong is ordered to go and find our luggage. There's a buzz amongst the passengers waiting to board the plane as they watch what's happening to us. Yong staggers off the baggage truck with our backpacks and drops them on the runway. I rush over, hoist my pack on my back and lead him away, biting back tears of vexation. Yong's mouth is twisted in disappointment.

The policeman points to a hotel about half a kilometre from the runway and orders us to go there.

'Yong, what's going to happen to our passports?'

'Yeah, let's get them back.'

Yong's passport was our reward for six months of running around. After all that effort, to have it confiscated by a drunken policeman is unbearable. We wait for him on the road to the hotel.

'I've gotta get that passport back!'

When the other passengers have finished boarding, the policeman walks over to us. 'What, you two still here? Hurry up and get the hell out of here!'

'Can't we have our passports back?'

'Shut up! Beat it! Or else I'll confiscate them forever.'

We're utterly helpless. Tears of exasperation stream down Yong's face, and the best I can do is to glare at the policeman with contempt.

'You understand, eh? You're going to prison!' he roars. We hear the plane behind us, taking off as we walk towards the airport hotel, utterly dejected.

At the hotel we're forced to pay the exorbitant sum of 50 yuan for a room for one night. Immediately we enter the room, Yong breaks down in tears.

'Shit! The mean bastard! He gets drunk and wants to fuck with people! Throwing his weight around just because he's the airport police – he's probably only after money!'

'That type just puts a noose round his own neck. I'm sure we'll have the last laugh.'

'Why do I always get such a rough deal! I've caused you so much trouble. Aya, I'm so, so sorry.' Yong prostrates himself at my knees, still weeping.

'What about phoning Lhasa Public Security and explaining the situation? Isn't there anything we can do?'

But such a proposal is meaningless – the law simply does not exist in China. It's the individuals in charge of their own little power domains who hold the whip. How do you deal with this kind of thing?

After a while Yong calms down and wipes the tears away. 'I'm going to talk it over with him,' he says, and goes off to find the policeman.

It turns out that this policeman, like Yong, is from Henan Province. But this fact doesn't change anything, and he refuses to treat us leniently, instead demanding a bribe of 500 US dollars. Grudgingly, Yong hands it over. This is daylight robbery: a policeman, for no reason whatsoever, abuses his power under the influence of alcohol and baldly pulls off this appalling stunt. I feel wretched with helplessness, but at least we've recovered our passports. We've already used up almost all our money – obtaining the passport itself consumed a great deal of it – and the little we have left is just enough to cover the cost of air tickets from Guangzhou to Japan.

20 August. Morning. This time, the policeman makes no objections when we board the plane. The incident has affected us both deeply, though, and neither of us feels the least bit happy when we finally arrive in Chengdu. Until we leave China, there's no knowing what might happen; only when the plane takes off and we cross the border will I feel peace of mind at last.

24 August. The morning after arriving in Guangzhou, we set off for the Japanese Consulate. There's a large crowd of Chinese already lined up outside the Garden Hotel where

the consulate is located, but when we explain our situation, we're admitted immediately.

The moment I step inside the consulate and set eyes on bespectacled, kindly Vice-Consul Hokari, I feel a flood of relief wash over me, as if we've reached shelter at last, and the sole place in China where reason prevails.

'We want to go to Japan to get married. Here is Yong's passport. We have all the necessary documentation.'

'Eh? Haven't you completed the marriage formalities in China yet? If you're applying for a visa with just a passport, it'll take quite some time.'

'No, I don't believe it! I enquired about the procedures at the Japanese Embassy in Beijing. They told me that the quickest way was to get a passport for the purpose of marriage and apply for a visa. So we just got the passport and didn't register our marriage.'

'The embassy probably assumed that going through marriage formalities in China would take an extremely long time. Because the two of you are still not legally married here, the visa application will have to be for the purpose of visiting a friend. In which case we will have to send the documentation to the Foreign Ministry in Tokyo, and, let me see ... if you're lucky, it will take two or three months. But it could be six months or more. It's even possible a visa may not be granted.'

This news shocks us profoundly. All this way, ever since Beijing, we've trusted in what the embassy told us. I should have asked in more detail ... but there's no use beating myself up about it now.

'I don't suppose there's any other way?' Yong asks, looking exhausted.

We rapidly explain the situation to Mr Hokari, and the routine manner with which he dealt with us initially is replaced by a show of sympathy.

'Well, I'm afraid the fastest way is still to complete the marriage formalities here and send the paperwork to the Foreign Ministry. After that we can send it to the city office where Miss Goda's family register is held, and Cao Yong can be recorded as her husband. Then if we receive a copy back by post, a visa can be issued straightaway.'

'Could you write us a list of all the necessary documents, please?'

'A Chinese certificate of marriage and notary's certificates.'

'And there really isn't any other way?'

'I can't give any guarantee as to how long it will take if you apply for a visa to visit a friend. Those are the regulations. There's nothing else I can do.'

Mr Hokari shakes his head. We thank him and leave the consulate feeling dismayed. Yong's face is ashen, his gait unsteady.

'If we have to register our marriage, then we need to go back to Lhasa,' he says and promptly collapses on the grass at the edge of the road. He sits there in silence a while, then abruptly jumps to his feet and races over to the bushes where he throws up violently. When the nausea passes, he lies down on the grass, exhausted.

We have very little money left. If we don't get to Japan quickly, we won't be able to go anywhere.

'Perhaps I can register the marriage in my home town,' Yong mutters.

'In Henan?'

'Yeah, I might be able to ask someone for a favour.'

We go to a restaurant to fortify ourselves. But Yong falls down onto the bench with a thud before putting even a single bite in his mouth.

'Hey! What're you doing? Get up!' the waitress shouts at him.

'He's not well, you fool!' I scream back at her. A deep anger at her heartlessness stirs within me. She shouts more abuse and disappears in a huff. Eventually Yong sits up.

'Let's go to Guangzhou Station and buy tickets to Xinyang.'

The station is incredibly jammed as usual, with a miscellany of people thronging the square: *mangliu* – peasants who 'float' in from the countryside seeking work in big cities like Guangzhou – squatting on the ground; beggars clutching children; families who can't find work camping out, sometimes for days; emaciated old people; men looking for the opportunity to pick pockets; people waiting for their trains to depart. We search for the ticket touts in the melee.

'We won't be able to get hard sleepers to Xinyang, so we'll just have to buy them as far as Zhengzhou.' Yong approaches one of the touts. The man goes off to consult with his cronies and returns with two hard-sleeper tickets to Zhengzhou in his hand.

'How much?'

'Three hundred yuan for the two.'

'You're joking! Come on, you can do better than that.' Yong takes his time, negotiating with several touts, and eventually purchases tickets for the train leaving tonight.

We go to the Telegraph Office and send a telegram to his parents, then go to the youth hostel where we've left our belongings. We stuff only the essentials into a small backpack and leave the rest of our luggage at the hostel reception.

We set off for the station again in time to catch the night train. Only yesterday we arrived in Guangzhou, and here we are leaving again.

1. HOMECOMING

25 August. We set off north again, thoroughly fed up with being jolted around on Chinese trains. I gaze out at the drab landscape of the Chinese interior – the bleak square brick buildings and the desolate yellow earth that goes on forever. This depressing scene puts me in mind of the first time I visited Beijing and was hugely disappointed. After a week I felt such an aversion to the place that I became almost neurotic. Buses were packed like sardine tins with passengers pushing and shoving, conductors haranguing them at the tops of their voices and people with garlicky breath spitting everywhere. I was cheated by a black-market money-changer and ignored by shop attendants whenever I tried to buy anything. I got left behind by the bus when I went to the Great Wall, and all I could see in the Forbidden City were people's heads. At the time I swore I'd never come back.

The train heads for Henan, birthplace of the Yellow River culture, one of the world's four great civilizations.

'I'm not especially fond of Xinyang because I only ever lived there a short time. I was already at university when my father changed jobs and moved there, and after that I went off to Tibet,' says Yong. 'Although I came home a number of times, I was never in the house for more than two days at a stretch. My father still worships Mao. When I'm with him, we only ever argue. If I can, I want to show you Xinxian, where I was born. It will have changed a lot though ...'

'I want to meet your parents at least, so I'm glad we're going to Xinyang.'

26 August. We pass the night in a hard sleeper and arrive in Xinyang before noon. Yong's father and oldest brother, Cao Zhi, are waiting with a joyful welcome when we leave the small station.

'*Ni hao, ni hao*!' We exchange greetings, then they call a motor tricycle and we all pile in.

'Papa, this is Aya. Her Chinese is good, isn't it?'

'Oh yes, that's right! Good girl, good girl.' His father smiles and praises me as if I'm a small child. He appears to have much to say to this son he hasn't seen in a long time, but I find it all difficult to follow – Yong has switched from standard Chinese to a local dialect.

'Number Four, I need to tell you that your mother recently suffered a cerebral hemorrhage.'

'What! Is she all right?' Yong is instantly pained.

'Now don't you go worrying her too much. She's resting at home.'

This part of Henan is a bleak industrial landscape of rows of buildings made from concrete and brick. There's nothing special or different; only the brick buildings stand out. I stare at the dreary townscape as we bump along the yellow-brown gravel road in a cloud of dust.

After about half an hour the motor tricycle turns sharply and arrives at a cluster of concrete-and-brick buildings; this is Yong's father's work unit, the Non-metallic Materials Research Institute. We walk through the grounds to their home, whereupon Yong's mother, who's been eagerly waiting for us outside, rushes over with unsteady steps.

'Mama!' Yong drops his luggage with a thud, races over to her and squeezes her hands. His mother's eyes glisten as she wordlessly studies his face. I'm moved and painfully reminded of my own mother, who's been caused so much distress by her unfilial daughter.

Yong's parents live on the ground floor of a two-storey brick building. The kitchen is in an annexe at the front, and at the rear is a small garden where they keep chickens and grow vegetables. The spacious living room contains a small television and sofa. It's a typical Chinese dwelling, with concrete walls painted white and pale green. We sit down at the table and Cao Zhi pours tea.

Yong's father begins to speak with a grave expression: 'Number Four, Cao Yi has been sent to jail.' This is Yong's second-oldest brother.

'What! How on earth did that happen?'

'You know he was with the Xinxian Tobacco and Liquor Corporation, right, and hadn't been on good terms with the county magistrate for a long time. Well, it seems that man was looking for an opportunity to get Cao Yi, so he sued him for embezzlement. Cao Yi was given a nine-year sentence for a crime he didn't commit.'

Yong jumps to his feet, shouting, 'Why couldn't he

escape! Isn't there something we can do? Ask somebody to help or something – isn't there anything?'

'Escape! What are you saying? We'll trust in the government and leave it up to the courts!'

'But there isn't any kind of law in this country, is there? Papa, why don't you open your eyes!'

Yong's father will be fifty-seven this year but looks much older. So does his mother. They both underwent severe hardship during the Cultural Revolution, and now worries about their sons being tossed about by the vagaries of politics have added to the strain. Yong doesn't say a word about our marriage registration. We can go back to Lhasa and get it done there.

'Number Four, are you all right? Do you have money? I can give you 2000 yuan if you want.'

'I'm fine, Papa. Nothing's wrong. You'll need money for Cao Yi. You need to concentrate on getting him released.'

An oil painting by Yong hangs on the wall. It depicts a bridge in some woods and is painted in the imposing tones of the Barbizon School. Yong's teenage fascination with Millet caused him to paint little else but rural landscapes imbued with a calm, peaceful air, exploring subjects such as child shepherds and villages at evening. In these paintings I sense his yearning for a paradise always beyond reach.

'That's a bridge I liked in my home town,' he says. 'I painted it just after I started doing oils. This is a nomad in Qinghai Province from when I travelled there as a university student. These are drawings from my wandering days.' One by one, Yong begins extracting drawings from an enormous collection stowed in a large wooden trunk. Some are of peasants taking a break from their work, sketched when he stayed in a village during his journeys through the countryside. They're drawn in charcoal on rough paper, but these are the faces of living people. Their vitality is tangible; the firm, accurate lines revealing warmth in the stern expressions of the peasants, their skin wrinkled as old tree bark. They're deeply moving. This collection, with its vibrant portraits, is the foundation of Yong's work.

We go into the bedroom to speak to his mother, who's lying down.

'Mama, we're going to get married and go to Japan.'

Yong's mother smiles and squeezes my hand. 'That's good,' she murmurs, still clasping my hand. 'I can close my eyes in peace now,' she continues, and shuts her eyes as if she's spent all her remaining strength.

'Mama, what are you talking like this for? Snap out of it! I may be going to Japan, but I'll be able to come back.'

'Number Four, come back soon, then.' Tears cloud her eyes. I guess she's caught between worry over her son's future and wanting him to be near.

Yong's mother has a calm, peaceful face with a resigned look you wouldn't see in a Japanese woman in her fifties. She lived through the Second Sino-Japanese War, the Cultural Revolution and many other periods of turmoil, yet even now she can't have a quiet life; instead she has constant worries about her children's futures. Yong decides not to say anything more to her about our situation. To me he says, 'Aya, I have to go to Lhasa. I'll go alone and register our marriage.'

29 August. After three nights in Xinyang, we leave for Tibet. We climb into a motor tricycle with Yong's father, who's accompanying us to the station. Cold rain falls even though it's summer.

'Mama, look after yourself. I'll be fine. I'm sure it'll go well for Cao Yi. Don't worry too much. We'll be back soon.'

'Number Four, Number Four!' Yong's mother stands in the cold drizzle, crying out to him as if this is all too much to bear.

'Mama, hurry and get back inside. Mama!' Yong urges loudly as we depart.

'Number Four, my son!' She sobs and takes a couple of faltering steps as if to chase after us.

'Mama, go back inside!' Tears stream down Yong's face. His mother's figure grows smaller and smaller, until eventually she disappears into the bleak landscape.

We take our leave of Yong's father and board the train. It's the start of another trip of more than 2000 kilometres. The tiny figure of Yong's mother standing in the rain remains etched in my mind's eye.

2. THE MARRIAGE CERTIFICATE

2 September. Morning. Once again we arrive in Golmud. We rent beds at the city guest house, then head straight for the bus station and buy one ticket for the Lhasa bus leaving at two in the afternoon. Once this is done, we go to a Muslim restaurant as usual, looking for the energy boost that Hui food always gives us, but Yong doesn't have much of an appetite.

'I'll try to complete the formalities on my own, and I'll send telegrams to the guest house to let you know how it's going.'

'Is it all right? Can you manage? Is it really possible to register a marriage without both of us being present?'

'I'll give it a go. If I take your passport and a copy of your family register, I think I can swing it. If you go back there, somebody's bound to inform on us and you'll be put under surveillance all over again.'

A little after two the Lhasa bus departs, taking Yong with it.

'Wait for my telegram! I'll be back soon!'

The moment he leaves, all of the strength drains from

my body, and I trudge wearily back to the dreary concrete guest house. How long will it take to register our marriage, I wonder. Just getting Yong's passport took a month and a half. Now that I think about it, ever since I arrived in Beijing back in February, he and I have barely been apart. Except for the two days when I was in Hong Kong getting my visa, we've been constantly in each other's company, travelling, eating and sleeping under the same roof. It feels like we've been together for many years.

I sigh as I sit on my bed by the window in the dormitory room. Other foreigners are also staying here – from Hong Kong, Taiwan and France – and all are planning to go to Tibet. They're here because, even though there hasn't been the slightest relaxation of martial law, the Chinese media are still reporting that Tibet is open and that foreign tourists can travel freely. Tourists take these reports at face value and come all the way to Golmud, just like we did. When they arrive, however, they learn that martial law hasn't actually been lifted and are forced to revise their plans. Most disappear on the bus to Dunhuang, but others – encouraged by tantalizing suggestions from the Public Security Bureau that travel permits can be issued to groups of three or more, or that if they wait another week they'll be able to enter Lhasa – stay put. It sounds to me like nothing more than a ploy to relieve tourists of their money, but many travellers stay on in the ugly guest house of this utterly boring town for one or even two weeks in the hope of journeying to Tibet.

4 September. Morning. I find a telegram from Yong waiting for me at the service desk; he's arrived in Lhasa and is

struggling with bureaucratic procedures. He says he misses me. As he's used up all his contacts and connections obtaining his passport, registering our marriage and getting notary's certificates as well isn't turning out to be easy. To make things even harder, he has little money left for bribes.

Three days later, in the afternoon, the guest-house receptionist comes into the dormitory and hands me a telegram: 'Procedures complete. Arrive 8th. Yong.' I never dreamt he could do it so quickly! Too excited to sleep, I lie awake all night waiting for morning to come.

Next day, I'm sitting on my bed alone in the dormitory when Yong blows in just before noon. 'Aya! It's done! We're all set now!'

Wild with joy, we hug each other. When I take a closer look at Yong, however, I notice that he's become terribly thin; his stomach is sunken, there are dark circles under his eyes and he has a deep scratch at the base of his nose.

'What happened to your nose?'

'It's nothing. Let's get going to Guangzhou straightaway.'

His expression is cheerful as, without resting, he picks up his luggage and we head for the train station. We're able to buy hard-sleeper tickets astonishingly easily at the ticket window. There's one snag, however: the price is twice what it was! We ask why and are told that this is one of the measures in place to restrict people's movements since Tiananmen Square; all bus, train and airplane fares doubled in September. What an outrageous price hike!

We board the 1.43 p.m. train for Xining with relief. 'Thank goodness! We'll be able to get the visa for Japan now.'

'I still can't believe it myself, that I could get it all done so quickly.' Yong pulls the marriage certificate out to show me.

'So this is the famous Chinese marriage certificate.'

This unique item must be produced by couples whenever they stay at guest houses or hotels. The bright red certificate inside a thick plastic cover is incredibly gaudy, with the words 'Marriage Certificate' and the gold-embossed character for 'Double Happiness' surrounded by a dragon and phoenix. At more than twice the size of a passport, it's rather large to be carrying around. That aside, the main problem for us is the photograph inside, which we took in haste before Yong left for Lhasa; wearing the hemp clothes we'd had made up in Dali that make us look like beggars, and with wildly dishevelled hair, the overall impression we give is rather fearsome – almost like a bandit and his wife.

'It's an amazing certificate.'

'I got everything done.' Yong shows me the sheaf of notary's certificates and smiles.

'It wasn't easy, I bet. You're thin again. And that nose, how did that happen?'

'I fell over.'

'What?'

'The bus stopped at the Tuotuo River near Mt Tangula. I bought a bowl of beef-noodle soup at a canteen and was about to start eating, when I suddenly fainted with the bowl in my hand. My face hit the ground hard, and I got this scratch on my nose. Some kind people carried me onto the bus, where I lay for several hours before coming to.'

Thank goodness. If they hadn't carried Yong to the bus, he would've frozen to death.

'I hardly ate the whole time I was in Lhasa, spending all day every day running around getting the certificates organized. To be honest, when I went there I didn't know what I was going to do. But I was lucky. When I went to the Notarial Office, the person in charge was a guy called Lü. "Aren't you Teacher Cao?" he asked. I was surprised, because no bureaucrat has ever addressed me in such a respectful manner before. I wondered what he wanted from me. But then he said, "Don't you remember? You used to teach my son," and I recalled one of my students called Lü, who'd been more enthusiastic about painting than any of the others.

'Lü told me, "My son has always held you in high regard. He's always saying that no-one in Lhasa can equal your oil painting. We heard the recent rumours about your situation. Bring the necessary documents for your application to me." He got the certificates ready in no time! And my friend Tudaji did all the English translations in a single evening.'

It was nothing short of a miracle.

This time our journey takes us via Xining to Luoyang, where we call in to see Yong's sister, Cao Qing, and retrieve the slide films of the Guge Kingdom that he left with her for safekeeping. Then, on the evening of 13 September, we board a train for Guangzhou.

3. DEPARTURE

We're both excited during the two-night journey to Guangzhou, but time drags heavily. On 15 September we arrive at a little past five in the morning. We rent a private room at the youth hostel to rest until the Japanese Consulate opens. Despite our fatigue, we can't keep still.

Impatient with the slow-moving hands of the clock, we wait until ten before hailing a taxi for the Garden Hotel building. Hearts pounding, we jump out of the taxi when we get there and race up to the consulate entrance.

'Closed for Respect-for-the-Elderly Day' announces a notice stuck to the door. The Japanese flag is flying, but the gates are firmly shut. I'd completely forgotten about Japanese public holidays. When I think about it, tomorrow is the third Saturday of the month – a day when Japanese public facilities are closed – and the day after that is a Sunday, of course.

'Japan sure has a lot of public holidays!' Hopes dashed for the moment, we head back to the hostel.

On the Monday, the consulate's heavy gates open at last.

Consul Seno and Vice-Consul Hokari interview us, and we submit the necessary documents.

'You've certainly had a hard time. Well done!' Mr Hokari promises to put the application through as quickly as possible: 'We'll post the papers to the Foreign Ministry in Tokyo and ask to have them sent on to the municipal office where Miss Goda's records are held. When we receive a copy of the register with Cao Yong's name recorded on it, we can issue a visa the same day.'

This consulate is just heavenly!

'There are a lot of fake marriages between Chinese and Japanese people these days, and plenty of brokers who make money out of them as well. Not to mention the stream of illegal immigrants from Fujian Province who pose as Vietnamese refugees. It's been causing major problems in Japan. Anyway, that's why these procedures are so complicated, and I'm sorry to have to trouble you with this, but ...'

We must fill in a strange document explaining our 'Motive for Marriage'. We do so feeling a bit bewildered.

Consul Seno, who speaks fluent Chinese, carefully reads the newspaper articles about Yong's exhibition. 'These paintings are amazing.'

'This one was confiscated by the Beijing Public Security Bureau.'

'I hope you will continue your work in Japan. Would you both like to come and have dinner at my home one day soon? I'm sure you haven't had Japanese food in a while, Miss Goda.'

'Thank you very much. By the way, how long will it take to get the visa, do you think?'

'We'll send the papers by express so they'll arrive at the Foreign Ministry on the 21st. After being checked, they'll probably reach the municipal office where your records are held around the beginning of October.'

'Thank you for your help,' we say, and leave the consulate.

'We have to wait a month before we can get the visa?'

'Why can't they stamp it for us right away, seeing as how they know everything they need to know?'

'We'll just have to wait – there's nothing else we can do.'

Our money is running low – there may not even be enough left for two tickets to Tokyo. Back in the hostel we count it again. 'One hundred and thirty thousand yen, three hundred dollars ... and a few yuan.' If we're careful, we should be able to get by. We shift from the private room to a dormitory in the hostel and decide to economize on food as well.

On 24 September, just as we're beginning to feel thoroughly fed up with life in Guangzhou, Vice-Consul Hokari telephones us at the hostel.

'Consul Seno would like to invite you to dinner this evening. Can you come?'

'Thank you very much. We'd love to!'

'In that case, I'll come and pick you up at six.'

Mr Hokari comes to fetch us as promised and takes us to Consul Seno's flat in the Garden Tower. We're taken into a spacious drawing room together with Mr Hokari and his wife. The experience is like stumbling across an oasis in the middle of a desert; I feel dizzy when I step onto the high-quality woollen carpet, and when I sit down on the soft, velvety sofa, I feel so out of place that I can't relax. After the rigours of our seven-month journey, I know we must be quite a sight with our unkempt hair, faded clothes and worn-out shoes – me with my Tibetan bone necklaces and bracelets – yet we're given a warm welcome and don't notice a single glance of disapproval.

When I'm served a small Japanese bowl of rice and miso soup, tears suddenly well up. 'Japanese food …'

But Yong doesn't seem to like food that tastes of the sea.

'From what I hear, you've had an extremely rough time, haven't you?'

'Yes, we've been on the move constantly for the last seven months. With the uprising in Lhasa and Tiananmen Square, China has been in unbelievable turmoil this year.'

'But you managed to make it this far, that's the main thing.'

Yong presents Mr Seno and Mr Hokari with rubbings of the stone Buddhas in Guge to show our gratitude.

25 September. After visiting Consul Seno's home, the streets of Guangzhou strike me as gloomy and dirty. Yet I feel this milieu is more in keeping with the person I am right now. We're searching for a money-changer in order to exchange dollars for Chinese money: we can get more than double the rate for foreign money on the black market than we could at the bank. After calculating how much we'll need for plane fares and expenses after arriving in Japan, Yong doggedly goes around to all the money-changers looking for the best possible deal.

'Seven hundred and fifty yuan for a hundred dollars.' A young Uighur, one of many in the Guangzhou black market, offers a very good rate indeed.

'I'll change 200 dollars. Give me the Chinese currency first.' Yong receives 1500 yuan from the Uighur. I quickly check the bundle of notes and signal that it's okay. Yong hands over 200 dollars and the transaction is complete. But at that moment, five or six Uighurs come out of nowhere and surround us.

'Oy, change some more!' they demand, closing in and jeering, although you wouldn't expect that they could use violence on this crowded shopping street.

'Beat it! We're not changing anything with you! Give me back my dollars,' Yong yells, then snatches the dollars from their hands and thrusts the yuan back at the same time. The Uighurs grumble threateningly.

'We'll look for another money-changer.' This time we search for a Han and find an old woman at a roadside stall.

'Let me see. There are a lot of counterfeit notes around these days.' She puts two hundred-dollar notes under a light and stares at them long and hard. 'Look here! This is fake! Don't you try and cheat me!' The old woman's face reddens with anger and she throws the American money back at Yong.

'You must be joking! My dollars ... they can't be fake! It's not possible!' Yong looks at the money and his face pales. His money has been switched for fake notes! The ink is much lighter than on genuine notes, and although it isn't obvious in the dark, under a light there's no mistake.

'Ah, you must have let the Uighurs touch your money then. That was foolish. Those counterfeit notes sell for 10 Hong Kong dollars each in Hong Kong,' the old woman says, showing some sympathy now.

We hurry back to the place where the Uighur gang had been, but they're long gone of course. We have to respect their technique – it all happened so fast. The Uighurs' skill in counting money in front of you, then dextrously extracting several notes, is well known amongst travellers, but we hadn't even considered the possibility of being taken in so easily ourselves. Like true professionals, these guys are never idle when it comes to studying new methods of trickery.

'Shit! Let's use this to get back at the Uighurs next time.' Yong bites his lip in chagrin. But there's no crying over spilled milk – what could be truer?

26 September. A short walk from the youth hostel is the White Swan Hotel. This four-star ultra-modern hotel, with rooms costing as much as 600 US dollars a night, has restaurants, a café terrace and a gallery that sells ink paintings amongst other artworks. We're on a reconnaissance trip to the gallery. Completely shut off from the outside world, an artificial air of orderliness pervades the luxurious interior bustling with foreign tourists – why, we could almost be in Tokyo! I instinctively feel allergic to the atmosphere.

'I want to try and sell some ink paintings here,' says Yong.

We're chatting and looking around the gallery when an attendant notices us and yells, 'Get out!', chasing us like beggars. Many places in China are off limits to ordinary citizens, including luxury hotels, restaurants, Friendship Stores and other amenities for foreigners. Locals are humiliated and turned away, but nothing is ever said to

foreigners, no matter how grotty they might look. We'd
been speaking Chinese, hence the appalling treatment.
Fuming with resentment, we leave the gallery and go to sit
on the terrace.

The loss of 200 dollars was an enormous blow – even
the youth hostel is an expense we can barely afford
anymore – and Yong has been racking his brains for a
solution. He has some Korean paper, ink and brushes with
him to paint pictures to sell in case of emergency. But he
seems in no condition to do that now. If we're even more
careful with the money we have, we'll get by. Only a little
bit longer to go.

The weather's been hot and humid, but now that
September is nearing its end, a fresh breeze has begun to
blow. I can't help but think longingly of the thin, clean, dry
air of Tibet.

28 September. We're still at the youth hostel, living frugally.

'Come to think of it, there's an artist I made friends
with in Tibet, Wei Kejian, who should be here in
Guangzhou,' Yong remembers. 'I don't know his address,
but we could get it at the Academy of Fine Arts.'

At the academy office we learn Wei Kejian's address;
then we find his house easily in a corner of a housing
estate on East Nonglin Road in the Dongshan district. He
and his wife, Xiao Chuan, give us a warm welcome.

'Hey, you know me better than that! Why didn't you get
in touch when you came to Guangzhou before? Idiot! You
don't need to be staying in guest houses. Come and stay
with us, pronto! There're four rooms, so you can have one
to yourselves. It won't be any trouble.'

Wei Kejian and Xiao Chuan are both involved in the arts; he's an abstract painter and she's a sculptor. His parents are high-ranking Party members, and he's obviously well off. The couple have a television, a video machine, an audio system, a sofa, even a telephone that can make international calls – something only the privileged few are allowed in China.

October comes and I ring my parents to give them Wei Kejian's telephone number. I've caused them so much worry – there aren't adequate words to apologize.

'We pray that you'll come back safely. When the register extract arrives here, I'll send it on straightaway,' my mother tells me.

'When we get to Japan, we'll have to look for part-time work,' I say to Yong.

'Fine. I can do anything,' he laughs.

5 October. We visit the consulate to see whether my register extract has arrived. Mr Hokari admits us with a smile.

'The papers still aren't here, but there's a letter from your mother.' I slit open the envelope and find the letter folded around 100,000 yen!

'Now that's gutsy – sending cash through the post!' Yong whoops in admiration.

All this time, I haven't been able to bring myself to mention money to my mother. But she's guessed our dire situation and sent us some, knowing that if she posted it care of the consulate it would escape inspection. Her thoughtfulness fills me with gratitude.

'If we're careful, we can get by until we reach Japan.

Let's use this money to get to Hokkaido. We have to say thank you.'

6 October. Evening. My mother telephones me at Wei Kejian's house.

'Now you can come home at last, can't you? We're waiting. Actually, I phoned to tell you that the Dalai Lama has been awarded the Nobel Peace Prize.'

We've heard nothing at all about the Dalai Lama. Ever since Tiananmen Square, China has been on the receiving end of strict sanctions from the United States and other countries.

13 October. My register extract is delivered to the consulate at last. Mr Hokari is just as thrilled as we are.

'Usually it takes three days to issue a visa, but as a special exception we'll issue yours today.' *Thwack*. Consul Seno stamps a visa with the words 'Spouse of Japanese National' into Yong's passport.

'This is just like being handed a prison release. At last we can get out of jail!' We thank Mr Seno and Mr Hokari and bound outside, jumping for joy. 'I don't believe it! Can I really leave the country? Is this for real?' Yong asks me over and over in wonder.

'Yes, you can. But let's not get too excited until we actually arrive in Tokyo.' I don't want to let myself get too elated; so many times in this country I've had my hopes raised only to be plunged back into despair. I can't bear to go through that again.

We walk to an airline office near Guangzhou Station and buy two tickets to Tokyo for the next day on Japan

Airlines. In the evening we pack our bags and bid farewell to Wei Kejian and Xiao Chuan. 'But … you never know, we might be back.'

'I'm sure things will work out. Come on, let's toast your departure from China.' Wei Kejian and Xiao Chuan open some champagne.

I pass a restless night without sleeping. We leave for the airport before daybreak. People are gathering, but check-in hasn't begun yet.

At last it does. Yong is afraid that his name may be on a blacklist and that he'll be arrested, but the inspections go smoothly and we enter the waiting room without difficulty. Then we board the plane. Yong is still worried that he'll be grabbed by an attendant and hauled off. But nothing happens. The plane moves down the runway. In tandem with the sounds of take-off, China grows smaller and more distant with each passing moment.

'Are we in the air? Have we left China yet?' Yong gazes out the window, his face still unbelieving. I feel slightly anxious too.

A short time later, we're in the transit lounge of Kai Tak Airport in Hong Kong.

'Is this Hong Kong? Are we over the border?' Yong asks me repeatedly.

'We crossed the border all right. This is Hong Kong. See? Look around you. It's different, isn't it?' Capitalism is in the air – you can smell it. Kai Tak overflows with an abundance of luxury goods, rows of glittering products in colours so bright they almost hurt the eyes. Yong starts to believe me at last. When we take off from

Hong Kong he finally lets himself relax and feel safe.

I think back over the events of the last eight months; it seems such a long, long time, as if years have passed. Never have I experienced such a long eight months in my life. Never have I experienced such a rollercoaster of emotions.

'Yong, there's something I realized in China.'

'What's that?'

'I think I'd never known true hatred or anger before. In China, I understood what those emotions are.'

'Are you saying there are places in the world where people don't feel hatred and anger?'

Yes, there are places in the world where people don't feel hatred and anger, but they don't feel genuine happiness either. I wonder how Yong, who brings with him the spirit of Tibet, will feel in Japan, that island nation of mild, gentle, subdued, indulged people. This time it will be his turn to experience an unfamiliar world.

The plane begins to descend. Between the gaps in the clouds appear a neatly partitioned landscape, an angular coastline, boxy-looking housing estates, square blocks of greenery and countless tiny cars driving along perfectly straight roads.

'Look, Yong. That's Japan.'

AFTERWORD

Eighteen years after these events took place in China, I am happy that this book has now been published in English.

After arriving in wintry Tokyo with barely a penny between us, Cao Yong and I looked around for part-time jobs. The work we eventually found, in this country where there is much prejudice towards foreigners, was digging archaeological sites and cutting grass at the Aoyama cemetery.

But even in a foreign country Cao Yong was able to soon flex his talents as an artist, and in bubble-era Tokyo he began to undertake the demanding work of painting giant murals on commercial wall-spaces. He also worked day after day without let up on his own paintings and was eventually able to hold an exhibition in Tokyo. His talent was recognized and he earned himself a place in the Tokyo art world. Yet ... the apartment in Tokyo, and indeed the whole country of Japan, turned out to be too small for him.

Several months after we arrived in Japan, we learned that the seven paintings confiscated by the Public Security Bureau in Beijing had been burned.

In the summer of 1992, Ahuang, the dog we left behind in Lhasa, was shot and killed. Ahuang had become the leader of a pack of dogs at Tibet University, and one moonlit night she led her gang in an extraordinary attack on a large pig in the grounds. Such a thing was unheard of, and we later learned from Husheng that this is why she was shot by university security down by the Lhasa River.

The following year, Cao Yong was finally able to get a visa to the United States on the strength of his artistic achievements. We traveled around America and discovered California, a place that seemed like an 'oxygen-rich Tibet' to us.

In May 1994, Cao Yong moved to America to live, and during the course of that year I began to write *Tao*. This book is the result of Cao Yong's enormous encouragement and cooperation.

Cao Yong held his first one-man exhibition in America in a Soho gallery in the autumn of 1994. By the summer of 1996 he obtained a green card. Galleries began to accept his work and he managed to establish a foothold for himself in America. Then our time spent together, since that first chance meeting, came to an end.

Cao Yong now continues to live like a bird of passage, soaring beyond borders and racing to wherever his heart takes him.

I'd like to take the opportunity here to thank all the people who took care of us and supported us. Forgive me for not naming names, but to everyone who encouraged and did their utmost to help Cao Yong in his work, who collected his paintings, who assisted him in painting the murals on-site, the art museums and galleries, and everyone in the media and other places who showed him their understanding, and all our friends who have supported us in spirit -- to all of you I offer my deepest and most sincere thanks. And then, to my parents in Hokkaido, who have always watched over me with generous hearts, I thank you truly.

I would also like to take this opportunity to offer my deepest thanks to everyone involved with this English edition of *Tao*: to Philip Gwyn Jones of Portobello Books who has made publication in English a reality; to Andrea Belloli, for her work in editing the English version; and to Alison Watts, for her long and enthusiastic involvement in bringing this translation to fruition.

On 27 November 1993, Cao Yong's mother, Cai Dewei, passed away at the still young age of 58. May she rest in peace. If she could only see the achievements of her fourth son now, I think she would be overjoyed!

Aya Goda

August 2007

For news about current and forthcoming titles
from Portobello Books and for a sense of purpose
visit the website **www.portobellobooks.com**

encouraging voices,
supporting writers,
challenging readers

Portobello
BOOKS